First-Person Journalism

A first-of-its-kind guide for new media times, this book provides practical, step-by-step instructions for writing first-person features, essays, and digital content.

Combining journalism techniques with self-exploration and personal storytelling, *First-Person Journalism* is designed to help writers develop their personal voice and establish a narrative stance. The book introduces nine elements of first-person journalism—passion, self-reporting, stance, observation, attribution, counterpoints, time travel, the mix, and impact. Two introductory chapters define first-person journalism and its value in building trust with a public now skeptical of traditional news media. The nine practice chapters that follow each focus on one first-person element, presenting a sequence of "voice lessons" with a culminating writing assignment, such as a personal trend story or an open letter. Examples are drawn from diverse nonfiction writers and journalists, including Ta-Nehisi Coates, Joan Didion, Helen Garner, Alex Tizon, and James Baldwin. Together, the book provides a fresh look at the craft of nonfiction, offering much-needed advice on writing with style, authority, and a unique point of view.

Written with a knowledge of the rapidly changing digital media environment, *First-Person Journalism* is a key text for journalism and media students interested in personal nonfiction, as well as for early-career nonfiction writers looking to develop this narrative form.

Martha Nichols cofounded *Talking Writing*, a nonprofit digital magazine. A longtime writer, journalist, and editor, she is a faculty instructor in journalism at the Harvard University Extension School. She is also the editor of and a contributor to *Into Sanity: Essays About Mental Health, Mental Illness, and Living in Between*.

First-Person Journalism

A Guide to Writing Personal
Nonfiction with Real Impact

Martha Nichols

Routledge
Taylor & Francis Group

LONDON AND NEW YORK

First published 2022
by Routledge
2 Park Square, Milton Park, Abingdon, Oxon OX14 4RN

and by Routledge
605 Third Avenue, New York, NY 10158

Routledge is an imprint of the Taylor & Francis Group, an informa business

© 2022 Martha Nichols

"Hurricane Warnings" originally appeared in *Into Sanity: Essays About Mental Health, Mental Illness, and Living in Between* (Talking Writing Books). A few sections of *First-Person Journalism* have also been adapted from previously published work in *Talking Writing* by the author: "How I Became a First-Person Journalist," "What Journalists Can Teach Memoir Writers," and "What's a Flash Essay?" In all cases, the author owns the copyright.

British Library Cataloguing-in-Publication Data
A catalogue record for this book is available from the British Library

Library of Congress Cataloging-in-Publication Data
Names: Nichols, Martha (Editor-in-chief of Talking writing), author.
Title: First person journalism : a guide to writing personal nonfiction with real impact / Martha Nichols.
Description: London ; New York : Routledge, 2022. | Includes bibliographical references and index. |
Identifiers: LCCN 2021024109 | ISBN 9780367676483 (hardback) | ISBN 9780367676476 (paperback) | ISBN 9781003132189 (ebook)
Subjects: LCSH: Journalism—Authorship. | Authorship.
Classification: LCC PN4775 .N475 2022 | DDC 808.06/607—dc23
LC record available at https://lccn.loc.gov/2021024109

ISBN: 978-0-367-67648-3 (hbk)
ISBN: 978-0-367-67647-6 (pbk)
ISBN: 978-1-003-13218-9 (ebk)

DOI: 10.4324/9781003132189

Typeset in Bembo
by Apex CoVantage, LLC

To my students

Contents

Preface

Personal journalism for challenging times

On January 6, 2021, when supporters of then-President Donald Trump stormed the U.S. Capitol building in Washington, I was most convinced something terrible had happened by the frantic journalists I saw on TV. There was ABC's Martha Raddatz, voice straining from behind her coronavirus mask, gesturing sharply in the darkness at National Guardsmen unloading from buses. At one point, studio anchor George Stephanopoulos interrupted her: "Constitution Avenue, Martha, usually the site of the inaugural parade."

"It-it. . . ." Raddatz shook her head. "It is just *appalling* to look down Constitution Avenue and just see nothing but red-and-blue lights—of law enforcement."

American broadcast journalists on the scene like Raddatz were corroborating what viewers felt, not simply reeling off facts. The reporters and their news organizations were also gathering more facts, and many feature analyses of why the Capitol riot took place followed. But if the event being reported is a government insurrection—and the outcome involves high emotion because social norms have been violated—journalists provide a moral compass with their own response. They convey feelings along with facts. Otherwise, it's tough to arrive at what the facts mean, especially if the meaning of an event depends on your political or cultural perspective.

In *First-Person Journalism*, I advocate for nonfiction storytelling that reveals the individual perspective behind the byline. That's not to say all news reporting should turn into personal blog posts or commentary. The standard third-person news story fills our basic need for information: we want to know what's happening and how it affects us. In news reports, personal digressions from a writer are unnecessary and can be downright annoying.

Yet once the *who-what-where-when* has been reported, we also want to know *why*—and interpreting the world and its many challenges is often subjective. Even if a third-person voice in a news analysis sounds neutral, it isn't always more reliable. Journalism is a collective enterprise, one aimed at informing the public, but as a profession it's also far from perfect, and that same public has become skeptical of the press. It's here that a first-person perspective can deepen the reporting and writing of feature stories, engaging readers in new ways.

Why is there confusion about first-person journalism?

The first-person approach I emphasize is a hybrid of traditional reporting and literary nonfiction, and at times, it may seem as if I'm arguing with both. Well, I am, because I'm also arguing with myself. The digital era has trounced all over my long-held beliefs about the truthfulness of what I read, see, or hear in the media. Propaganda now blurs with news, and not just on alt-right sites. Celebrities masquerade as authentic until they're canceled or they revise their stories. This ethical squishiness—of identity, of performing for influence, of disguised bias—continues to undermine the public conversations we need to have and keep having in a troubled world.

For anyone now publishing work labeled "nonfiction" or "true," it's time to rethink what those terms mean. Consider all the perspectives on contentious topics such as race, gender, religion, politics, medicine, climate change—much of what people talk about in their public and private lives. Self-awareness about our own biases is the starting point for credible nonfiction.

Reporters do have gut reactions to what they witness. Yet "first-person journalism" may still sound like an oxymoron to many. Here are typical responses I've heard from peers and students:

- *Journalists are supposed to be disinterested observers.*
- *A reporter's personal point of view doesn't matter.*
- *Getting personal inevitably introduces bias.*
- *All biases are bad.*

Bias in reporting *is* bad, especially unconscious biases. The problem is that all humans are biased, including journalists. And the omniscient, dispassionate stance of traditional reporting no longer serves fractured audiences in a globally connected landscape.

Meanwhile, literary nonfiction writers and other artists often fail to understand the bedrock importance of accuracy for readers. With the growing interest in creative nonfiction classes and personal storytelling comes a less welcome confusion about facts. Reporters who insist on the need for objectivity may be ignoring digital reality, but misconceptions I've heard from literary nonfiction writers are more disturbing:

- *It's okay to massage the facts of your own story.*
- *Emotional truth matters more than what actually happened.*
- *An event in the past doesn't need to be pinned down in time or to its historical context.*
- *Just quote one expert and you've proven your point.*

In the chapters to come, I'll underscore the ethical purpose of journalism, which I believe applies not only to first-person feature articles but also to literary essays, personal narratives, and any form of topical nonfiction. Ethics in journalism may seem to be no more than aspirational or of less importance than artistic goals, but we ignore this aspiration at our peril.

How can first-person journalism build trust?

Anyone reading this book knows we're living in a post-fact world, one in which distrust of the media is on the rise. Take the 2020 Pew Research Center report on public skepticism of the press. This study of attitudes about news media among 10,000-plus Americans indicates the impact of U.S. political divisions. But beyond partisanship, it points to more specific problems: "not only do many people see news outlets as opaque in how they produce their stories and choose their sources, but a large majority—72%—say news organizations do an insufficient job explaining to the public where their money comes from."

Beyond a lack of transparency about techniques and sources, however, other findings of this Pew report uncovered longstanding issues that have eroded faith in journalism:

> Many Americans remain skeptical toward the news media, questioning not only the quality of journalists' work but their intentions behind it. For instance, no more than half of U.S. adults have confidence in journalists to act in the best interests of the public. . . . And the public is more likely than not to say that news organizations do not care about the people they report on.

My heart sank when I first read that assessment, but it also signals how individual journalists and news organizations can improve their approach to readers. Three-quarters of the people surveyed said they were open to improvements in journalism that would make it more credible. "Being transparent about corrections is another area where the public says news organizations have an opportunity to gain trust," the Pew report adds.

What stands out most for me, though, is the subjective quality of caring about people. Some respondents noted the personal connections they make with local news or with stories about topics they relate to. An empathetic approach is engaging to readers, but journalists often spend more energy battling the outrage of those who dislike them. Thick skins are a job requirement, but imperviousness to what other humans feel has real drawbacks. Beneath the familiar omniscient tone of a reporter interpreting the news, many viewers and readers may hear something else: *I know more than you do, average citizen, so I don't care what you think or feel. You have no right to question what a news expert says.*

This hypothetical reader reaction isn't meant as an excuse for pandering—the kind of false reassurances, trumped-up relatability, or circus of squabbling pundits that already clog news feeds. But while media-literacy programs can help address misunderstandings about how journalists do their jobs, I suggest more emotional literacy on the part of the press. Too often, desperate calls from reporters for more media literacy are code for *teach those dumb fools to listen to us*.

People don't easily change their perceptions, and unfortunately, digital disinformation shapes those perceptions. However, questioning news outlets is not the same as promoting wild conspiracy theories. Many respondents in the Pew survey said skepticism of the media is healthy. Indeed, questioning institutions and those in power amounts to what good reporters do, and the best journalism encourages people to think critically about information. It also treats them as participants in the public conversation, not passive consumers of whatever they're told.

One of the most obvious ways to flip the traditional terms is to write a feature or an essay based on personal experience. True stories like this can speak directly to audiences, forging emotional connections that feel convincing. Yet first-person journalists do more than write about themselves or speak on behalf of their identity groups. The most radical quality of first-person journalism is its transparency in exposing an individual writer's uncertainty.

When you care deeply about a topic, you're more likely to communicate what's at stake to your audience. Caring doesn't disqualify you from doing journalism—it may even lead you to ask different and better questions than a dispassionate observer would. But the fact that you care can also inspire you to question yourself and your initial assumptions.

In *First-Person Journalism*, I'll keep returning to the value of revealing the limits to what you know as well as the mistakes you may have made. Good journalists strive for accuracy, so admitting to an error in public can seem like an embarrassing failure. We're supposed to appear confident and authoritative, not uncertain. But in this book, I'll encourage nonfiction writers of all kinds to reframe an admission of uncertainty as proof of humanity.

Acknowledgments: Not just one voice

In *First-Person Journalism*, you'll learn a bit about me. After years of teaching, editing, and writing, I have a particular perspective on the growth of digital journalism at its best and worst. I'll tell personal anecdotes and express opinions. I never intended this work as an encyclopedic guide to reporting, fact checking, or story formulas. Instead, I've highlighted the nine elements of first-person journalism that have mattered most to me in my own nonfiction.

Yet the book is not about me, nor is it based only on my perspective. First off, my students in the journalism program at Harvard University Extension School have greatly influenced the lessons presented here. There's no better way to test assignments than in the classroom, but more than that, I've learned so much from the questions students ask. I acknowledge their hard work as writers and the lively discussions we've had for more than a decade.

I also thank my fellow editors and contributors at *Talking Writing*, the digital magazine and nonprofit organization I cofounded in 2010. In addition to my classroom teaching materials, several of my "First Person" columns from *Talking*

Writing have been incorporated into this book. Karen Ohlson, my longtime editor, was enormously helpful with some early chapters. And one *Talking Writing* mentor deserves a special nod: Michael Steinberg, who himself founded the journal *Fourth Genre* in the late 1990s, was one of our first board members. Mike, who has since passed away, encouraged me to promote innovative approaches to nonfiction.

As for other nonfiction writing guides, I'd like to assign a few favorites here as required reading, just as I've done in my classes over the years: William Zinsser's *On Writing Well*, Phillip Lopate's *To Show and to Tell*, and any of Roy Peter Clark's books, especially *How to Write Short*. I quote these wise guides on occasion in this book because they're all so eminently quotable.

When it comes to writing instruction and journalism practice, of course, there are many shoulders to stand on. *The Elements of Journalism* by Bill Kovach and Tom Rosenstiel has long been a touchstone for me. Michael Caulfield's *Web Literacy for Student Fact-Checkers* is a terrific resource for nonfiction writers in the digital realm. Two other recent books provide a provocative look at what truth on the public record really means: Lewis Raven Wallace's *The View From Somewhere: Undoing the Myth of Journalistic Objectivity* and Kevin Young's *Bunk: The Rise of Hoaxes, Humbug, Plagiarists, Phonies, Post-Facts, and Fake News*.

I'll nod to Joan Didion and James Baldwin along the way, too. Their fierce self-scrutiny is another kind of guiding light for *First-Person Journalism*. For the same reason, I acknowledge an earlier generation of feminist journalists, essayists, and scholars who shaped my thinking as I came of age: Adrienne Rich, Maxine Hong Kingston, Nora Ephron, Audre Lorde, Susan Brownmiller, Jill Nelson, Terry Tempest Williams, and many more. I don't have space here to distill what I've received from each, but I thank the collective Sisterhood.

Finally, I honor the patience of my husband and son, as well as the pod of good friends who provided so much emotional support and intellectual stimulation in 2020. During that tough year, I wrote much of *First-Person Journalism*, and the book is inevitably imbued with what we and others felt. The coronavirus pandemic, mass protests, the contested U.S. presidential election—it may all fade in time, but the real world leaves a personal imprint on everyone.

April 2021
Cambridge, Massachusetts

Sources

"'Busloads' of National Guardsmen Head to Capitol Grounds," reported by Martha Raddatz, *ABC News*, January 6, 2021. www.abcnews.go.com/US/video/busloads-national-guardsmen-head-capitol-grounds-75097621

"Americans See Skepticism of News Media as Healthy, Say Public Trust in the Institution Can Improve" by Jeffrey Gottfried, Mason Walker, and Amy Mitchell, Pew Research Center (Journalism and Media), August 31, 2020. www.journalism.org/2020/08/31/americans-see-skepticism-of-news-media-as-healthy-say-public-trust-in-the-institution-can-improve/

Part I

What is first-person journalism?

The value of a first-person journalism perspective has as much to do with a writing approach as the final product. If you think your job is to talk about more than yourself, then the whole process—from conceptualizing the idea to doing research to interpreting what you discover—becomes richer, deeper, and more self-critical.

DOI: 10.4324/9781003132189-1

1 How I became a first-person journalist

Writing and reporting true stories

When Tom Wolfe's *The New Journalism* came out in 1973, I was 15. At the time, I wasn't reading his arguments about why the "pale beige tone" of news writing needed a kick in the ass. But I was greatly influenced by Hunter S. Thompson's fast-and-loose, imagination-fueled reports from the field, especially when they lined up with my countercultural desire to tear down the walls. I was a bookworm kid in California who loved glitter rock, *The Electric Kool-Aid Acid Test, Fear and Loathing: On the Campaign Trail '72,* and *Slouching Towards Bethlehem.*

I grew up thinking the truth was what you shaped for yourself.

In *The New Journalism*, Wolfe touted nonfiction with a literary twist, complete with vivid characters and scenes that incorporated dialogue, even internal monologue that represented what a subject might have been thinking or feeling. "[H]ow could a journalist, writing nonfiction, accurately penetrate the thoughts of another person?" he asked, before exuberantly providing his own answer: "interview him about his thoughts and emotions, along with everything else."

Back then, this cavalier approach to journalism suited me fine. My other bookish loves were novels—big fat facsimiles of the real world. I enjoyed immersing myself in seamless plots, suspending disbelief. In high school, my goal was to be a novelist, and a science-fiction novelist at that. I would be a master of imagined worlds—detailing everything from an alien planet's biology to its history of colonization—and stay far away from chronicling the emotional thicket of my actual experience.

In hindsight, my young writing goals were way off base. I was meant to be a journalist, but I backed into it, even getting a master's degree in creative writing first. My jump into magazine journalism in the early 1990s was pure chance—a job that opened up when I needed one—but it also turned out to be the right match for the way I think about the world.

In the 1960s and 1970s, the New Journalists were part of a revolution against the Powers That Be. Like these revolutionaries, I wanted to change the terms of truth-telling and who got to control history. Despite their macho posturing, I was on board—a young feminist writer who followed their trail almost without question, as did many of the journalists and editors of my era.

DOI: 10.4324/9781003132189-2

Then the World Wide Web happened, profoundly changing how writing reaches readers and unleashing a creative torrent of "truth-telling" from all sides.

Oh, the irony. (*The irony!!!!!*—as Wolfe would crow.) Now, after decades as a magazine editor and writer, I'm confronting the inadequacy of the novel-like journalism I used to love. I'm wrestling with its messy legacy in creative nonfiction classrooms. And I'm concerned about what's been lost in the digital age with the implosion of traditional journalism, including basics like verification of facts and attribution.

I still believe in personally inflected journalism that's liberated, as the New Journalism was, from false claims of objectivity. Like so many digital readers, I'm more convinced than ever by personal stories. But in anything labeled nonfiction, I no longer trust colorful characters who sound like they're mouthing dialogue in a novel. With only a few exceptions, I don't like when the writer telling the story seems intent on distorting reality. Hunter Thompson was a brilliant reporter, questioner, brooder—all qualities I admire in first-person writing—but his "I" was mostly a fictional creation.

The "gonzo journalism" Thompson popularized decades ago (the term was coined to describe one of his early pieces) involved a highly subjective perspective on the events being reported. In many ways, it is the genesis for what I call first-person journalism. While Thompson, Wolfe, Gay Talese, and other New Journalists are now far in the rearview mirror for younger readers, their style greatly impacted generations of journalists who came after them. In academic settings, the New Journalism continues to influence contemporary ideas about nonfiction writing and personal authenticity.

Here's what troubles me: Thompson and his peers had no problem massaging what they observed to suit their own purposes, often setting up events to "report" on them or otherwise ignoring facts. Many bloggers and literary nonfiction writers have now absorbed this license to reshape the observed world, leaning on the techniques of fiction writing and poetry to create narratives that are too loose with the truth. When it's clear to readers why certain facts (such as names) have been changed, the result is still truthful; readers understand the need for anonymity. But as an editor and a teacher, I've observed how often factual information is incorrect or its sources unclear in work submitted to me. With misinformation proliferating at an alarming rate in digital media, I've come to believe that *all* nonfiction writers need to take responsibility for getting the facts right.

That's why in *First-Person Journalism* I embrace the passionate involvement of a first-person perspective combined with the truthful substance of journalistic research. You'll now find first-person pieces in the daily news, as well as in magazines that favor long-form features and investigations. Just a few examples from the past decade:

- Shane Bauer's "My Four Months as a Private Prison Guard," a 2016 investigative report for *Mother Jones*.

- Alex Tizon's "My Family's Slave," a 2017 personal narrative in the *Atlantic* about the Filipina domestic servant who came to the United States with Tizon's family.
- Kelley Benham's "Parents of Micro Preemie Face Heart-Wrenching Decisions," a 2012 first-person account in the *Tampa Bay Times*, the first of a Pulitzer-nominated series about her daughter.
- "A Most American Terrorist: The Making of Dylann Roof" by Rachel Kaadzi Ghansah, a 2017 award-winning feature in *GQ* about the young white man who shot nine Black people dead in an AME church in Charleston, South Carolina.
- "In Harm's Way: A Plague of Unsolved Femicides Haunts Mexico," a 2020 investigative feature in *Harper's* by Seth Harp.
- "Getting the Vaccine Along With a Glimmer of Hope," a 2021 first-person piece by Hannah Wise, a *New York Times* editor at the time, that, in describing how she burst into tears when getting the coronavirus vaccine, breaks down the fourth wall between producing news and what it feels like as a participant.

Other guides to writing personal nonfiction emphasize gripping narratives, lyrical imagery, artfully reconstructed memories, inspiring anecdotes, or (at worst) inventions that leave out key facts to promote a brand. With *First-Person Journalism*, I highlight the journalism part. For me, facts should never be fudged. Beautiful language, humor, the quest for deeper truths—none of these qualities justifies changing what actually happened unless you, the writer, come clean with readers and, most important, with yourself.

In this introductory chapter, I establish the hybrid nature of first-person journalism—its versatility and appeal—which is why journalists and their readers benefit when they give themselves permission to use the first-person voice. Then I nod to one of the biggest potential problems: dumping too much personal information in public. Claiming your story *and* questioning what it might mean to others is a challenge. More than that, you need to cultivate self-awareness, investigating your motivations in a way that at times may resemble doing therapy, even if the end result isn't a personal story.

Back when I believed I could shape the truth, I was a naïve teenager. But my beliefs about writing were also shaped by a cultural milieu that's long since vanished. In the era of digital misinformation, nonfiction writers need to do more than tell readers what they want to be true. They need to establish their own credibility as storytellers.

Defining first-person journalism

As I came of age in the 1970s, my love for first-person nonfiction really blossomed when I discovered Joan Didion. "I had better tell you where I am, and why," Didion writes at the beginning of her essay "In the Islands," part of her iconic 1979 collection *The White Album*. From the first paragraph, we know she's in Honolulu with her husband and three-year-old daughter, waiting for news of a possible tidal wave. Then:

> We are here on this island in the middle of the Pacific in lieu of filing for a divorce. I tell you this not as aimless revelation but because I want you to know, as you read me, precisely who I am and where I am and what is on my mind.

This kind of personal scrutiny in nonfiction is no longer surprising. It's become the gold standard for magazines such as *Vanity Fair, Rolling Stone, GQ, Esquire*, and the *New Yorker*. On digital sites, the truth-talking "I" voice is now everywhere: in commentary and personal essays, in blog posts, long-form nonfiction, and social media. These days, first-person features pop up on the print front page of the *New York Times*.

It's an exciting trend, one I wouldn't have predicted in the early 2000s, let alone the 1970s. Yet as the years roll on and digital media consolidates its hold on publishing, the boundaries have grown ever more slippery, with first-person nonfiction pieces labeled as "Opinion," "Feature," "Essay," "Personal History," or a think piece under "Ideas."

Writing in the first-person voice isn't a binary choice: on or off. There are many variations on using "I" in nonfiction. Some writers drop into a personal pronoun only to explain how they did the reporting; some open with a personal anecdote but focus on other people; some use their own story throughout to exemplify a universal experience. What ties all these variations together is the first-person voice.

Still, you may well be wondering if topical feature articles, personal essays, and creative nonfiction all qualify as first-person journalism. My short answer is yes—with a few important caveats. Let's start with the basics, defining the following related categories and the threads we'll weave together in *First-Person Journalism*.

Journalism: The stock definition is that journalism is about reporting and presenting news of the day. The confusion comes in pinning down what news is or how it's told. Journalists document real-world events as they're happening, but they also interpret them. Print magazines, in particular, have always been hybrid forms, mixing third-person articles, reviews, and how-to pieces with first-person essays or columns.

What matters is a quality that the American Press Institute says distinguishes journalism from other forms of media: "its purpose, [which is] to provide people with verified information they can use to make better decisions" about the world they live in. At its best, journalism has an ethical purpose and intent to inform, one that relies on facts. But this purpose doesn't only depend on quoting experts or tracking down sources. A powerfully told personal story can inform readers, too, as long as it's factual. According to *The Elements of Journalism*, "journalism is storytelling with a purpose." Authors Bill Kovach and Tom Rosenstiel (the latter was executive director of the American Press Institute from 2013 to 2021) then add: "The first challenge is finding the information that people need to live their lives. The second is to make it meaningful, relevant, and engaging."

Memoir: Dictionary definitions of memoir call it an autobiographical account or a narrative based on a writer's own experience. Because this can encompass everything from celebrity confessionals to posts by influencers pitching products to literary reconstructions to out-and-out fakes, memoir as a form rarely qualifies as journalism. As indicated by the word itself, most of these first-person narratives are based on memory, which isn't the same as a factual account based on the public record.

The focus of memoirs—one writer's life—also isn't journalistic in any traditional sense. Still, aspects of memoir writing are part of first-person journalism, especially if the point of telling a personal story is to expose readers to a world they've never seen before: that is, to inform, document, and interpret. These techniques include witnessing events from a first-person perspective, evocative descriptions, and self-reflection.

Creative nonfiction: This broad term covers memoirs, personal essays, and other literary nonfiction narratives. Creative nonfiction and first-person journalism may seem to be the same thing, and there are many overlaps. But they are distinct genres, taught and practiced in different settings. Not all such "true stories, well told"—the tagline of *Creative Nonfiction* magazine—are written in the first-person voice; it's the emphasis on artistic impact and literary craft that's common in this genre. On the website of *Creative Nonfiction*, founding editor Lee Gutkind says the "goal is to make nonfiction stories read like fiction so that your readers are as enthralled by fact as they are by fantasy."

Defining nonfiction this way, however, often masks unconscious biases against journalism (it's too prosaic, lacks nuance, is obsessed with literal facts). As Gutkind argues, "It is possible to be honest and straightforward and brilliant and creative at the same time." Indeed, you don't have to sacrifice art when writing first-person journalism, and many creative nonfiction writers adhere to factual accuracy. And yet, if your intent is to immerse readers in a narrative that feels like fiction—rather than to alert and inform them—that doesn't mesh with the purpose of journalism.

Feature: In journalistic outlets, feature stories are anything that doesn't qualify as a breaking news report—human-interest stories, "explainers" of hot topics, an analysis of news events, lifestyle stories, profiles, and personal essays. They've also traditionally been called soft news, compared with hard news, but that opposition doesn't bother to disguise a whole slew of gender biases that have long relegated too many features to heart-tugging emotion, advice, and so-called female troubles.

In *First-Person Journalism*, we'll break apart that opposition. My perspective is that of a magazine editor rather than a news reporter, so my focus will be on the impact of personal nonfiction on readers, not on how to do investigative reporting. My lessons focus on the craft of writing first-person features rather than books, although I'll refer to book-length nonfiction in some examples. (I also consider many podcasts, documentary films, and other multimedia stories to be first-person journalism.) Regardless, this isn't just another guide to writing magazine articles. Throughout, I'll highlight the value of thinking through your attitudes about a topic—and cultivating self-awareness of your biases—no matter how much of your own story ends up in a final piece.

Didion herself is famous for a detached personal voice rather than emotional expressiveness, and her style of standing back to observe the self has influenced many younger writers like me as much as, if not more than, Hunter Thompson's most feverish prose. Literary first-person essays, such as her "In the Islands," are often given another label—*reportage*—yet another indication of what a hybrid this kind of writing is.

Presenting a personal perspective and maintaining enough distance to cite facts may appear to be two very different approaches to storytelling. Yet these supposed opposites coexist just fine in first-person journalism. While a few traditionalists may cling to the hoary distinction between hard and soft news, this artificial divide gets creakier with every passing second. When journalists meld head and heart, it can lead to first-person storytelling that not only hooks readers but also impacts public debate. Consider writers as varied as Helen Garner, Ta-Nehisi Coates, Alex Tizon, and Lindy West.

So, what *is* a first-person feature story? Simple as it sounds, this is the basic equation: *Facts + Personal POV = Story*. But regardless of format—personal narrative, personal essay, or topical article—such features don't just use the "I" voice. They join research and reporting with the person telling the story.

It's a potent combination. First-person journalists acknowledge their biases up front, identifying who's behind the "I." And they link their own stories to larger themes, incorporating direct observation, quotes from outside sources, statistics, and other information on the public record. That's what makes the collage of "In the Islands" first-person journalism. It moves from Didion's personal situation to accounts of the Royal Hawaiian Hotel's privileged history and the Punchbowl—a U.S. military cemetery on Oahu, where she observed graves being dug for American soldiers killed in Vietnam.

Permission to say "I"

In his classic guide *On Writing Well*, William Zinsser referred to the "transaction" writers establish with readers. This is akin to a writer's contract with the reader, but I like Zinsser's practical sense of an emotional exchange in which both parties benefit. "Ultimately," he noted, "the product that any writer has to sell is not the subject being written about, but who he or she is." Zinsser added:

> I often find myself reading with interest about a topic I never thought would interest me—some scientific quest, perhaps. What holds me is the enthusiasm of the writer for his field. How was he drawn into it? What emotional baggage did he bring along? How did it change his life?

News reporters, doctors, and other professionals are called on to describe people and events with clinical detachment. They document what they observe, providing necessary detail with as much objectivity as possible. Not every nonfiction piece needs a personal perspective; news reports are news reports. But feature writing is about interpreting events and complex topics for readers. Good features express a point of view whether they're told in the third-person or first-person voice, and those written with clinical detachment are rarely illuminating. In today's media, they can even feel less true than a more biased account because the writer's response seems apathetic or deliberately concealed.

And yet, a 2019 feature on the *Open Notebook* site, "Journalists as Characters," quotes *New York Times Magazine* contributing writer and former *Essence* editor Linda Villarosa as saying: "I really hate writing in first person. . . . I was trained not to rely on it. I use it sparingly, usually pushed by my editor or when there's no way around it."

"I don't know how much we lose by inserting ourselves in stories," writer Eve Fairbanks, a contributing editor at the *New Republic*, told the *American Journalism Review* in 2014, "[but] I think we lose something when we write mainly about anecdotes that already happened in our own lives instead of going out and seeking stories."

That's only true if first-person reporting is considered an either/or choice. Too often, reluctance to use "I" simply indicates how tough old constraints are to shake off. Beyond how nervous-making it is to venture from behind a safe byline to describe your own health crisis, say, traditional journalism has long exhorted reporters to avoid "I." We're supposed to tell other people's stories, not our own. More than that, old attitudes about the need for objectivity, neutrality, and detachment in reporting still hold sway. Using the first-person voice is often penalized as unacceptable advocacy or partisanship.

Fear of using the first-person voice hasn't yet died out in journalism programs, even if it's tough to ignore the popularity of first-person storytelling in the digital realm. I've heard too many old-school journalists categorize anything that involves a writer's personal story as memoir, which is both an oversimplification of a whole literary genre and a snub of the potential that first-person journalism has to engage readers. Bias has always been a dirty word in journalism—not to mention "aimless revelation"—yet the bias revealed in first-person accounts is often the thing that makes them ring true.

Writing with an "I" underscores that the person telling the story of how they were scammed, or observed a disaster unfold, or talked with a grieving survivor, or decried this week's government mess is a *real person*, not a masked voice professing disinterested authority. This real person has biases and cultural affinities of their own. This person explains how "I" did the reporting, directly addressing readers' questions about claims of fact and why a story should matter to them.

Those questions from readers are reasonable. It's tempting to blame Fox News and the rise of digital opinionating for the current crisis in misinformation. There is a crisis, and more writers than ever seem confused about what constitutes the truth in a first-person story. But while I've never been a willing Fox viewer, distrust of the media goes back long before cable news, let alone sophisticated digital news sites or apps that make it easy to fake almost anything in the virtual landscape.

First-person storytelling isn't just an approach to be used for unscrupulous influence or an easy fix to attract eyeballs. For many of us, the barriers to telling our own stories are internal. In "Up From Pain," *New York Times* columnist Charles Blow grapples with early sexual trauma and his own adult sexuality. In this short but powerful essay, adapted from Blow's 2014 memoir *Fire Shut up in My Bones*, he puts it this way:

> Daring to step into oneself is the bravest, strangest, most natural, most terrifying thing a person can do, because when you cease to wrap yourself in artifice you are naked, and when you are naked you are vulnerable.
>
> But vulnerability is the leading edge of truth. Being willing to sacrifice a false life is the only way to live a true one.

Achieving such vulnerability on the page is one of the goals of this book. Indeed, it's the ultimate goal woven throughout the lessons in *First-Person Journalism*, but it's not the only reason to use the first-person voice. Sometimes permission to say "I" means giving yourself permission to speak at all or to take back that permission from those who want to silence you. It can be a lifelong undertaking, especially when racism, sexism, ageism, and every other form of discrimination have denied writers a platform.

Vulnerability is the leading edge of truth. Digital media now offers many more outlets for speaking up in blogs, online magazines, and niche news sites and through social-media movements like #MeToo or #BlackLivesMatter. Yet exposing your life in this way can be uncomfortable, even scary, depending on who's reading or listening.

In the end, writing with an "I" takes guts.

Is it ever *too* personal?

The bravery required of speaking truthfully relies on self-awareness. Before you question anyone else, question yourself: your biases, your privilege (or lack of privilege), your position in the social hierarchy. But beyond the value of acknowledging differences in point of view for readers, cultivating self-awareness also helps combat one of the main downsides of personal nonfiction: talking about everything that's *ever* happened to you *ever*, including yesterday's bad tuna sandwich.

I did this . . . I think this . . . I FEEL that . . . I'm the center of the universe!!!

We've all winced when friends or relatives or strangers at bus stops dump too much information (TMI) on us. TMI has now become part of the vernacular. Hearing too many personal details seems to be the cost of communicating in digital publishing and social media. At the same time, writers of first-person nonfiction are also expected to expose themselves in a way that feels honest to readers. That's an edgy line to walk.

Relentless TMI gives personal preoccupations the same weight as universal problems. Admittedly, I'm not a millennial, but I dislike the hothouse quality of tell-all essays by many younger writers, especially those in which they imply "if I remember it this way, it *must* be true" or it's simply "my truth." At worst, revealing private experiences in a public forum invites a nasty kind of voyeurism.

For the pros and cons of overly personal writing, consider Natasha Chenier's "On Falling In and Out of Love With My Dad," published in *Jezebel* in 2015. This short essay about becoming sexually involved with her formerly estranged father went viral minutes after it appeared. Not surprising, given the lead: "My biological father wanted to have sex with me from the first moment he laid eyes on me."

Chenier bravely reveals a lot about her emotional state once she becomes attracted to her father at nineteen. Early on, she says, "I was filled with an unmatched horror. I can't really begin to describe it." However, describing this experience in specific ways *is* the point. So is explaining—and questioning—why she felt so compelled to tell the story in public, something Chenier doesn't get across. Instead, she tries to connect the "hottest hate and . . . intense disgust" that people feel when hearing about parent-child incest, especially of the father-daughter kind, to male power and its cultural tropes. She argues that "genetic sexual attraction is normal," if a set-up for abuse, ending with: "And to the victims of their abuse, I want to say what I have finally been able to understand myself: that my attraction, and what it led to, was not my fault."

Much as I believe it wasn't her fault, post-traumatic stress is enormously complicated. It can prompt you to forget what happened or to blab to anyone who'll listen. Given my own experiences of early trauma, I'm not convinced by glosses like "I have finally been able to understand myself" or arguments about the patriarchy.

In the 2015 commentary "The First-Person Industrial Complex" in *Slate*, Laura Bennett opens by describing Chenier's piece, using it to illustrate a growing and problematic trend. Bennett reports that Chenier came to regret going public, especially given the impact on her mother's family and this young writer's own sense that the editors only accepted her pitch because it was about a personal trauma. Bennett argues:

> First-person essays have become the easiest way for editors to stake out some small corner of a news story and assert an on-the-ground primacy without paying for reporting. And first-person essays have also become the easiest way to jolt an increasingly jaded Internet to attention, as the bar for provocation has risen higher and higher.

Yet by 2017, *New Yorker* staff writer Jia Tolentino was proclaiming that "The Personal-Essay Boom Is Over," detailing how the trend of first-person essays like "Ten Days in the Life of a Tampon" (tagged as "Gross Things That Happen to Your Body" in *Jezebel*) had gone bust. Tolentino notes:

> There's a certain kind of personal essay that, for a long time, everybody seemed to hate. These essays were mostly written by women. They came

off as unseemly, the writer's judgment as flawed. They were *too* personal: the topics seemed insignificant, or else too important to be aired for an audience of strangers.

She locates the trend in the rise of sites like *Gawker*, *Jezebel*, *Salon*, *Vice*, and the *Awl* circa 2008 and its ending in the demise of many of them. Tolentino, herself a former *Jezebel* editor, is right about the limitations of such prurient accounts, but her focus on what went wrong is too narrow. Taking down such ultra-confessionals is easy—like shooting tampons in a trashcan—when you confine them to online content meant to get readers clicking on ads. But essay writing and the impulse to tell your own story haven't evaporated just because an exploitative publishing model has.

Let's try a different approach by redefining *personal essay* as a form of first-person journalism. As such, it's far closer to Joan Didion's sharp self-scrutiny than overwrought TMI. Despite the way the essay has been lumped into a catch-all category for overly intimate stories, it has a much longer history in literary nonfiction. The tradition of writing about yourself harks back to at least the sixteenth century and Michel de Montaigne, the writer-philosopher who popularized the term "essay." The story goes that he retired from his life as a French public servant and nobleman in 1571 to focus on writing "essais" that were based on observing himself.

In French, an *essai* is an attempt or a trial run, a way to study a problem, not a discourse about fixed knowledge. Known for his slogan *Que sais-je?* ("What do I know?"), Montaigne used his essays to explore the endlessly evolving sense of who he was and what he believed. As he wrote in "Of Books":

> What you have here is purely an essay of my natural parts, and not of those acquired: and whoever shall catch me tripping in ignorance, will not in any sort get the better of me. . . . [T]he confession of ignorance is one of the finest and surest testimonies of judgment that I know.

Montaigne leaped from such self-reflection to historical anecdotes and quotes to observations and memories, a heady and personal mix that still animates literary essays today. He wrote about everything from smells to liars to educating children to vanity, circling around from his personal point of view to universal experience. Sound familiar? In *First-Person Journalism*, I have no problem with personal essays delving into taboo topics like sex and religion—essays can be about anything—but what makes good first-person essays so powerful is a quality I associate with journalism: questioning.

It may seem as if readers want to know every speck of dirt, but in personal nonfiction, dumping too much dirt can feel unmoored, as if the writer-victim is shouting for help and readers are stuck watching a train wreck happen. With effective first-person journalism, however, conveying that you've thought through your own motives as a writer, that you're aware of the impact your story will have, makes readers feel they're in safe hands. When you question your own experience, a "confession of ignorance," as Montaigne wrote centuries ago, can paradoxically indicate your good judgment as an observer, anchoring your perspective in the uncertain reality we all share.

Self-reporting: "What do I know?"

TMI remains a problem, of course. A grisly account that's been spun to increase the shock value but leaves readers in an incomprehensible pit isn't satisfying or emotionally honest. Responsible journalism may document horrors, but it doesn't dismiss real-life complexity or stick us with the feeling of *Huh? Well, I guess life sucks.*

On social media and among my younger feminist students, too many discussions of personal writing assume that it's inherently political or empowering to express whatever you feel in the moment. By this reasoning, the act of writing it all down and pushing "publish" on a blog provides a new kind of openness.

Feminist though I am, I don't believe the personal is inevitably political. Nor is it a sufficient explanation for why readers should care. I want interpretation, critical thinking, and a bigger view of the world than the interior of somebody's head. Journalists, for all their flaws, are trained to provide the *who-what-where-when* specifics of their observations. In a first-person feature, they make clear who the "I" is and why that "I" is telling the story. They approach information sources with necessary skepticism, whether it's a politician, Mother Teresa, or themselves.

Back in the early 1970s, Tom Wolfe wrote disdainfully about the "I" voice, saying that journalists of old had "often used the first-person point of view—'I was there'—just as autobiographers, memoirists and novelists had":

> This is very limiting for the journalist, however, since he can bring the reader inside the mind of only one character—himself—a point of view that often proves irrelevant to the story and irritating to the reader.

Wolfe's solution was to write journalism as if you're writing a novel, turning your sources into characters with their own thoughts and feelings. That's an approach many contemporary creative nonfiction writers take, yet as I'll address in more detail in the next chapter, there are ethical hazards in relying too much on fiction-writing techniques. And at the practical level of selling stories, readers and editors do want more revelations about the writers themselves in these digital times. Whether this hews to the ethical purpose of journalism depends on the questions a writer poses.

In "How Personal Essays Conquered Journalism—and Why They Can't Cut It," a 2014 *Washington Post* opinion piece, Eve Fairbanks offers a more nuanced take than her ironic title implies. But she echoes Wolfe, arguing that one of the fantasies "perpetuated by the first-person essay boom is that people's own account of their lives are always the most interesting accounts." Fairbanks adds:

> Reading the wave of first-person essays, I often wish the writers had an interlocutor visibly present in the piece, someone to ask more questions and provide an outside view.

A skeptical attitude on a writer's part certainly makes for better reporting. But this argument assumes that news organizations or an "outside view" have no biases of their own. In fact, traditional journalists are often blind to their cultural attitudes—a point New Journalists like Hunter Thompson, no stranger to TMI, repeatedly pounded home. In his scathing 1994 obituary of Richard Nixon, originally published in *Rolling Stone*, Thompson referred to "Objective Journalism" with ill-disguised contempt:

> Some people will say that words like *scum* and *rotten* are wrong for Objective Journalism—which is true, but they miss the point. It was the built-in blind spots of the Objective rules and dogma that allowed Nixon to slither into the White House in the first place. . . . You had to get Subjective to see Nixon clearly, and the shock of recognition was often painful.

An outside observer isn't necessarily more astute or honest as a reporter. If a writer's biases are unconscious, as they often are when a third-person feature reinforces sexist or racist assumptions, it may sound authoritative, but it's far from truthful.

The key is to ask hard questions about your own biases—to be that self-aware interlocutor—and to learn to question your own experience. I call the process *self-reporting*, which affects both the way you research what really happened in a personal story or events you've observed and the way you present that story to readers.

How to use this book

First-Person Journalism is a guide for anyone interested in writing personal non-fiction. Using the "I" voice in both a factual and an engaging fashion is challenging for all writers of true stories—journalism and other writing students, working journalists, memoirists, podcasters, bloggers—a challenge I'm now inviting you to take with me.

The value of a first-person journalism perspective has as much to do with a writing approach as the final product. If you think your job is to talk about more than yourself, then the whole process—from conceptualizing the idea to doing research to interpreting what you discover—becomes richer, deeper, and more self-critical.

In practice, this approach requires a variety of lessons from different angles. You'll get to try out different ways of voicing your observations or ideas, and if a given exercise doesn't click for you, then move on to the next. Trying, failing, revising, rethinking—these are all part of the process for becoming a good self-reporter.

I can't just exhort you to be a personal truth-teller (although I will do some exhorting). When I teach journalism students, I begin with baby steps. I emphasize what an excellent tool a first-person perspective is for providing the reporting context: *How did I get this information? Why do I trust this source? Why does this story matter?* Many readers now want to know how the reporting was done in investigative features; there's pressure on all news organizations to be more transparent. So, giving yourself permission to say "I" to describe your reporting is a good place to start writing more personally.

With students who want to write memoirs or personal essays, however, I emphasize the journalism basics: pinning down when something happened, who it happened to, where it happened, the specific chronology of events, the actual words somebody said. Verification, fact checking—and, most especially, effective attribution—may seem too pedestrian for anybody touched by the literary muse, but for nonfiction writers, these lessons are the foundation for presenting a credible true story.

This book highlights four related mental tools for the first-person journalist: self-awareness, an eye for details, active response, and questioning (see Box 1.1). Throughout the lessons, you'll develop these tools in order to begin reporting from a personal perspective in a fresh way. You'll use a *process notebook* to encourage self-awareness, an eye for details, and questioning. You'll write *response papers* to build an active response to everything you read, experience, and observe.

Box 1.1 Mental tools for first-person journalists

Self-awareness
Understand and acknowledge your biases.

Active Response
Engage passionately with the world.

An Eye for Details
Avoid abstractions—describe everything vividly.

Questioning
Examine why you believe what you do.

The next chapter, "The Ethics of Personal Reporting," delves into some of the thornier issues around truthfulness and subjectivity, especially the problem of faking yourself by creating a fictional "I" to tell a story. The rest of *First-Person Journalism* is devoted to nine practice chapters, each of which focuses on an element of first-person journalism (see Box 1.2). An endnote about witnessing with empathy closes the book, along with a compilation of "25 Rules" for first-person journalism that I touch on throughout.

The practice chapters include a sequence of warm-up exercises—called *voice lessons*—to help develop specific writing or reporting skills. Each chapter also presents a full writing assignment at the end. If you complete the lessons in every chapter, you'll have written many kinds of first-person pieces, such as a how-to article, an open letter, and a personal essay. By the time you reach the concluding chapter of *First-Person Journalism*, you'll have generated many additional ideas for features and essays, too.

Box 1.2 Elements of first-person journalism

Passion
Self-reporting
Stance
Observation
Attribution
Counterpoints
Time Travel
The Mix
Impact

In addition, the practice chapters are organized into three parts that correspond to the steps of the feature-writing process: "Developing an Active 'I' Voice," "Reporting Beyond the Self," and "Storytelling to Make an Impact." They provide a basic curriculum sequence for teachers and students to follow if the book is used in a classroom setting.

But reporting and writing a feature often overlap, and individual writers using *First-Person Journalism* don't need to work through the parts in order. Some lessons may spark you more than others. For instance, chapters on the elements of observation and attribution may initially be of more interest to journalism students. Those that emphasize storytelling elements like time travel may grab literary nonfiction writers.

Still, I strongly suggest that everyone begins with the first three chapters in the "Active Voice" part—"Locating Your Passion," "Investigating Yourself," and "Establishing Your Stance." They are the framework for first-person journalism, and developing an authentic first-person voice matters for all nonfiction writers. It will matter to the editors you pitch with story ideas and, most of all, to your readers.

In *First-Person Journalism*, I call on our better natures as nonfiction writers and journalists, because writing truthfully comes down to witnessing and interpreting the world. It is "storytelling with a purpose," in Kovach and Rosenstiel's phrase. Journalism as an institution—and as practiced in a real world of dwindling resources—has failed many times to live up to its ethical purpose. Yet that purpose matters more than ever, and it's often well served by first-person perspectives. Because evocative writing can increase a story's impact, my lessons also cover literary techniques for narration, description, and self-reflection. Engaging and entertaining readers is a journalistic goal, too. Throughout this book, we'll connect storytelling with two *true questions:*

1   *What makes a personal voice believable?*
2   *What makes my first-person story accurate?*

If you find yourself feeling defensive about my emphasis on ethics over art-fulness in nonfiction, I'd nudge you to ask these questions yourself. A defensive reaction indicates an emotional hot button, something you may need to explore, if not resolve. Whether or not you think of yourself as a journalist, establishing your credibility in the digital realm matters for the next generation of nonfiction writers, and credibility is about honesty. That's especially true of writers telling their own stories.

Why gonzo got it wrong—and right

For me, the valuable legacy of the New Journalism is not its overreach into fiction but its move toward complex self-examination and expression. It's not Hunter Thompson's exaggerated gonzo persona, "Raoul Duke," screaming across the desert in a narcotics-packed convertible hallucinating about giant bats. Rather, it's the Hunter Thompson who declared, in the opening note for his book about the 1972 presidential campaign, that his goal was to write "as close to the bone" as he could get.

In "Fear and Loathing in the Bunker," a 1974 commentary published in the *New York Times* after months of Watergate coverage, Thompson moved between childhood memory and his adult reflections. Recoiling from "the horror of American politics today" and the "burned-out hack" politicians running the show, he asked, "How long, oh Lord, how long?" Then he pushed it farther:

> And how much longer will we have to wait before some high-powered shark with a fistful of answers will finally bring us face-to-face with the ugly question that is already so close to the surface in this country, that sooner or later even politicians will have to cope with it?
>
> Is the democracy worth all the risks and problems that necessarily go with it?

Almost half a century later, these questions make me shiver with their prescience, their bitterness. They are definitely close to the bone. More important, though, Thompson then connected his fist shake at God with his own unknowing culpability at ten years old, when he worked for a milkman in Louisville, Kentucky:

> But every once in a while, on humorless nights like these, I think about how sharp and sure I felt when sprinting across those manicured lawns, jumping the finely-trimmed hedges and hitting the running board of that slow-cruising truck.
>
> If the milkman had given me a pistol and told me to put a bullet in the stomach of any slob who haggled about the bill, I would probably have done that, too. Because the milkman was my boss and my benefactor. . . . On a "need to know" basis, the milkman understood that I was not among the needy. Nor was he, for that matter. We were both a lot happier just doing what we were told.

Here, I feel the ghost of real pain. It's the same true voice I hear lifting off the page when students in my journalism classes respond to the world around them in unique, personal ways. A nonfiction writer's voice is always constructed, but sometimes its authenticity only rings out in response to events beyond the self.

I can't think of a better antidote to the digital media sphere we now confront. We're steeped in corporate interests that project themselves as the hip good guys, in virtual spaces where writers like Thompson have long since been co-opted and personal authenticity is easily faked. I'm a first-person journalist because I know I should question my own assumptions as well as the facts. I don't always like it. It can be extremely unfun when the facts prove me wrong. But if I admit I'm wrong and wonder why, that's when I move past the chimeras that mask so many truths.

It's just my humble opinion, but when a nonfiction writer expresses doubts, readers get permission to ask their own questions. First-person journalism isn't only informative and entertaining—the traditional hallmarks of journalism—or close to the bone. It's illuminating. It exposes our weaknesses in getting at the truth. For me, this shared vulnerability is what makes us human. Even in the midst of so much private information slopping over into public spaces, honest self-examination is far too rare, the most radical of fist shakes. It's where the real truth-telling begins.

Sources

The New Journalism by Tom Wolfe (Harper & Row, 1973).

"My Four Months as a Private Prison Guard" by Shane Bauer, *Mother Jones*, July/August 2016. www.motherjones.com/politics/2016/06/cca-private-prisons-corrections-corporation-inmates-investigation-bauer/

"My Family's Slave" by Alex Tizon, *Atlantic*, June 2017. www.theatlantic.com/magazine/archive/2017/06/lolas-story/524490/

"Parents of Micro Preemie Face Heart-Breaking Decisions" by Kelley Benham, *Tampa Bay Times*, April 17, 2013; originally published in December 9, 2012. www.tampabay.com/news/health/medicine/parents-of-micro-preemie-face-heart-wrenching-decisions/1264963/

"A Most American Terrorist: The Making of Dylann Roof" by Rachel Kaadzi Ghansah, *GQ*, August 21, 2017. www.gq.com/story/dylann-roof-making-of-an-american-terrorist

"In Harm's Way: A Plague of Unsolved Femicides Haunts Mexico (Letter From Ecatepec)" by Seth Harp, *Harper's*, March 2020. www.harpers.org/archive/2020/03/in-harms-way/

"Getting the Vaccine Along With a Glimmer of Hope" by Hannah Wise, *New York Times*, February 6, 2021. www.nytimes.com/2021/02/06/world/vaccine-first-person.html

"In the Islands" from *The White Album* by Joan Didion (Farrar, Straus and Giroux, 1979), p. 133.

"For a Generation, Writing in Joan Didion House Style" by Antonia Hitchens, *Wall Street Journal Magazine*, February 2, 2021. www.wsj.com/articles/joan-didion-style-what-i-mean-essay-11612282938

"What Makes Journalism Different Than Other Forms of Communication?" from "Journalism Essentials" on the American Press Institute website. www.american-pressinstitute.org/journalism-essentials/what-is-journalism/makes-journalism-different-forms-communication/

"Engagement and Relevance" in *The Elements of Journalism* by Bill Kovach and Tom Rosenstiel (Three Rivers Press, 2007/2014; originally published 2001), p. 189.

"What Is Creative Nonfiction?" by Lee Gutkind, Issue #0, "Online Only," *Creative Nonfiction*
website. www.creativenonfiction.org/online-reading/what-creative-nonfiction

On Writing Well by William Zinsser (HarperCollins, 2006; originally published in 1976),
p. 5.

"Journalists as Characters: Using First-Person Narration to Drive Stories" by Knvul
Sheikh, *The Open Notebook*, April 30, 2019. www.theopennotebook.com/2019/04/30/
journalists-as-characters-using-first-person-narration-to-drive-stories/

"Vice, and the Trend of First-Person Journalism" by Dustin Levy, *American Journalism Review*,
December 1, 2014. www.ajr.org/2014/12/01/vice-trend-first-person-journalism/

"Up From Pain" by Charles Blow, *New York Times*, September 19, 2014. www.nytimes.
com/2014/09/21/opinion/sunday/charles-blow-up-from-pain.html

"On Falling In and Out of Love With My Dad" by Natalie Rose Chenier, *Jezebel*, February
17, 2015. www.jezebel.com/on-falling-in-and-out-of-love-with-my-dad-1686108276

"The First-Person Industrial Complex" by Laura Bennett, *Slate*, September 14, 2015. www.
slate.com/articles/life/technology/2015/09/the_first_person_industrial_complex_how_
the_harrowing_personal_essay_took.html

"The Personal-Essay Boom Is Over" by Jia Tolentino, *New Yorker*, May 18, 2017. www.
newyorker.com/culture/jia-tolentino/the-personal-essay-boom-is-over

"Ten Days in the Life of a Tampon" by Moe, *Jezebel*, May 7, 2008. www.jezebel.com/
ten-days-in-the-life-of-a-tampon-388226

"Me, Myself, and I" by Jane Kramer, *New Yorker*, August 31, 2009. www.newyorker.com/
magazine/2009/09/07/me-myself-and-i

"Montaigne on Trial" by Adam Gopnik, *New Yorker*, January 8, 2017. www.newyorker.com/
magazine/2017/01/16/montaigne-on-trial

"Of Books," Chapter X of the second book of *Essays of Michel de Montaigne*, edited
by William Carew Hazlitt, translated by Charles Cotton (originally published 1877;
available through Project Gutenberg). www.gutenberg.org/files/3600/3600-h/3600-h.
htm#link2HCH0067

"How Personal Essays Conquered Journalism—and Why They Can't Cut It" by Eve Fairbanks, *Washington Post*, October 10, 2014. www.washingtonpost.com/posteverything/
wp/2014/10/10/how-personal-essays-conquered-journalism-and-why-they-cant-cut-it/

"Fear and Loathing in the Bunker" by Hunter S. Thompson, *New York Times*, January
1, 1974. www.nytimes.com/1974/01/01/archives/fear-and-loathing-in-the-bunker-no-
questions-asked-the-cheap-dream.html

"He Was a Crook" by Hunter S. Thompson, *Rolling Stone*, June 16, 1994. www.theatlantic.
com/magazine/archive/1994/07/he-was-a-crook/308699/

2 The ethics of personal reporting

Establishing what's true—and what isn't

I've always been an impatient reader. Way back in the seventh grade, I searched the La Vista Junior High School library shelves with one goal in mind: a first-person narrator. I loved stories told by the characters themselves. I relied on them to take me away from the strip malls of Hayward, California.

In the early 1970s, I decked myself in orange tie-dyed pants. I wore granny glasses, parting my hair in the middle, a dead ringer for John Lennon. I wasn't hip—at all—which is why I was in the library, but that's how I came across John Christopher's science-fiction series. I can't pinpoint exactly when I picked up *The White Mountains*. But I remember sunlight streaming through utilitarian windows, turning pages, hitting the first-person jackpot: *The clockman had visited us the week before, and I had been permitted for a time to look on while he cleaned and oiled the Watch. . . .*

As a tween, I would have said "I" stories were easier to read. Decades later, the adult-me says first-person stories feel more real. The trouble is that the realness conveyed by using a first-person voice doesn't make a story true. *The White Mountains* is labeled science fiction—a fictional boy in a fictional world describes the arrival of the clockman. As readers, we don't enter the book expecting this description or anything else that happens to be real. It's the writer's imagined world that hooks us.

The difference between nonfiction and fiction is not merely one of style. At the most basic level, nonfiction is about true events and fiction is made up. If you're writing a true story, then the experience you describe should be something that really happened at a particular time in a particular place. Rule 1: *Do not knowingly change facts or the sequence of what happened.* Once you do that, you're writing fiction.

Obvious as this distinction may seem, I can't tell you the number of times I've had to emphasize this definition of nonfiction with students. When I conclude (I like to think) with panache or at least irrefutable logic—*otherwise, you're writing fiction*—too many students do the equivalent of slapping their foreheads in shock.

In this chapter, I'll explore the tension between subjectivity and factual accuracy when writing nonfiction with an "I." Two broad trends—the increasing debate about objectivity in newsrooms and the rise of literary nonfiction in creative-writing programs—call for a frank discussion of ethics in personal

DOI: 10.4324/9781003132189-3

reporting. Since the New Journalism of the 1960s and 1970s, literary techniques have filtered into journalistic writing, and many writers no longer hide their biases behind the god-like reporting voice. That's a good thing. At the same time, ideas about what constitutes journalism are dramatically shifting. Traditional newspaper models have unraveled, and many readers are turned off by displays of omniscient expertise by journalists. That's a challenge.

My own biases should be obvious by now. I've never assumed news organizations were presenting an objective view of women, people of color, or anyone else who's traditionally been left out the publishing mainstream. I like passion and personal stories. But in *First-Person Journalism*, I'll keep returning to the need to stick to the facts, because too many literary writers, oral storytellers, postmodernists, and political operatives argue that our perception of reality amounts to more than "just the facts." Of course it does, whether it involves me asserting how I felt in junior high school or a U.S. president claiming his blamelessness. The truth will always be shaped by the person telling it. Yet that doesn't mean facts are irrelevant.

Even if many of us no longer trust experts, there's still a commonsense consensus that the truth is based on observed reality. Few people applaud fakes done to gain influence or to rip off consumers. When I ask students why they care about journalism, I hear an earnest desire for facts, not philosophical concerns about the nature of truth.

It's when the reality bending is unintentional that personal honesty gets slippery. Such honesty often involves admitting to your own uncertainties and biases in public—not a natural stance for the press. And yet, much as some reporters grumble about first-person stories, I value the straight-talking approach of journalistic prose and its reliance on what can be observed in the real world. In first-person journalism, I call this the *active "I" voice*, a way of speaking directly to readers that does not fake who the writer is.

Using the active "I" can be an antidote to many fictionalizing tricks that undercut the truthfulness of personal storytelling, whether in essays or in a celebrity influencer's Instagram account. Indeed, when feature writers narrate the "facts" of something they didn't witness, they can end up fictionalizing reality just as much as if they'd conjured the clockman. Take the following fiasco.

He said, she said

In November 2014, *Rolling Stone*, that longtime hotbed of New Journalism, published "A Rape on Campus" by Sabrina Rubin Erdely, setting off a storm of outrage. Erdely opened her now-infamous 9,000-word feature with a shocking narrative reconstruction of an alleged gang rape at a University of Virginia frat party. It was told from the point of view of the supposed victim, Jackie. Just days after publication, critics began poking holes in the factual basis of Jackie's story, and a few months later, in April 2015, *Rolling Stone* retracted the whole piece.

In its lengthy 2015 report on what went wrong, the Columbia School of Journalism points to the problem here of confirmation bias—of a reporter expecting to find something, then putting too much stock in a story told by a single unreliable source who confirmed her own attitudes. Unconscious bias no doubt set this reporter off in the wrong direction. But the narrative form of her opening scene—like fiction, it was meant to immerse readers in the action and to outrage them—also established expectations that couldn't be fulfilled.

What if Erdely had instead opened by framing events in her own voice? After the fallout from this story, I've long wondered what would have happened if the exposé began with her first-person perspective rather than a depiction of a rape and its victim that could have been ripped from a crime novel. Erdely did inject her first-person perspective into later sections of her feature. She visited the campus, made her own observations, talked to other people—and I wish she'd opened with something like this:

> *When Jackie told me, I was horrified. Her story shifted over time as she told it, but I wanted to believe her, because I thought something bad had happened to this young woman. Exactly what and how is the tricky part—but that's the trouble with abuse that occurs in the shadows. It ends up being "he said, she said," with those who have more power controlling the story. It's always about whose story you'd rather believe.*

That paragraph exists only in my imagination, of course. But such self-expressiveness isn't necessarily a sign of weakness or bad reporting. With hot-button topics, journalists always have attitudes, and most readers know that nobody is a completely objective observer. Owning up to the limits of your own knowledge can make the necessary point that we humans often get the facts wrong.

The limits of objectivity

Truth is a loaded word, whether it involves the facts of a major news story or the historical record. This book is a practical guide, so I'll only nod to a few turning points that have led to more subjectivity in journalism. I won't review the literature on truth in storytelling, which goes back at least to Thucydides. Many historians, philosophers, and journalists have trod this ground before me, including Lewis Raven Wallace in *The View From Somewhere*, a 2019 book that challenges "the myth of journalistic objectivity." As Henry Luce proclaimed with the founding of *Time* magazine in 1923: "Show me a man who thinks he's objective, and I'll show you a man who's deceiving himself."

In their influential guide *The Elements of Journalism*, which debuted in 2001, veteran journalists Bill Kovach and Tom Rosenstiel note that critics have been bashing journalistic claims of objectivity for decades on both ends of the political spectrum. (Wallace points to the conservative Luce, as well as abolitionist Horace Greeley, legendary Black editor T. Thomas Fortune of the *New York Age*, and a host of other muckrakers.) For Kovach and Rosenstiel, interpretation of facts for readers is basic to what journalists do. "The impartial voice employed by many news organizations—that familiar, supposedly neutral style of newswriting—is not a fundamental principle of journalism," they write, then follow up with this clincher:

> Journalists who select sources to express what is really their own point of view, and then use the neutral voice to make it seem objective, are engaged in deception. This damages the credibility of the whole profession by making it seem unprincipled, dishonest, and biased.

In the early 2000s, Jay Rosen of New York University and *PressThink* started calling the neutral voice the "View from Nowhere" (a phrase he attributed to the philosopher Thomas Nagel). Ron Rosenbaum put it more colorfully in 2002: "The third person is like the Great and Powerful Oz of journalism—a schlumpy little guy hiding behind a curtain, exaggerating his omniscience." Rosenbaum wrote this in a column about what was wrong with journalism teaching, at a time when the industry had begun yet another round of soul searching. Citing the "Fallacy of Third-Person 'Objectivity,'" he adds:

> Over and over again in J-school classes, students who had internalized this theology would ask me plaintively, "How can you justify using the first person—isn't the third person more 'objective'?" Or, literally, "Are you sure it's O.K. to use the first person?" I almost felt as if I were in Oliver Twist's orphanage: "Please, sir, can I have my voice?"

Part of what Rosenbaum calls the theology of journalism has to do with newsroom protocols. Not so long ago, beyond colorful columnists and some op-eds, self-references got the chop. After all, according to the doctrine of objectivity, journalists are supposed to be dispassionate observers. Except that feature writers (and their editors) always choose which facts and quotes to use. Such shaping doesn't make an article more objective, and when telling a gripping story takes precedence over verifying facts or providing context, readers are right to feel manipulated.

There's been muted discussion of first-person journalism for years in the online world, although in the past it's been cast as journalists stepping out of the way and letting sources tell the story, much in the manner of documentary filmmakers. At the Poynter Institute's website, Amy Gahran wondered as far back as 2005:

> Assuming that first-person, on-the-scene accounts of newsworthy events are likely to play a growing role in "the news," what advice could professional journalists offer to citizen journalists to make their accounts more useful to a wider audience?

Focusing on what's "useful," however, undercuts the value of taking an active, transparent role in the story you're reporting. First-person journalism means more than regurgitating what you observe or stepping out of the way to livestream citizen videos. In digital media, we now have far more access to raw documentation, whether it's images, video, or social-media reactions shared online. Yet journalists are still in the business of making meaning of raw footage, and it's here that a real sea change is underway.

Since 2013, the Black Lives Matter movement has spotlighted how much the so-called neutral voice is, in fact, a privileged white voice. Mass protests over the killing of George Floyd in May 2020 by Minneapolis police, caught on video by horrified bystanders, precipitated calls for change in many newsrooms, including the *Washington Post, New York Times*, and *Los Angeles Times*. In "A Reckoning Over Objectivity, Led by Black Journalists," a June 2020 opinion piece in the *New York Times*, Pulitzer-Prize winner Wesley Lowery makes clear why ignoring other perspectives has eroded factual accuracy:

> Since American journalism's pivot many decades ago from an openly partisan press to a model of professed objectivity, the mainstream has allowed what it considers objective truth to be decided almost exclusively by white reporters and their mostly white bosses. . . . The views and inclinations of whiteness are accepted as the objective neutral. When black and brown reporters and editors challenge those conventions, it's not uncommon for them to be pushed out, reprimanded or robbed of new opportunities.

This call for institutional change is not directly about permission to use the first-person voice. It focuses on inequities: the need to hire more writers of color and to reconsider who gets to decide which stories the public hears or what the actual facts are. A new generation of reporters embraces advocacy journalism to report on social injustices. In *The View From Somewhere*, Wallace also argues for bringing in perspectives long considered "deviant." One of few openly transgender journalists, Wallace describes being fired from the staff of American Public Media's *Marketplace* in early 2017 after publishing a personal blog post on *Medium* titled "Objectivity Is Dead, and I'm Okay With It." Remaining neutral, Wallace underscores in *The View From Somewhere*, doesn't equal good reporting:

> It is this idea of a detached, impartial journalist that I take the strongest issue with, and argue vehemently against, pushing instead for transparency and self-awareness.

Wallace freely admits to "the element of confirmation bias" in *The View From Somewhere*, given the book's focus on reporters who did and have bucked the hallowed status of objectivity. But such self-awareness also underpins first-person journalism. It indicates a new strategy, based on voice and emotional response, for countering the implicit biases that influence traditional coverage of contentious topics.

Other trends—such as the immersive focus on ordinary lives found in Walt Harrington's *Intimate Journalism* or calls for empathetic journalism to help humanize underprivileged communities—also point to the value of personal reporting. Still, I'm struck by the openly subjective way Wallace and others frame their own stories or the personal stories of sources. It's here that journalism stumbles into literary nonfiction.

Liars, thieves, and postmodernists

Not all stories benefit from subjectivity. Far too many commentators use personal stories to prove everything from new diet schemes to election fraud to claims that climate change isn't real. The tendency to skip over facts or other points of view is very human, but that doesn't excuse nonfiction writers of any stripe from avoiding them. When you add the first-person voice, the challenge intensifies. Most of us believe our own version of events; it takes pushing to question what we think we already know.

For this reason, professional journalism emphasizes fact checking and oversight. Working journalists are used to being edited. Editors vet story ideas, sources, and other evidence. Writers often end up consulting multiple sources that are never mentioned in an article itself. But even when there's an editorial process in place, it can go awry. "In retrospect, I wish somebody had pushed me harder," Erdely is quoted in the Columbia Journalism School report as saying of her editors at *Rolling Stone*.

But then there are the outright liars and thieves. In *Bunk*, Kevin Young's deeply researched 2017 history of "The Rise of Hoaxes, Humbug, Plagiarists, Phonies, Post-Facts, and Fake News," he spends almost a hundred pages of a long book on infamous journalistic fabrications from the 1990s and early 2000s. For Young, the fall and rise of a glitzy magazine writer like Ruth Shalit—who, when exposed for plagiarizing and faulty fact checking, used computer accidents and her girlish inexperience as an excuse—are harbingers of our current post-fact crisis. At the end of one chapter, Young notes that "when your first instinct at the sign of national tragedy is to tell your phone, not tell someone using that phone: then you have become as fictional as the world that you've created."

As he emphasizes, the most glaring fakes by white millennial reporters often involved false narratives about Black people, especially Black men as over-sexed predators. (At the time of this writing, Young directs the Smithsonian's National Museum of African American History and Culture.) He castigates Shalit's embrace of 1990s "racist chic" at the *New Republic*, but for him, Stephen Glass personified the "bland" male whiteness of that era, playing to the biases of an audience who easily believed his hackneyed stereotypes of everything from homeless guys to tech entrepreneurs.

Some critics have compared Erdely's mistakes in "A Rape on Campus" to those of Glass and other journalistic cons or plagiarizers like Shalit, Jayson Blair, Michael Finkel, and Jonah Lehrer. In November 2016, Erdely and Wenner Media, *Rolling Stone*'s publisher, lost a defamation suit brought by a former dean at the University of Virginia. But despite the harsh judgment (the jury awarded

$3 million in damages), there's still no clear evidence that Erdely intentionally lied to readers.

Comparing her to Glass, in particular, isn't fair. The subject of "Shattered Glass," a 1998 *Vanity Fair* exposé by Buzz Bissinger (and a 2003 movie of the same name), he spun a whole series of intricate fabrications—"the most sustained fraud in modern journalism," Bissinger claims. These days, Glass has competition in conning, but at the time, top editors at *Harper's* and the *New Republic* were taken in by his faked sources and websites. Even his fact-checking lists were designed to fool those vetting his stories.

Way back in the 1990s, I remember reading a *Harper's* first-person piece by Glass about his alleged experiences with telephone psychics. It read like a funny literary short story, which made it sound more convincing. Did I believe that amusingly stylish "I" voice at the time? Well, no—but I wanted to.

Such fictionalizations and the rise of "deep fakes" in digital media require constant vigilance. Yet writing off the disaster of "A Rape on Campus" to fakery ignores the real ethical hazards in this kind of magazine journalism: a lack of self-awareness in the way you're doing the reporting, an approach that presents the truth as objective when it's not.

In late 2020, the retraction of a "core" part of *Caliphate* by the *New York Times* underscores how confirmation bias and a highly opinionated reporter can influence the way a story is told. In *Caliphate*, a marquee 2018 podcast series hosted by award-winning terrorism reporter Rukmini Callimachi, *Times* editors acknowledged later that provocative claims by a dishonest source hadn't been corroborated at the time. The Canadian man in question told Callimachi and her team he'd joined ISIS in Syria, executing nonbelievers until he escaped. But two years after *Caliphate* episodes featuring him aired, he was arrested in Canada for lying about being a terrorist.

If factual errors made by journalists are now getting more public exposure, literary nonfiction has gone through its own chest-thumping stages—denial, anger, bargaining, depression, acceptance—about what the truth means. Here, again, I won't provide an exhaustive review of the "memoir craze" that began in the 1990s. I'll only highlight how the popularity of memoirs like Mary Karr's 1995 *The Liars' Club* drove a steady increase in nonfiction classes taught by creative-writing instructors.

The public comeuppance of James Frey in 2006 for fictionalizing aspects of his memoir *A Million Little Pieces*, a pick for Oprah Winfrey's book club, led to lots of nervous discussion in literary circles about how exacting you had to be. Frey had claimed he did serious jail time, among other tough-guy things, when in fact he hadn't. On her TV show, Winfrey turned on him in righteous anger, asking, "Why would you lie?" Frey apologized. Then Winfrey herself apologized a few years later for "ambushing" him. The upshot? His book, remarketed as a novel, is still in print. The movie version starring Aaron Taylor-Johnson and Billy Bob Thornton came out in 2018.

And creative nonfiction and memoir remain popular genres for both readers and aspiring writers. "Demand Booming on College Campuses for Creative

Writing," a 2017 AP story, reports that the number of creative-writing courses in general at Yale, for instance, had doubled over the previous five years. The story quotes Yale's creative-writing director, Richard Deming, as crediting the new interest to social media and saying, "This act of expressing one's voice in a public way—some people feel that they want to add craft, they want to hone those skills and take it to a place of more intensity."

Journalism schools, in contrast, saw shrinking enrollments during much the same time period, although interest perked up after the election of Donald Trump in 2016. Even so, more students are drawn to nonfiction classes in creative-writing programs, which focus on craft rather than the journalism basics of research and credible sourcing.

Despite the Frey outing, literary writers continue to play around with facts. Some have done this to tweak conventional sensibilities about truth and narrative. Others argue that history and the public record are themselves fabrications that reward those in power. As a second-wave feminist, I'm drawn to such arguments, and in writing this book I've had to confront my own discomfort with factual nitpicking. Authors I greatly admire, like Vivian Gornick, have defended fictionalizing scenes and dialogue in their memoirs.

"I embellish stories all the time," Gornick told Madeleine Schwartz in a 2014 *Believer* interview. "I do it even when I'm supposedly telling the unvarnished truth." In that same interview, she put it baldly—"So I lie. I mean, essentially—others would think I'm lying. But you understand. It's irresistible to tell the story." Gornick, a literary critic and one-time journalist at the *Village Voice*, shrugged off the need for "actuality," noting the aesthetic reasons for constructing a first-person narrator: "[O]n the page I create a consistency, a voice that must sound really reliable; whereas in person I am free—obviously!—to sound every which way."

Creating a reliable "I" voice is essential for first-person journalism. We all have public and private selves, and first-person writers do need to make decisions about how much to reveal about the internal forces driving them. But the honesty I'm calling for involves informing readers of how much you're *willing* to tell. Such transparency can establish that you aren't conveying your whole messy self. There's no need to fictionalize what you'd rather not say, let alone deceive readers intentionally.

I now balk when a writer doesn't clearly indicate to readers which parts of a nonfiction story have been imagined. Much as progressive literary writers may hate to admit it, plagiarists, con artists, and alt-right news outlets aren't the only culprits behind proliferating misinformation. Decades of postmodernism in academia have contributed to reader confusion about the need for facts or who is responsible for facts on the public record. It's here that nonfiction storytellers stumble into faking themselves.

Fictional selves versus true selves

Many journalists know how to write moving stories, vivid narratives, and artful descriptions. Yet in literary circles, first-person features are often called everything *but* journalism. (I've heard at least one writing instructor talk about a "*Modern Love* column personal kind of thing.") This vagueness about an author's intent can mislead creative nonfiction students into thinking that revising reality is acceptable. For this reason alone, journalists have a lot to teach other nonfiction writers.

Journalists also have a lot to learn about the art of self-expression, given how much they resist diving into their own muck. But in my experience, creative nonfiction writers and oral storytellers are the most confused about fact versus fiction. They're plagued by the insidious notion, promulgated by all those academic debates in the classroom about artistic truth, that a good story matters more than an honest "I" voice.

As a writer, I know personal honesty is one of the most difficult things to pull off in a public venue, especially if your goal is to entertain. But it's unethical to knowingly change a story you say is true. You're not only writing fiction; you *are* lying. You may believe saying "I" makes it so, but there are countless ways to hide behind that pronoun.

Describing your own life is hard. There's the uncertain nature of memory, with the story of what happened changing with repeated tellings. There's the difficulty of establishing a contemporary "I" who looks back, telling the story of a younger self. Then there's the temptation to change the action so it's more exciting or funnier or inspiring—to buff up what you did in order to come off better or to avoid being judged. We're all the heroes of our own stories, which inevitably leads to personal mythmaking.

Consider the work of David Sedaris, a popular first-person storyteller for everyone from *This American Life* listeners on NPR to *New Yorker* readers. Yet as far back as 2007, investigative reporter Alex Heard in the *New Republic* took on Sedaris's made-up facts. Regarding a North Carolina state mental hospital Sedaris says he volunteered in as a teenager (as recounted in "Dix Hill" from his 1997 collection *Naked*), Heard didn't believe some of the wilder anecdotes— and when he asked one registered nurse who'd worked there at the time about them, she replied of Sedaris: "He's lying through his teeth!" She pointed Heard to "the more obvious factual errors," such as photographs of the hospital in the 1970s that don't match the author's lurid description.

More telling, Heard tracked down Sedaris himself, noting that the author was "admirably open to fielding my most obnoxious questions about the hard-to-believe things I had found in some of his stories. He admitted that he had pumped up the Dix episode to tell a funnier yarn." This is Heard's response:

> That seems beyond the boundaries of comic exaggeration. It's fine to use absurdly embellished descriptions for laughs—this is an essential tool for any humorist. If I write, "I was so hung over, I threw up my own skeleton," you know I'm kidding. It's not fine to pretend—in a long and detailed scene—that you performed outlandish, dangerous tasks at a mental hospital when you didn't.

Sedaris has a distinctive first-person voice, and his use of humor could reflect who he really is. But his "realishness" has received repeated scrutiny in the press. Even if he's admitted to fictionalizing aspects of his own story, such a casual attitude toward crafting a larger-than-life persona has now affected (and infected) more than one generation of nonfiction writers. In *Bunk*, Kevin Young tellingly connects flat-out fake memoirs like Frey's with literary nonfiction that emphasizes individual subjectivity over fact:

> Once, the point of memoir or nonfiction like James Baldwin's or Joan Didion's was to say, *Look at me* as a way of saying *Look at us.* . . . Today's memoir all too often says, *Look at me and look no further.* Worse, it says, *Looky what happened to me.* And if it didn't happen, why not make it up?

With the rise of fakery and misinformation in digital media, intellectual debates about the truth don't address why readers have become so skeptical of journalists. Neither does the need to entertain a restless, screen-glazed audience. Letting yourself off the hook for facts is often just a rationalization for not doing enough research. That goes for reporters, as well as postmodernists. In academia, we can get into epistemology, but in the real world, most of us still prefer straight talk to nonfiction writers reconstructing reality to fit whatever an audience wants. Amid so many competing voices working hard to gain your trust—or to fool you—I believe readers are looking for honest self-reporters.

Embracing the active "I"

In my library anecdote at the opening of this chapter, I pinned down the place and time period in my life, but I tell you I'm not certain of the exact year ("the early 1970s"). Nor do I whip up a dramatic scene in which young Martha pulls *The White Mountains* off a library shelf, because I don't remember doing that.

I will admit to being tempted to write that scene. I did include a few specifics (a quote from *The White Mountains*, tie-dyed pants, granny glasses), but for those, I checked what I recalled. I stuck in the direct quote only after tracking down *The White Mountains* to verify that it's told in the first person. And I have photographic documentation of 13-year-old me. In a La Vista Junior High yearbook picture taken in the library, I sit hunched forward with shaggy hair and glasses, wearing those ugly pants and looking extremely ill at ease.

Compared with literary nonfiction instruction, the craft of first-person journalism has a lot to do with pinning down external reality. But it's also about creating a trustworthy first-person narrator. One signal quality of first-person journalism is an active "I" voice. This voice is conversational, part of the real world rather than elliptical, passive, or prone to internally driven claims unsupported by factual evidence (Box 2.1).

Box 2.1 What's a trustworthy "I" voice?

- There's a conversational rhythm.
- It's intimate, engaging with the reader.
- But it's also dispassionate, questioning everything.
- It actively responds to the world, events, ideas.
- It can be contrary, argumentative, ironic.
- It almost certainly conveys mixed feelings.
- But it comes to conclusions and offers insights.
- The voice is as honest as possible—a truth-speaker.

While *First-Person Journalism* focuses on feature writing and essays, you'll also find terrific examples of the active "I" voice in memoirs. For instance, in the award-winning bestseller *Educated*, Tara Westover makes sense of an array of confusing personal experiences just as first-person feature writers make sense of competing opinions. She opens the first chapter of her 2018 memoir by admitting how much her memory has played tricks on her:

> My strongest memory is not a memory. It's something I imagined, then came to remember as if it had happened. The memory was formed when I was five, just before I turned six, from a story my father told in such detail that I and my brothers and sister had each conjured our own cinematic version, with gunfire and shouts.

This imagined scene prefigures her coming of age in Idaho, in which she has to reconstruct her own belief system to escape her survivalist family in their off-the-grid cabin. Her father's "story" was about Ruby Ridge, when white supremacist Randy Weaver and his family faced off in another Idaho cabin against the FBI. The siege went on for days, with several people killed. A cautionary tale as told by Westover's father, it fed his anti-government paranoia. Yet Westover herself grew up questioning it all, and her consistent tone and response to the world in *Educated* is a unifying force for readers.

Box 2.2 True questions

What makes a personal voice believable?

What makes my first-person story accurate?

What will readers expect when they read this story?

How do I know what I know?

In Chapter 1, I posed two *true questions*, and to those I'll add a third and fourth: "What will readers expect when they read my story?" and the classic "How do I know what I know?" (Box 2.2). Just as our behavior as social beings affects others, the stories we tell impact those who read them. An ethical first-person journalist treats them as fellow humans with questions of their own—and a right to ask questions.

"I know this because" is a powerful statement. Readers want to believe in your "I." They may disagree with your claims, but they'll keep reading if you provide good evidence in addition to moving them emotionally. The key is to be honest about why you believe what you do and to let them know when you're imagining or dreaming about events rather than documenting reality. In Phillip Lopate's essay "The State of Nonfiction Today," part of his excellent 2013 writing guide *To Show and to Tell*, he frames it like so:

> We may never be in possession of the truth, but as nonfiction writers we can try to be as honest as our courage permits. Honest to the world of facts outside ourselves, honest in reporting what we actually felt and did, and finally, honest about our own confusions and doubts.

This could be my credo for *First-Person Journalism*. The best first-person stories do include flights of imagination, gorgeous descriptions, and detailed memories. My "I" voice here doesn't reveal every aspect of who I am or how I experience the world. But most readers understand that a nonfiction writer isn't reproducing an exact replica of life or the inner self. The truth comes in self-awareness about your limitations as an observer and empathy for your audience, even if you think they'll argue back.

The truth comes in not faking yourself. I feel very old-fashioned saying this, but I'll take the risk: be honest. Tell readers who you are and your reasons for saying *this story is true*. One of the biggest services we truth-tellers do is to reveal we're not all-knowing. So, explain why you care enough to question yourself and to keep discovering more with every story you write.

Sources

The White Mountains by John Christopher (Simon & Schuster, 1967).

"Rolling Stone and UVA: The Columbia Graduate School of Journalism Report" by Sheila Coronel, Steve Coll, and Derek Kravitz, *Rolling Stone*, April 5, 2015. www.rollingstone. com/culture/culture-news/rolling-stone-and-uva-the-columbia-university-graduate-school-of-journalism-report-44930/

"Rolling Stone and the Backlash Against Advocacy Journalism" by Martha Nichols, *VIDA: Women in Literary Arts*, June 4, 2015. www.vidaweb.org/rolling-stone-backlash-advocacy-journalism/

The View From Somewhere: Undoing the Myth of Journalistic Objectivity by Lewis Raven Wallace (The University of Chicago Press, 2019).

"Both Sides Now: The Myth of Media Objectivity" (review of *The View From Somewhere*) by Ari M. Brostoff, *Bookforum*, December/January 2020. www.bookforum.com/print/2604/the-myth-of-media-objectivity-23759

The Elements of Journalism: What Newspeople Should Know and the Public Should Expect by Bill
    Kovach and Tom Rosenstiel (Three Rivers Press, 2007; originally published 2001 and
    updated in 2014), p. 83.

"The View from Nowhere: Questions and Answers" by Jay Rosen, *PressThink*, November 10,
    2010. www.pressthink.org/2010/11/the-view-from-nowhere-questions-and-answers/

"Columbia's J-School Needs to Consider Trollopian Retooling" by Ron Rosenbaum, *Zoned
    for Debate*, Number 1, 2002, a New York University "webforum." (The column originally
    appeared in the *New York Observer*, August 26, 2002.)

"Can First-Person Accounts Be 'Journalism'?" by Amy Gahran, Poynter Institute website,
    August 3, 2005. www.poynter.org/reporting-editing/2005/can-first-person-accounts-
    be-journalism/

"Rancor Erupts in 'LA Times' Newsroom Over Race, Equity and Protest Coverage"
    by David Folkenflik, *All Things Considered*, NPR, June 15, 2020. www.poynter.org/
    reporting-editing/2005/can-first-person-accounts-be-journalism/

"A Reckoning Over Objectivity, Led by Black Journalists" by Wesley Lowery, *New York
    Times*, June 23, 2020. www.nytimes.com/2020/06/23/opinion/objectivity-black-jour-
    nalists-coronavirus.html

"Objectivity Is Dead, and I'm Okay With It" by Lewis Raven Wallace, *Medium*, Janu-
    ary 27, 2017. www.medium.com/@lewispants/objectivity-is-dead-and-im-okay-with-
    it-7fd2b4b5c58f

Intimate Journalism: The Art and Craft of Reporting Everyday Life by Walt Harrington (Sage
    Publications, 1997).

"The Empathetic Newsroom: How Journalists Can Better Cover Neglected Communities"
    by P. Kim Bui, American Press Institute website, April 26, 2018. www.americanpressin-
    stitute.org/publications/reports/strategy-studies/empathetic-newsroom/

"Journalism and the Power of Emotions" by Lene Bech Sillesen, Chris Ip, and David Uberti,
    Columbia Journalism Review, May/June 2015. www.cjr.org/analysis/journalism_and_the_
    power_of_emotions.php

Bunk: The Rise of Hoaxes, Humbug, Plagiarists, Phonies, Post-Facts, and Fake News by Kevin
    Young (Graywolf Press, 2017), pp. 122, 316, 338–339, 341.

"CORRECTING THE RECORD; *Times* Reporter Who Resigned Leaves Long Trail of Decep-
    tion" by Dan Barry, David Barstow et al. (public admission of Jayson Blair's fabrications
    and plagiarism), *New York Times*, May 11, 2003. www.nytimes.com/2003/05/11/us/
    correcting-the-record-times-reporter-who-resigned-leaves-long-trail-of-deception.html

"Jonah Lehrer Remembers the Moment His Career Was Shattered" by Benjamin Mul-
    lin, Poynter Institute website, February 6, 2017. www.poynter.org/ethics-trust/2017/
    jonah-lehrer-remembers-the-moment-his-career-was-shattered/

"*Rolling Stone* Settles with Former U-Va. Dean in Defamation Case" by T. Rees Shapiro and
    Emma Brown, *Washington Post*, April 11, 2017. www.washingtonpost.com/local/educa-
    tion/rolling-stone-settles-with-u-va-dean-in-defamation-case/2017/04/11/5a564532-1f
    02-11e7-be2a-3a1fb24d4671_story.html

"Five Years on, the Lessons From the *Rolling Stone* Rape Story" by Lucia Graves, *Guard-
    ian*, December 29, 2019. www.theguardian.com/society/2019/dec/29/rolling-stone-
    rape-story-uva-five-years

"Shattered Glass" by Buzz Bissinger, *Vanity Fair*, September 1998 (updated in 2007). www.
    vanityfair.com/magazine/1998/09/bissinger199809

"*New York Times* Retracts Core of Hit Podcast Series *Caliphate* on ISIS" by David Folkenflik,
    Morning Edition, NPR, December 18, 2020. www.npr.org/2020/12/18/944594193/
    new-york-times-retracts-hit-podcast-series-caliphate-on-isis-executioner

"Author Is Kicked Out of Oprah Winfrey's Book Club" by Edward Wyatt, *New York Times*, January 27, 2006. www.nytimes.com/2006/01/27/books/27oprah.html

"Oprah Apologizes to James Frey," video from *The Oprah Winfrey Show*, OWN, May 17, 2011. www.oprah.com/own-oprahshow/oprah-apologizes-to-author-james-frey-video

"Where Is James Frey in 2019?" by Johnny Brayson, *Bustle*, December 5, 2019. www.bustle.com/p/where-is-james-frey-in-2019-the-a-million-little-pieces-author-is-plenty-busy-19400852

"Demand Booming on College Campuses for Creative Writing" by Michael Melia, *AP News*, April 7, 2017. www.apnews.com/article/286ad20c060f4e57b545d1dcd5793c44

"The State of American Journalism Education" in *Above and Beyond: Looking at the Future of Journalism Education* by Dianne Lynch, a Knight Foundation Report, 2015. www.knight-foundation.org/features/je-the-state-of-american-journalism-education/

"A Trump Effect at Journalism Schools? Colleges See a Surge of Admissions" by Nick Anderson, *Washington Post*, September 16, 2018. www.washingtonpost.com/local/education/a-trump-effect-at-journalism-schools-colleges-see-a-surge-in-admissions/2018/09/16/18497156-b2b2-11e8-a20b-5f4f84429666_story.html

"We Knew We Were Not Liberated and Were Never Going to Be Liberated. But We Knew What Liberation Was," an interview with Vivian Gornick by Madeleine Schwartz, *The Believer*, March 24, 2014. www.believermag.com/logger/2014-03-24-we-knew-we-were-not-liberated-and-were-never/

"This American Lie" by Alex Heard, *New Republic*, March 19, 2007. www.newrepublic.com/article/63463/american-lie-midget-guitar-teacher-macys-elf-and-thetruth-about-david-sedaris

"The David Sedaris Dilemma: A Fine Line Between 'Realish' and Real" by Paul Farhi, *Washington Post*, May 13, 2012. www.washingtonpost.com/lifestyle/style/david-sedariss-exaggerations-in-memoirs-npr-nonfiction-program-raise-questions/2012/05/13/gIQA-m9QONU_story.html

Educated: A Memoir by Tara Westover (Random House, 2018), p. 3.

To Show and to Tell: The Craft of Literary Nonfiction by Phillip Lopate (Simon & Schuster, 2013), p. 13.

Part II

Developing an active "I" voice

Question your own kneejerk reactions while also passionately engaging with the world. Don't stuff a story with fancy language or melodrama or your cleverness just to impress an audience. Fabrication and self-deception easily become habitual. Instead, respond to everything you encounter. The rust on your car door. The swirl of opalescent light on a puddle after it rains.

DOI: 10.4324/9781003132189-4

3 Locating your passion

What do I want to write about?

Back in the 1980s, while I worked as an educational software developer, I took classes at San Francisco State University for my master's degree in creative writing. I reveled in the mix of logic and creativity, yet it was also a time of reckoning for me as a young writer. In my graduate workshops, I tried out a cavalcade of literary styles and personas, none of which felt like a good fit. I loved writing but felt trapped by the expectations of an academic program and my own desire to create new worlds.

One morning, I was struck by a simple realization. I recall standing in my bedroom, staring down at piles of notes on my yellow milk-crate nightstand. They were all about a science-fiction novel I was also writing, undercover and half-ashamed, the thing that obsessed me far more than any literary short story or poem I'd done for school. And then it came: *I should write what I want to read.*

I liked poetry and Flannery O'Connor, but I loved science fiction. I loved *Star Trek.* I loved long, complicated social novels like *Middlemarch, Bleak House,* and *Anna Karenina.* The classic *New Yorker* short story bored me. I did *not* love Thomas Pynchon or Ann Beattie, much as I'd been trying to channel their style into a novel about another planet.

This realization is now self-evident, but it wasn't at the time. As I stared at my scribbled notes, it hit me with visceral force. I didn't go on to publish the novel, but I did learn a lesson that's mattered far more in my writing career. My over-stuffed fictional plot incorporated topics that still obsess me: gender construction, social hierarchies, inequality, biases in storytelling. There, I found my passion as a nonfiction writer.

Passion, the element of first-person journalism we'll explore in this chapter, is a big part of what makes an individual writer's voice feel authentic, and locating your passion doesn't start with what other people want. It starts with what *you* care about.

In learning how to write essays and cite academic sources in school, most of us have been trained to write objectively about facts. We use the dry language of academic researchers or try to sound more intellectual with fancy words—or, if we're accustomed to social media, we use marketing clichés that are a stand-in for real feeling. We're not prisoners of our passions so much as we're prisoners of the opinions of others. We write what we think we're supposed to write,

DOI: 10.4324/9781003132189-5

which can stop us dead as storytellers. We don't tell personal stories that engage readers because we don't trust our own feelings.

Of all the inner baggage first-person nonfiction writers carry, this can be the heaviest. Much of digital publishing now reinforces shallow emotional responses. Writers and readers end up trapped between chirpy life-hacking advice and ironic commentary. We've become accustomed to cute or faux-angry memes or gorgeous photos of influencers living gorgeous lives. We click our likes in an instant, then move on.

None of this has real impact, even if you appreciate the gorgeous photos or nod to the irony with a wink emoji. Self-help cheerleading can be so generic it appears machine-generated (and just might be). And much as a self-aware ironic perspective can be fun, it's emotionally distancing. It makes it easy for first-person storytellers to avoid strong feelings or to create a polished illusion of control. At worst, such superficial writing exhibits a lack of compassion for others who do express their feelings.

In this first practice chapter, I'll take you through a sequence of *voice lessons* to help identify story ideas that matter to you. Some ideas will be based on your personal interests; others may emerge through writing about strong feelings. Locating your passion as a writer is harder than casting a judgmental, ironic eye on the world, but it's how genuine joy, grief, or desire light up your words—and light up your readers. Personal storytelling requires you, the writer, to be emotionally involved.

Chapter 3 also introduces two key practices in this book: the *process notebook* and *response papers*. In many lessons, I'll ask you to reflect on an exercise in your notebook. What you write in that notebook isn't meant for an audience. It's a tool for digging deeper into what you're thinking and feeling. The same goes for responses to readings by published writers. Unlike book reports or academic essays, your response papers are meant to be personally voiced and passionately engaged with your reading.

Don't bore yourself

Let's start with generating ideas. As a practical matter, this can seem daunting, especially if you're just starting out as a freelance journalist or blogger. Recently, when I did a Google search on the phrase "blogger's block," I turned up more than half a million results. Even veteran journalists hit dry spells, but as we'll see, ongoing research habits, unsexy as that sounds, often come to the rescue.

There are bad approaches to idea generation, though, especially when it comes to first-person authenticity. They invoke "hacks" for what you "should" do in order to keep other human users and Google happy. They often involve posting daily online, doing boatloads of social media to drive traffic (aka readers) like virtual cattle to your site, and consulting apps to track the most popular keywords and topics in online searches.

A bullet list of hacks based on apps—not to mention all the reasons why I *should* be writing all the time to build an audience—makes this writer rebel. It highlights what I'm *not* doing. It assumes that blocks can be broken by rationality or willpower alone, and it's not exactly original advice. In a 1903 essay titled

"Getting into Print," Jack London advised, "Don't loaf and invite inspiration; light out after it with a club." Anthony Trollope famously set daily word counts: 250 words every 15 minutes for three hours a day, according to his autobiography:

> This division of time allowed me to produce over ten pages of an ordinary novel volume a day, and if kept up through ten months, would have given as its results three novels of three volumes each in the year.

Ugh. There's no dearth of advice online in posts like "How Famous Writers Overcome Writer's Block and Reawaken Their Creativity" (its "7 strategies," from Trollope to Toni Morrison, are an "8 min read," *Medium* calculates). Trollope did write 47 novels.

The trouble is that quantity is not the only goal. The digital version of such advice often emphasizes tools for optimizing the process, as if a lack of inspiration is a technical problem to be solved. This is backward. If the point is inspiration, all the algorithms in the world won't get at the human quirks that drive a complex emotional response. Many of us have already internalized messages about pleasing others to be relatable. Now we've got Google to contend with and ever more demands to step up the pace. We fake it until we make it, but fakery is not how you come up with an authentic personal story.

As a journalist, I know that fakery is everywhere. Yet as a writing instructor, I believe faking yourself is a much more fundamental problem. Advice about churning out content as fast as you can—and relying on digital genies for ideas—results in eye-glazing posts that all sound the same.

And so we've arrived at an essential first-person rule: *Don't bore yourself.*

Apathy, a self-protective response, is the biggest block to coming up with genuinely inspiring ideas. Instead of ending up bored, try flipping the "Boredom Cascade" of thoughts around (Box 3.1). When you get to *Writing? OMG! It's scary*, that's your beginning. If you allow yourself to feel the fear, you're tapping into a personal experience that has real weight. Write about your fear, what it means, what it feels like in your hands and feet, what it makes you remember, and what scares you most. Write for five minutes or an hour, as much as you can tolerate and only for yourself. I bet you'll arrive somewhere you didn't expect—and you won't be bored.

Box 3.1 The Boredom Cascade

Writing? OMG! It's scary!

What should I do? What should I say?

Nobody cares what I have to say.

The things I like are stupid. They're boring.

I have to write about what other people like.

Now I'm bored.

You are your best idea machine. For example, I've had students in my journalism classes write about the phenomenon of Disney pin collecting because they were dedicated pin collectors. Others have examined their passion for a particular football team and what it means, their survivor's guilt after 9/11, or helping victims of sexual abuse as a front-line responder during the 2020 coronavirus pandemic. In all these cases, I gave them permission to write in the first-person voice about something they care about. But my ultimate goal was and is for them to give themselves permission.

Voice Lesson 1

1 **Your process notebook:** Start this notebook by making a list of your interests, whether it's Indonesian cuisine, artisanal beer, ice hockey, or makeup videos. Time yourself—take just a minute or so to jot down your interests (and no more than Trollope's 15 minutes). Go with your immediate gut feelings rather than over-thinking it.
2 **Sticky ideas:** Next, take a small pad of sticky notes and write each of your interests on a separate note—again, do it fast, using just one word or a few words per interest.
3 **Your idea room:** Then stick your notes all over your desk or around your bedroom. Et voilà! You've got a whole room of potential ideas.

Don't perform your emotions

Another block to tapping into your passions is a misconception about expressing feelings in writing. We're motivated to tell our own stories for many reasons, and sometimes writing leads to an emotional catharsis. At best, such stories are also cathartic for readers. But too often, emotion-drenched verbiage reads like a personal journal entry, insular and overheated and crammed with therapeutic platitudes. It lacks the self-awareness of what will make an individual story meaningful to others.

In coming to grips with personal trauma, there's great therapeutic value to private journaling and what psychologist James Pennebaker and others have called expressive writing. In the 2016 book *Opening Up by Writing It Down,* Pennebaker and his coauthor Joshua Smyth note in the first chapter:

> Whereas harboring secrets is potentially harmful, confronting our personal thoughts and feelings can have remarkable short- and long-term health benefits. Confession, whether by writing or talking . . . can neutralize many of the problems of secrets. Talking or writing about upsetting things can influence our basic values, our daily thinking patterns, and our feelings about ourselves.

I've long believed that first-person writing is therapeutic. But at a writer's conference a few years back, as I staffed the table for my literary magazine at the time and explained why I love personal stories, one woman sneered, "Writing is *not* therapy." She was middle-aged, white, with a mop of brownish hair; she probably wore glasses. Her appearance was similar to my own—she may well have been another editor or freelance writer—yet she treated me like a kid who didn't know any better.

Her vehemence took me aback, although it wasn't surprising given the professional focus of that conference. At the time, I think I said something noncommittal like "let's agree to disagree." Still, elitist comments such as this irritate me. *Of course writing is therapy. It always is,* I could have told her. And yet, if we'd actually had a real exchange, I would have then underscored another first-person writing rule:

The process of telling your story is not the same as the end result.

Too many young writers assume that the more emotionally they write about their lives, the better. After generating a bunch of words about what they feel, they hit "publish" for their post, without thinking about the impact of those words on anybody else. They're expressing themselves. That's what makes it authentic. Case closed.

Alas, no. A first draft of what you feel isn't the most authentic; it's usually the opposite. Finding your real story often involves a lot of lousy writing—therapy jargon ("I'm getting in touch with my inner child"), expositional glosses and clichés ("the world is full of winner and losers, but winning doesn't matter in the end"), pumped-up self-help ("I need to ratchet up the therapy transfer"), and feeling labels ("I'm so depressed, scared, hungry, [fill in the blank]"). In first drafts, most of us begin by performing our emotions. Even if we're scribbling in a private diary, we've all got an inner audience of judges or therapists. We say what we think they want to hear.

Here's another version of my previous writing rule: *No first drafts.* Self-editing is not the same as self-censorship. Don't confuse the writing process with the outcome. Personal stories that feel authentic in print are anchored by the self-awareness of the writer in revising, shaping, and cutting away all the junk that first emerges in the telling.

The therapeutic practice of expressive writing, as defined by Pennebaker and Smyth ("people typically write about an upsetting experience for 15 or 20 minutes a day for three or four days"), isn't the same as doing "morning pages" or freewrites to prime the creative pump. But confronting painful material might be what eventually leads you to a personal essay or an idea for a feature. If you release those secrets, you may also release your fear and shame, giving yourself permission to *start* writing.

Voice Lesson 2

1   **Express yourself:** In your process notebook, do 15 or 20 minutes of expressive writing—journaling about emotions or difficult experiences for therapeutic purposes.

2   ***Deep breaths:*** Take a 15-minute break at least (and a longer break is fine). If possible, stare out the window, take deep breaths, have a snack, or otherwise be kind to yourself.

3   ***Your second idea room:*** After your break, repeat Voice Lesson 1. Again, jot down a list of story ideas without thinking about it too much. Compare this list to your previous list. In your notebook, describe how the two lists differ and why you think they do.

Don't scream at readers

Expressing joy or pain in writing has long been viewed as problematic in topical nonfiction. For one thing, it's a challenge to the authority of traditional publishers and news organizations, and emotional language can be a legitimate fist-shake against the dry rules of academia. The current epidemic in exclamation pointing and ALL CAPS in social media illustrates just how much we humans want to express our feelings.

My college-age son tells me "nobody" of his generation uses periods in texts. According to him, the hard stop sounds too harsh or angry. Many older writers tell similar anecdotes about their kids, as Gretchen McCulloch confirms in *Because Internet*, her 2019 book about "Understanding the New Rules of Language." Informal digital writing generates an everchanging array of typographical conventions to convey emotional tone, and periods as markers of "passive-aggressive" attitude, she notes, had hit the zeitgeist by 2013. (A *New Republic* piece that year was titled "The Period Is Pissed.")

McCulloch, a linguist, focuses on how language evolves over time, and she's rightfully irritated by old-fashioned writing rules (or new-fashioned spell- and grammar-checkers based on those rules) that define "Proper English" or any other language. She distinguishes between the formal style of published writing—what older generations thought of as Writing with a capital W—and the informal style of the internet, which is more akin to spoken language. Think exclamation points; stretched words ("NOOOO!!"); and, of course, emoji, which we use "less to describe the world around us," McCulloch writes, "and more to be fully ourselves in an online world."

The idea of being fully ourselves online is lovely, yet it's also troubling. Self-expression is great in first-person nonfiction, but only if it rings true. The wonderful ease provided by virtual communication often reinforces emotionality for emotion's sake. It comes off as artificial because the context for an individual life is missing. Popularity, as defined by machine learning, tends toward extremes; that's what search algorithms are designed to promote. The result is that everybody seems to be feverishly worked up about everything and nothing. Too many digital writers scream whatever they think, as in:

It reinforces emotionality for emotion's sake!
It comes off as artificial!!
It's not about anything!!!!!!!!

This book *is* about something: personal nonfiction writing for magazines and other journalistic venues. Revising and editing are part of reporting craft, even if that restrains creative language use. We are social beings, and we're always performing for others in writing or speaking—but just because you can blurt a text in nanoseconds doesn't make it true or the best expression of what you feel. *First-Person Journalism* is not about the mechanics of writing style versus informal social-media posts. My emphasis is on first-person writers moving beyond platitudes to a deeper analysis of the world.

Given the constant churn of digital misinformation, such analysis has become crucial to the way we convey the truth to readers. In a sobering 2017 *Quartz* article, "This Is How Your Fear and Outrage Are Being Sold for Profit," Tobias Rose-Stockwell reviews research on how much emotional expression online has now been monetized via corporate-controlled algorithms. The algorithm for Facebook's News Feed, he writes, "is a robot editor [that] is far better at capturing attention than human editors." Social-media algorithms track what you do online, and as Rose-Stockwell notes:

> Emotional responses are one of the most prominent ways to gauge the value of a post, and the easiest things for the News Feed Editor to map, measure, and provide more of. These are emotional hijacks—based on affective engagement.

"Affective engagement" is the digital version of "if it bleeds, it leads" from print newspapering. The practice of going for the gut isn't new, but the impact of nonhuman algorithms deciding what to emphasize with no accountability is far more insidious. Rose-Stockwell cites a 2017 study by an online content marketing firm (BuzzSumo) of 100 million digital headlines, in which many that did best on Facebook included phrases like "make you cry," "tears of joy," "shocked to see," or "will make you."

In his useful online guide *Web Literacy for Student Fact-Checkers*, Michael Caulfield emphasizes "*Check your emotions*" when evaluating hot-button claims, especially in social media: "Every time content you want to share makes you feel rage, laughter, ridicule, or even a heartwarming buzz, spend 30 seconds fact-checking."

It's far too easy to be emotionally manipulated online or to do the manipulating. If you're writing online, you'll be influenced to emote—to do the digital equivalent of a scream—just to get attention. You may become an influencer yourself, reshaping who you are on Instagram or a blog to attract more followers, but such shapeshifting doesn't amount to authenticity. Instead of questioning what you really want, you let popularity float you along. If becoming a writer of true stories is your goal, you'll end up wiggling away from the "true" part, maybe unaware you've done so.

Regardless of internet norms, I use exclamation points sparingly, even in personal communication. I'm old school; I believe words should speak for themselves. And I don't want robot editors determining what I or my readers feel. In personal stories, there are often strong emotions at play—lust, greed, terror, outrage—but the writing that moves readers comes down to lived, difficult-to-quantify human experience.

Consider how *New York Times* columnist Charles Blow writes about his emotional response to sexual trauma. In "Up From Pain," a personal essay adapted from his 2014 memoir *Fire Shut Up in My Bones*, Blow opens by recalling a phone call from his mother when he was in college. She told him somebody wanted to talk to him, then passed the phone to an older cousin of Blow's. This man had sexually assaulted Blow when he was seven. Yet Blow recalls this cousin acting "as if nothing had ever happened," asking over his mother's phone, "What's going on, boy?" Blow's response:

> I don't recall saying anything or even hanging up. I flung myself down the stairs of the apartment, wearing only pajama pants and a T-shirt. I burst out of the door and bolted to the car.
>
> I was engulfed in an irrepressible rage. Everything in me was churning and pumping and boiling. All reason and restraint were lost to it. I was about to do something I wouldn't be able to undo. Bullets and blood and death. I gave myself over to the idea.

This is powerful emotional writing, but there's not an exclamation point in sight. Imagine that excerpt with exclamation points ("I burst out of the door and bolted to the car! I was engulfed in an irrepressible rage!"). As soon as you do, I hope it's clear how artificial the words now sound. For all the emotional intensity of what Blow is describing, his restraint in the telling is what keeps us with him. He manages the tricky balance of documenting what he feels yet reflecting on what it means.

If you're writing about traumatic experiences or anything that triggers strong emotions, it may feel natural to use exclamation points or ALL CAPS. But counterintuitive as it seems, conveying your passion for a topic often requires analytical distance, both in stating what you believe and in assessing facts. As a writer, honor the pause between feeling and thinking. Work with it, uncomfortable as it may be to second-guess why you're angry or laughing away a problem with an emoji. Passionate first-person nonfiction relies on more than chatty expressiveness. It requires self-reflection: the ability to question yourself and the way the world makes you feel *and* think.

Voice Lesson 3

1 **Exclamation editing:** Copy a recent piece of your own writing that has exclamation points into a new file. This piece can be anything from a published article or blog post to an email or a text message. In your file, remove all the exclamation points.

2 **Self-reflection:** Has the meaning of your piece changed just by taking out exclamation points or emoji? If so, why? In your notebook, describe any changes in tone and style.

3   **Response paper:** Read Charles Blow's "Up From Pain" and write a brief response. In one or two pages, discuss how his piece works and why it affects you, including any experiences of your own it sparks. (If you don't have access to Blow's *New York Times* column, try the electronic resources available through your local school or public library.)

Cultivating curiosity: Passion for facts

So, you're a journalist. You don't have any problem with all this emotional language stuff because it was beaten out of you on the job or in J-School. Journalists, rather than being saddled with exclamation-pointed feeling, have the opposite problem—insisting on the need to be objective and impersonal. It's another block to writing in the first-person voice, one I'll keep nudging those who shy away from "I" to get past.

But reporters who love the profession are also motivated by curiosity, and curiosity is at the heart of good first-person nonfiction. Asking questions is what you do in the pause between feeling—*yowza can this be happening I have no idea if this is real*—and thinking about the larger implications. First-person journalists balance feelings with facts, which may seem the opposite of passion. But the drive to find those facts can be very passionate, if not obsessive, especially when an investigation drags on for years.

Take Michelle McNamara and her quest to track down the identity of the elusive Golden State Killer—a name she gave a California sexual predator and serial killer who'd eluded the authorities for decades. In her 2018 book *I'll Be Gone in the Dark*, published posthumously, McNamara detailed her hunt through the records, sometimes conducted after midnight on a laptop in her daughter's playroom (husband Patton Oswald pieced together a few sections of the book—which became a 2020 HBO documentary series—from her notes). McNamara wasn't a working journalist but part of a growing number of amateur true-crime researchers who obsess over cold cases. Yet she meticulously recorded every lead she checked and detective she interviewed:

> I scoured thousands of pages of 1970s-era police files. I pored over autopsy reports. That I should do this surrounded by a half-dozen stuffed animals and a set of miniature pink bongos didn't strike me as unusual. I'd found my searching place, as private as a rat's maze. Every obsession needs a room of its own. Mine was strewn with coloring paper on which I'd scribbled down California penal codes in crayon.

The Golden State Killer began as the "East Area Rapist" in Sacramento and elsewhere in the mid-1970s, then morphed into the "Visalia Ransacker" and the "Original Night Stalker" in Southern California in the early 1980s. But McNamara's investigation and the splashy moniker she came up with to snag public attention helped keep the case alive. Joseph James DeAngelo was finally arrested in April 2018 after her death. DeAngelo, an ex-cop, was pinned down because the police gained access to his genetic information through the open-source site GEDmatch.

Cultivating curiosity isn't just an intellectual exercise. Too many aspiring first-person writers avoid research, as if the only endpoint is an academic paper. Yet no matter how personal your story, tracking down the facts often leads to the unexpected, and unexpected twists aren't boring. Delve into all the weird, offbeat facts, then get down what the weirdness means to you and other people. Far from canceling out passion or personal storytelling, curiosity brings your passions to life.

Good nonfiction story ideas feel electric as you're working on them. You grab hold, and it's hard to let go. When you start down the reporting trail, you'll hit dead ends, but you'll also be excited, even disturbed by what you uncover. Prosaic as it sounds, reporting and doing background research is the best way to generate new story ideas.

Here's an example of my own, based on two lists of ideas I came up with while practicing Voice Lessons 1 and 2 in this chapter. For the first round, I set a timer for two minutes and jotted down a list of my interests on a piece of scrap paper. My first list appears in Box 3.2. These topics are all personally meaningful—I'm a birder, and I grew up in California. "Teaching," "journalism," and "books" are professional and personal interests. Others sprang to mind because of my circumstances at the time: sheltering in place with my husband and son in the spring of 2020 in Cambridge, Massachusetts, during the rise of the coronavirus pandemic. I craved a stay at a retreat center; I was taking long bike rides to get outside and work off the stress.

Most of the ideas remain unfocused, however. I could write hundreds of features about "journalism" or "parenting," for example, and no one story could cover every nuance of such broad topics. To focus them, they need specific hooks.

Box 3.2 Martha's list, round one

birds

Italy

California

parenting

cooking vegetarian gourmet

biking—aerobically

needlepoint/cross-stitch

teaching

journalism

books

women's studies

travel writing

clouds

yoga

retreat centers

After making the first list, I spent 20 minutes doing expressive writing in a notebook, as instructed in Voice Lesson 2. This journaling exercise surfaced a lot of raw emotion, stuff I'd never want others to read. When I finished, I needed the 15-minute break I took—again, following my own instructions.

It was early morning, a little chilly. I wore polar fleece and flip-flops on my back deck, sipping coffee and taking in neighboring backyards from two floors up. My heart rate slowed. I watched two robins that had built a nest on the fire escape above our deck. They flapped and darted between nearby tree branches, chattering angrily at me.

After my break, I again set the timer for two minutes. I made a second list of things that interest me (Box 3.3). Some of these topics are broad, too, but now many have emotional hooks. My curiosity was sparked—by those territorial robins, by wondering what other birders were doing during the lockdown, by my own vexed relationship with my mother. I've put stars next to the ideas I'm most intrigued by.

Box 3.3 Martha's list, round two

birding during the pandemic
bird behavior:

territorial!

nesting

different bird calls = emotions? ★ ★

nut-based sauces—replacements for cheeses
identifying migraine triggers—for me and generally
complicated mother-daughter relationships:

how do people describe mothers in social media? ★ ★

bad mom comments vs. good comments?

how many say "I hate my mother"? ★

taboo feelings
physiological response to anger ★

This is the beginning of the feature-story process. The next step is to Google around for a few minutes. For example, on a May morning in 2020, when I did a Google search with my desktop computer on "nut-based sauces replacements for cheeses," I got more than 41 million results. A quick skim through the first three pages (the most popular or relevant results Google came up with for me) yielded 12 recipes and approximately equal numbers of "how-to" articles about the best dairy-free cheeses.

It all seemed standard-issue and repetitive, indicating a possible story opening for me. But when I refined my search to "what do vegans think of dairy-free cheese?," I turned up a 2019 first-person feature by *Guardian* reporter Elle Hunt—"To Brie or Not to Brie: Can Vegan 'Cheese' Taste as Good as Dairy?" Hunt's piece examines the nondairy trend in cheese-obsessed England, focusing on the response to a "plant-based cheesemonger" (La Fauxmagerie) in London. In this case, 15 minutes of research got me a solid source I could use in my own American take, if I decided to write such a story. Or maybe it just tells me I need a fresh angle. At least the idea hooks me far more than "The Best Vegan Cheese Substitutes."

My second list is only a starting point. We'll delve into additional self-reporting techniques in Chapter 4. Still, I generated 12-plus story ideas—and I did so with a relatively quick personal writing exercise, not by tracking popular hashtags. You don't have to spend weeks studying a new trend or reporting on events to come up with ideas. Rather than forcing yourself to write 250 words in 15 minutes, try this:

Spend that same 15 minutes on researching a topic you like.

Keep track of what interests you when you're responding to a voice lesson or anything you may be researching. Put a star beside it, a checkmark, an emoji; highlight it in your file of notes. *Be expressive when nobody else is watching or reading.* My italic emphasis underscores that good ideas come from your own curiosity, not anybody else's. Document your excitement and the questions that won't let you go.

Voice Lesson 4

1   ***Your hooks:*** In your notebook—or wherever you've made lists of things that interest you—go wild with emojis and stars to indicate the ideas that hook you most. Make a new list of ideas in your notebook, if you'd like to start over.
2   ***Research generator:*** Spend 15 minutes researching one idea online. Do you have a new angle to explore? To build up your Googling muscles, you might also research the same idea in 15-minute increments for three days in a row.

Responding to the world

Let's return to the mid-1980s, when the Age of Irony and Artifice (and Madonna) was still new. I lived in a house with roommates in the Richmond District of San Francisco, which was in the City's fog belt. I grew desperate for the sun. Our house, sandwiched between other narrow pastel houses, was close enough to the ocean for us to hear foghorns at all hours. I had to park my orange VW Dasher on the street, sometimes blocks away, and I kept flooding the carburetor because of the humidity.

Most days in the spring and summer, I'd drive down Highway 280 until I emerged from that monolithic gray fog bank. This usually happened at the

Trousdale Drive exit, near the top of the Sawyer Camp Trail in Millbrae. I still retain images of poppies and wild irises blossoming along the bike trail in spring, of reworking poems or stories in my head as I pounded down the hill near the freeway. I'd reach the dam—*silver or translucent? turquoise or aquamarine?*—running shoes tap-tap-tapping, curving out of direct sunlight into the dappled woods. *Eucalyptus? Live oak? Red-fleshed manzanita?*

These are fond memories, but they're also steeped in anxiety. In my graduate creative-writing workshops, I was hyper-aware of being judged. I agonized about not being literary enough to get my master's degree. The second-person "you" voice had become trendy then, a point of view I found pretentious. *You walk down the street, observing your red stilettos beside his size-12 Hushpuppies. You are in love, you tell yourself, but you are unconvinced. His feet are so big. He is a moose. You are a gazelle.*

Never a shrinking violet (or a gazelle), I avoided such silly plays for a professor's approval or the approval of student magazine editors. Still, when I didn't stick to the postmodern agenda, I got roasted in class. A fiction writer and teacher whom I greatly admired dismissed one of my protagonists as "neurotic." This same instructor reduced other women students to tears for writing too personally.

I wish I could say it was just my problem. But while I can't speak for all writers, I have since learned how common it is to feel caught between the joy of creation and the fear of failure. Take Stephen King's *On Writing* and his section toward the end titled "On Living: A Postscript." This is a harrowing personal account of the accident that almost took his life. In June 1999, a van slammed into King while he was walking along a Maine country road, which left him with a leg broken in multiple places, a torn-up knee, and other serious injuries. As King describes it, he was still recovering and in pain when he returned to the unfinished manuscript that became *On Writing*. As it was, he'd begun his craft guide in late 1997, then set it aside for more than a year.

In "On Living," King says that even before the accident, "Writing fiction was almost as much fun as it had ever been, but every word of the nonfiction book was a kind of torture." Despite his many bestselling novels, he'd been dogged by uncertainty. After the accident, when he finally got back to a semblance of a writing routine, King notes:

> There was no sense of exhilaration, no buzz—not that day—but there was a sense of accomplishment that was almost as good. . . . The scariest moment is always just before you start.

When nonfiction writers tell their own stories, describing the real world from a personal point of view, they are taking a risk. They can't hide behind fictional characters. The magnifying glass of a writing workshop or much larger audience will be trained on the actual person behind the "I." We need courage in the face of fears we all feel about being judged or unlovable. But revealing ourselves is not only cathartic; it's real. Personal stories at their best, like King's "On Living," convey the reality of being alive.

If you want to be a writer, what matters more than anything is responding to the world around you—emotionally, intellectually, viscerally. I still recall the smell of eucalyptus trees in the heat of that trail, the wild iris and orange-and-yellow columbines in spring ravines. I jotted lines of poetry with details I'd observed in my journal.

As I look back decades to that younger me, it's sometimes hard to remember what it felt like to be that age. But when I name the heat and the dust, the neighborhood I lived in, the highway that took me out of the fog, the specifics of the world bring that me back. Those details are my emotional hooks, and they are what determine my voice as a writer. It's all in the details, not just abstract words like "love" or "grief."

In Part Three of *First-Person Journalism*, we'll spend more time on developing good observational skills as a first-person reporter and on writing capsule descriptions. Chapter 4, "Investigating Yourself," digs into the process of self-reporting, getting into the nitty-gritty of confirming the specific details of your own life.

But for now, just pay attention to how you respond to daily events, books, articles, podcasts, movies, or any media you interact with. Think about the things you hate and the things you love. Acknowledge your passions, because they're grounded in your particular identity and perspective on the world.

Personal story: Write about a "wart"

1 **Your hate list:** In your notebook, make a list of "Ten Things I Hate." These items could be anything from noise to the Beatles to saccharine cat pictures. Don't be afraid to be contrary and humorous—and feel free to write a paragraph or more for each list item.

2 **Didion essay:** Read Joan Didion's "In Bed" from *The White Album* about her struggles with migraines. (If you don't have access to Didion's well-known essay, try the electronic resources available through your local school or public library.)

3 **Your "wart" story:** Write a short personal story about a "wart" in the manner of "In Bed." Your wart could be one of the things you hate, a health issue, or something else. Focus on your own experience but include a few research references to make your points.

Sources

"Writing Is the Art of Applying the Seat of the Pants to the Seat of the Chair," *Quote Investigator*, September 24, 2015. www.quoteinvestigator.com/2015/09/24/chair/

"Getting into Print" by Jack London, originally published in *The Editor*, 1903; see *No Mentor but Myself: Jack London on Writers and Writing*, edited by Dale L. Walker, Jeanne Campbell Reesman (Stanford University Press, 1999).

"The Last Chronicle of Barset" in *An Autobiography of Anthony Trollope* by Anthony Trollope (quote on p. 237 taken from 1912 edition by Dodd, Mead & Company—it was originally published posthumously circa 1883).

"Trollope Trending" by Adam Gopnik, *New Yorker*, April 27, 2015. www.newyorker.com/magazine/2015/05/04/trollope-trending

"How Famous Writers Overcome Writer's Block and Reawaken Their Creativity" by Nicole Bianchi, *Medium*, November 6, 2017. www.medium.com/the-mission/how-famous-writers-overcome-writers-block-and-reawaken-their-creativity-7c604f73697c

Opening Up by Writing It Down: How Expressive Writing Improves Health and Eases Emotional Pain, Third Edition, by James W. Pennebaker and Joshua Smyth (Guilford Press, 2016; revision of 1997 edition by Pennebaker).

Because Internet: Understanding the New Rules of Language by Gretchen McCulloch (Riverhead Books, 2019).

"The Period Is Pissed" by Ben Crair, *New Republic*, November 25, 2013. www.newrepublic.com/article/115726/period-our-simplest-punctuation-mark-has-become-sign-anger

"This Is How Your Fear and Outrage Are Being Sold for Profit" by Tobias Rose-Stockwell, *Quartz*, July 28, 2017. www.qz.com/1039910/how-facebooks-news-feed-algorithm-sells-our-fear-and-outrage-for-profit/

Web Literacy for Student Fact-Checkers by Michael A. Caulfield (Pressbooks, 2017; updated in 2021; Creative Commons). www.webliteracy.pressbooks.com/

"Up From Pain" by Charles M. Blow, *New York Times*, September 19, 2014. www.nytimes.com/2014/09/21/opinion/sunday/charles-blow-up-from-pain.html

I'll Be Gone in the Dark: One Woman's Obsessive Search for the Golden State Killer by Michelle McNamara (HarperCollins, 2018), p. 1.

"The Creepy Genetics Behind the Golden State Killer Case" by Megan Molteni, *Wired*, April 27, 2018. www.wired.com/story/detectives-cracked-the-golden-state-killer-case-using-genetics/

"Golden State Killer Sentenced to Life in Prison Without Parole" by Michael Levenson, *New York Times*, August 21, 2020. www.nytimes.com/2020/08/21/us/golden-state-killer-sentenced.html

"To Brie or Not Brie: Can Vegan 'Cheese' Taste as Good as Dairy?" by Elle Hunt, *Guardian*, February 20, 2019. www.theguardian.com/lifeandstyle/2019/feb/20/to-brie-or-not-to-brie-can-vegan-cheese-taste-as-good-as-dairy

On Writing: A Memoir of the Craft by Stephen King (Scribner, 2000).

4 Investigating yourself

How do I know my own story is true?

Many people assume that writing in the first-person voice is easy. After all, this reasoning goes, you're only describing what's already in your head: feelings, opinions, memories of things that happened to you. You don't need to do outside research. It's a simple matter of pouring everything onto the page, like taking mental dictation—right?

If only. I'd love to push an inner button and let the story of my life just flow, except I know it takes more than that. The "it's easy" attitude ignores how difficult it is to write *well*—finding the language to express your thoughts effectively. More important, though, it fails to recognize the real challenge of writing in the first-person voice: finding the truth in what you remember and conveying who you are to other people.

Addressing readers in the "I" voice is actually pretty hard. Despite the exhibitionism of social media, most people have a tough time figuring out how to present themselves and what they want to say to an audience. My sweatiest times as a writer have involved interpreting my own response to a complicated event. *Why was I there? Why does it matter to me? How do I know that what I believe is true?* Writers misremember things all the time (as do most people), and we often mislead ourselves about our true feelings and biases. Yet probing those uncomfortable truths and messy facts is crucial for unleashing the powerful honesty that sparks the best first-person writing.

Self-reporting, the first-person element at the heart of this chapter, helps you to find the factual and personal truth in what you're writing. By making sure your own facts are right—and admitting when you can't be sure about them—you create a bond of trust with readers. And by developing self-awareness about your point of view, your credibility as a first-person reporter will shine amid a sea of impersonal experts, hand-wringing personal confessions, and staged photo shoots.

Paradoxical as it sounds, good first-person journalism is not just about you. It's about the way you observe and interpret the world. In other words, writing with an "I" doesn't give you a free pass to stay inside your head. You need to report on yourself as you would on somebody else, with both compassion and skepticism.

Self-reporting may seem like familiar territory for journalists, but for many reporters, questioning their own experiences can feel like a bushwhack through

DOI: 10.4324/9781003132189-6

impenetrable jungle. For literary nonfiction writers, turning personal material into stories is fine, but verifying facts? Yikes! Talk about a climb up Mount Everest.

If you're a literary writer, the idea of reporting on yourself may seem especially off-putting. Isn't the most beautiful personal writing driven by mysterious internal processes rather than prosaic facts? Yes and no. There are aspects to self-reporting that involve the unconscious, but not in the way you think.

Self-reporting encompasses your whole approach to investigating and writing a personal feature. In this chapter, we'll focus on fact checking and questioning yourself, but before you turn and run, let me reassure you: journalistic method helps offset the challenges. In the voice lessons that follow, I'll provide plenty of guidance on the first steps of self-reporting. Together, we'll begin investigating *you*.

Why memories are not facts

What's the very first thing you remember?

Even if you've never done such an autobiographical writing exercise before, somebody in your life has probably asked you about your first memory (maybe so often you can't help rolling your eyes). Here's my initial response to this prompt:

> *The very first thing I remember is the neighbor's roof blowing off. I was two or three years old, staying overnight at my aunt's house in Albany, New York. It was 1960 or 1961. After a big storm, I stood in my footie pajamas at her front door. It was the next morning, and with the screen open, the bright light made me squint. I stared at the wreckage of trees and downed power lines—and there it was, the house next door without its roof! Where did it go? I imagined it twirling through the clouds, all the way up to the stars. I felt giddy. I felt scared, thinking that could have been us, the wind whooshing through with a mighty roar, ripping away the sturdiest wood to expose my cousins and me asleep in our cots. I would have ridden the roof into the sky, alone, with no one to bring me home.*

As a personal story, this foreshadows a number of themes that feel honest to me. But would you call my account above nonfiction? I wasn't born with a recording device in my skull to document every moment of my life. What I'm remembering is the story I tell based on what other people have told me and bits and pieces of recalled feeling.

I may be conveying this memory through a child's eyes, but I'm far from sure the imagined parts about the roof are things I knew or thought as a toddler. Throughout my childhood, I watched *The Wizard of Oz* many times, and that spinning roof in the clouds could come straight from the movie. Even the footies might be based on seeing my pajama-clad self in old family photographs.

My story is both true and untrue, precisely because it is a *story:* an event reconstructed by my adult self with a beginning, middle, and end. The best nonfiction relies on such classic narrative strategies to engage readers, and that doesn't make all well-told tales false. But one of the most basic rules for a first-person reporter is this:

Memories are not facts.

Memories can provide engaging anecdotes; they can become the premise for a journey of self-discovery. But remembering an event doesn't make it factually true. Writers constantly reinterpret memories through the lens of everything experienced since. And that's okay. First-person journalism combines factual information with the person doing the writing, and what the person remembers is informative, too. Personal quirks, emotional intensity, biases—they're all part of how we respond to the world. Without such passion and sense of purpose on a writer's part, readers often remain disengaged.

The trouble is that writers screw up facts all the time, often unintentionally, which is why memory can wreak havoc with even an experienced journalist's story. In David Carr's *The Night of the Gun*, his 2008 memoir title refers to the night he thought a friend had threatened him with a handgun. Years later, as he and this friend chatted, the friend insisted Carr had the gun. Of his initial reaction, Carr wrote in the opening of his book:

> I am not a gun guy. That is bedrock. . . . I've been on the wrong end a few times, squirming and asking people to calm the fuck down. But walking over to my best friend's house with a gun jammed in my pants? No chance. That did not fit my story, the one about the white boy who took a self-guided tour of some of life's less savory hobbies before becoming an upright citizen.

A *New York Times* media columnist for many years, as well as a reporter in Minneapolis, Carr died in 2015 from complications of lung cancer. By then, he was a celebrated journalist who'd raised twin daughters as a single dad after regaining custody of them from foster care. And yet, he felt compelled to make sense of his earlier addiction to drugs, including crack cocaine. Calling memory a "courtesan" that "answers back with bullshit," Carr then argued that "there is a way, not to Truth, but to fewer lies":

> When I set out to write a memoir, I decided to fact-check my life using the prosaic tools of journalism. For the past thirty years, give or take time served as a drunk and a lunatic, I have used those tools with alacrity. I decided to go back and ask the people who were there: the dealers I worked for, the friends I had, the women I dated, the bosses I screwed over.

Carr discovered he was the guy with the gun; his book is an example of extreme self-reporting. But if the thought of interviewing an endless stream of past acquaintances and reviewing your own police records feels daunting, take heart. You don't need to be an extreme self-reporter to fact check your memories. I love the craft of journalism for many reasons, but I rely on it because it demystifies the art of nonfiction. Instead of forcing yourself to be a brilliant stylist from the get-go, just pin down the facts.

Voice Lesson 1

- **Your first memories:** In your process notebook, describe three of your earliest memories. A paragraph for each one is fine—150 to 200 words—although feel free to write at length. Describe at least one memory about an event on the public record (such as 9/11, a presidential election, a natural disaster, or a local incident).

Fact checking the basics

First, I'll play hard-bitten journalist. Memories aren't facts, but they usually contain pointers to factual information, and there's no excuse for fudging facts that are on the public record. It's one thing to draft what you remember in response to a writing prompt; it's quite another to publish a finished personal essay or post that hasn't verified dates, times, and locations—the *when* and *where* of good reporting.

Questioning the facts behind your own stories is the place to begin. Start by verifying the dates of a public event or how old you might have been at the time. Who else was present? Where did the event take place? Are you sure? This may all seem like a nonissue when it comes to your own life—you know what you know—except that almost everyone misremembers names, dates, and locations. Trust me, I'm an editor. I'm also a writer who's made plenty of mistakes myself.

Let's break it down with the description of my first memory, beginning with the basics of *when*, *where*, and *what*. Here are a few starting questions for this self-reporter: When exactly did the storm hit the east coast and can I verify that it happened? What kind of damage did it do? Were there reports of roofs blowing off in Albany or elsewhere? And when was *The Wizard of Oz* first broadcast?

As a self-reporting test in 2017, I pinned down two things almost immediately: when the storm happened (1960) and how old I was (two; I was born in March 1958). A quick Google search on "major hurricanes U.S." brought me to the National Oceanic and Atmospheric Administration's table of all hurricanes recorded from 1851 to 2015, including the states impacted, the category (strength) of a given hurricane, and its name. (NOAA's hurricane site has since been updated.)

From this, I found that Hurricane Donna, a Category-4 storm at its worst, bludgeoned the east coast all the way from Florida to Maine in September 1960. More digital sleuthing got me to NOAA's description of Donna on its "Hurricanes in History" page: "One of the all-time great hurricanes, Donna was first detected as a tropical wave moving off the African coast on August 29. It became a tropical storm over the tropical Atlantic the next day and a hurricane on September 1."

A caption on an archival photo from the *New York Daily News* noted that Donna's eye passed over Long Island on September 11, 1960, as a Category-2 storm with 100 mph winds. (Some more recent accounts compare Donna to Hurricane Sandy in 2012.) The storm hit Albany on September 12. A preliminary report in 1960 on Hurricane Donna from the U.S. Weather Bureau listed the following for New York and Albany: "Principal damage from Albany southward through Catskills. Severe small stream flooding in parts of Greene County. Apple crop severely damaged. Two deaths reported."

Full disclosure: As a kid, I wanted to be a meteorologist when I grew up. That Weather Bureau report, with its 50-plus pages of ALL-CAP, real-time bulletins issued by weather stations from San Juan to Boston, made for fascinating reading—or at least this record of a storm's passing and local observations piqued my curiosity.

But here's where the facts from outside sources don't quite gel into the straightforward picture I'd like to present. According to NOAA's "Hurricanes in History" page, Donna caused $387 million in damage in the United States and more elsewhere, especially in the Caribbean. But amid all the dry words about "property damage"—when the storm "slammed" New York City, the NOAA summary notes, "trees, signs, TV antennas, and utility lines" went down—I found nothing about roofs blown off houses in the five boroughs or in Albany upstate. The few reports I came across about destroyed or missing roofs came from Florida and other locations far to the south.

It's not clear how fast wind speeds were by the time Donna hit Albany, which is inland from Boston and north of New York City. The day before, there were reports of gale-force winds over Long Island, and areas in coastal New England reported gusts as high as 140 miles per hour. But the weather bulletin from Albany at 9 a.m. on September 12 predicted winds only in the 25-to-35 mph range with gusts up to 50 mph. My home in the Boston area often weathers gusts of 50 mph or more. How strong does the wind need to be to blow a roof off a house, especially a suburban ranch house not on the ocean?

Fact checking one more detail caught me off guard: *The Wizard of Oz*, originally released by MGM in 1939, was first broadcast on television in 1956, earlier than I'd thought. It became an annual TV event on CBS starting in 1959 until 1991 (in later years, it shifted back and forth with NBC). While I can't state definitively how many times I watched the movie as a child, it's likely I saw it at least ten times—and I may, in fact, have first seen it the year before Hurricane Donna.

So, I confirmed that a very big storm did indeed hit the east coast when I was two years old and that it had an impact on Albany. But when it comes to self-reporting, "just the facts, ma'am" only takes you so far.

Voice Lesson 2

1   **Your facts:** Choose one early memory from the first voice lesson—the one that lends itself best to fact checking. Go back over your description,

underlining (or highlighting) every place where you need to pin down a date, a location, or another basic fact.

2   *Google check:* Spend a few minutes Googling around to verify any facts that you can.

3   *Messy facts:* If this quick digital search (say, half an hour) doesn't yield or confirm the details you need to know, highlight the messier fact items in your draft.

Fact checking with family and friends

The information I've gathered up to this point came via the links Google turned up for me. Verifying the missing facts, if they're on the record at all, would involve digging through more local news stories, books, academic studies, or photos that haven't been digitized or aren't publicly available online. I'd need to travel to Albany to track down newspaper archives for 1960 (as of this writing, the digital archives for the *Albany Times Union* only go back to 1986 for selected stories). I could also interview a building engineer or meteorologist to figure out under what circumstances a roof blows off a house. I could get more familiar with the Beaufort Scale for wind speeds.

Then there's the other interview source for fact checking personal stories: family and friends. Long before I began this exercise, I'd asked the adults who were with me at the time about their memories of the storm. But as David Carr soon discovered, even if you try to grill family and friends like an investigative journalist (complete with digital recorder), such interviews come with an emotional charge. What other people recall is rarely an exact match with what you remember, especially if their point of view differs from your own. In my case, the memory about the roof comes from what older family members told me, yet their stories shifted as I grew older.

By the time I was in my twenties, I'd asked my mother repeatedly about the neighbor's roof, but she didn't remember it blowing off. Her memory was never good, and she often misinterpreted family stories. A visual artist, she died in 2013, diagnosed with Alzheimer's disease, unable to speak (although she could sing "Yellow Submarine," when prompted). My father, who passed away in 2014, didn't recall hearing about the roof from my mother, and I don't think he was with us in Albany then. His Parkinsonian ruminations weren't a reliable guide to reality, either.

Years ago, when I asked my aunt and uncle—it was their house in Albany—they told me they thought a neighbor's roof had blown off, but not next door, and it might not have been the whole roof. At least that's what I remember them telling me. My aunt died in 2012; my uncle passed away in 2017, and he suffered from dementia in his last years.

After my digital round of Hurricane Donna research, I began to think I'd conjured a Dorothy-like fantasy, not an actual memory. Still, as part of that exercise, I did email other family members to see if they remembered anything about the neighbor's roof. I heard back from several cousins (the children of my aunt and uncle), and that's when I realized my first memory can't be neatly pigeon-holed as false.

Three of my cousins confirmed that the roof blew off a neighbor's house—but it wasn't next door. They said it happened to the house across the street, or several houses down, so my two-year-old self could have seen the result from the open front door. My cousin Tom offered the most detailed interpretation, including why the roof might have come off with a relatively low wind gust. In 2017, he wrote:

> I wasn't alive in 1960, but did hear the stories. . . . I remember being told the roof blew off and flew over our house, and I believe there was still debris from it over the bank behind our house when I was little, some of which was put to use by me and my friends for purposes of building our tree houses (aka forts). . . . The roof on [the neighbor's] house was flat, which is very unusual in our area primarily because of the snow, so if the wind caught it right, it could take off like a wing and get airborne. . . . We have a lot of wind at our location.

If I wanted to take this farther, I could examine the house myself on a visit to Albany (according to Tom, who still lives nearby, the original neighbors are long gone). But the most telling—and realistic—part of his response is this:

> Maybe the "whole roof" was a bit of an exaggeration, since when I was older and the topic came up, it seemed to be less of an event than I had imagined. I would say it was probably a good-sized chunk of the roof, though. I also remember being told it was a tornado, not a hurricane, so I guess the tales become as we like to remember them and embellished a bit for effect or downplayed, depending on the audience and circumstances.

One other detail I can't confirm: those footie pajamas. Was I wearing them in September 1960? That's usually a hot month on the east coast. I've done a preliminary check of temperatures, and it appears Albany was only in the 60s (Fahrenheit) when Donna came through. So, maybe I did have on footies. Because they appear in other photos from that time period, I feel justified in using this detail; "footie" conveys how young I was.

But really, I don't know.

Voice Lesson 3

•   *What other people say:* Dig deeper into one of the messier facts you've highlighted: Contact family members or friends to see what they remember or if they have other leads you might follow.

Reporting on your "I"

What do your memories really say about you, the adult writer?

Potentially, a lot. They aren't facts in the journalistic sense, but vividly detailed memories can evoke the personality behind a narrator's voice. They hold emotional clues to the things a writer cares about or the way he or she interprets the world. Early memories aren't always tied to natural disasters or major traumas. My college-age son has told me he remembers as a baby pushing aside the zipper of a dark-green fleece shirt I often wore so that he could rest his cheek on the fuzzy cloth.

I also remember as a child watching JFK's funeral on television in 1963 while my little brother and I built marble towers with blocks. The following year, I recall a big girl running up and down the aisles of my school bus, shouting Barry Goldwater's name. In 1968, I watched RFK's assassination live because my dad, a political scientist, had let me stay up late to see the results of the California primary. These public events shaped me, as did growing up in the Bay Area during the 1960s and early 1970s.

As a first-person writer, I've found that the tension between personal memory and public events is what yields my most original work. And yet, the details I've just told you—where I grew up, my approximate age, my father's profession as a social scientist—convey a lot more about who I am than the first draft of my Hurricane Donna memory. They also clarify my biases as an adult observer and interpreter.

Those biases include the fact that I'm white, which is signaled as much by the details I leave out as those I keep in. I don't mention the death of Martin Luther King, Jr. I remember it, but I opted not to put it in. That's mostly because I watched Bobby Kennedy get shot in real time on TV, an event that terrified my father and me. Still, King's assassination happened only a few months before RFK's, as did riots around the country, and it provides context. I'm including it now, after posing some uncomfortable questions to myself, which brings up another essential rule for self-reporters:

We all have biases, and it's important to acknowledge what they are.

Just as memories aren't facts, they don't in themselves get across a writer's point of view. As David Carr made clear in *The Night of the Gun*, memories of a past self are not the same thing as the contemporary writer who's doing the writing. Your current context—how old you are now, where you live, what you've become—determines the way you remember anything or the details you share with readers.

When Carr wrote "I am not a gun guy," he was presenting his contemporary point of view to readers. Given that he didn't remember threatening a friend with a gun, the contrast between what actually happened and what he remembered creates the narrative tension in his memoir. His point of view is not that of his out-of-control self at twenty or thirty; as he observed, David Carr the Addict could not have written such a book. His first-person POV is that of a writer looking back, questioning all he's experienced, and interpreting his own story so that it's meaningful for readers.

In my Hurricane Donna memory, I do indicate the approximate date (the early 1960s), so readers can assume I'm looking back decades later. To some extent, the fanciful details about the bright light or imagining myself riding the roof through the sky illustrate how I view the world. But they don't clarify why this memory matters to me as an adult. In the initial draft, I have yet to indicate where I live now (the Boston area), where I grew up (California, not the east coast), and who my parents are.

In "On the Necessity of Turning Oneself into a Character," a chapter of Phillip Lopate's 2013 *To Show and to Tell*, he notes that first-person writers often assume their "I" says more about them than it does:

> In their minds, that *I* may be swimming with background and a lush, sticky past . . ., whereas the reader encountering it for the first time in a new piece sees only a slender telephone pole standing in the sentence, trying to catch a few signals to send on.

Boring as basic *orienting details* like your age and gender may seem to writers more interested in poetic descriptions, they are nonfiction bedrock for readers. We want to know who your "I" is immediately. We need you to orient us in order to grasp your point of view, which is surely shaped by how old you are, whether you grew up American or Chinese, if you're a Mormon or Muslim, or if you've ever been arrested.

Gone are the days when an author's biographical note at the end can stand in for revealing personal details. I've long believed that relying on a third-person bio note to explain a first-person writer's point of view—oh, *now* I see, she's Black . . . he grew up in Bosnia . . . she was an investigative journalist in Mongolia—is a cop-out. Author photos can do some of the obvious work, but readers may not see a photo. More important, physical appearance isn't the same as your identity or affinities. Whether it's clear what you look like, tell us who you are directly, especially if social class, gender, national citizenship, or any other aspect of yourself is relevant to the story being told.

The flip side of a vague "I" is the social-media tic of describing every passing thought or action. But a stream of words without context rarely conveys a writer's biases in an informative way. While many younger authors assume the act itself of writing in the first-person voice gives their work a point of view, a raw info dump doesn't point readers to what they want to know: why your experiences should matter to *them*.

In Chapter 1, I noted that Joan Didion refers to "aimless revelation" in her 1979 essay collection *The White Album*. Here's a bit more from her opening to "In the Islands," where she famously says of the personal details she presents:

> I tell you this not as aimless revelation but because I want you to know, as you read me, precisely who I am and where I am and what is on my mind. I want you to understand exactly what you are getting: you are getting a woman who for some time now has felt radically separated from most of the ideas that seem to interest other people.

Voice Lesson 4

1 ***Orienting details:*** In your notebook, list five key details about yourself: age, current occupation, where you live now, where you grew up, ethnicity or religious background.
2 ***Orienting readers:*** Mark places in your memory draft where you can add orienting details. Do you think adding these details will change the way you tell the memory? Why or why not? In your notebook, reflect on how much readers need to know about you.

Reporting on what you haven't said

When you begin to question what you remember and who you are, the reporting can take you down unexpected rabbit holes. The surprises are valuable to first-person journalists, sparking writers to connect a remembered personal event with a much larger topic or to define their point of view. But research rabbit holes also raise the question of just how much time any writer, even the most scrupulous self-reporter, should put in.

It depends on the kind of feature or post you're writing. A book-length memoir like Carr's *The Night of the Gun* can take years of research and writing time. But short feature articles that connect a personal experience to current research about a health problem, for example, don't require reporters to spend weeks or months digging into archives. The more you do this kind of writing and research, the better you'll get at knowing when to stop ferreting out facts and when to keep at it.

The reporting time I put into investigating Hurricane Donna took a few hours of Googling and some back-and-forth with family members. But other ideas percolated as I did the initial research, and I kept notes. This led me to eight questions with specific story angles (Box 4.1). It's hard to imagine these topics popping up in a search on trending hashtags. Wanting to know more about the hurricane is what drove the information I discovered, as did my particular interests. I'm a weather nerd and a journalist.

But the initial memory exercise also points up gaps in my story. In *To Show and to Tell*, Lopate puts it this way: "Facts have implications, which, it seems to me, are ignored at the nonfiction writer's peril. The whole plausibility of a nonfiction narrative may be undermined by altering or evading crucial details."

I invoke Lopate's "facts have implications" with many students and writers, because literary essayists often wrongly assume that key situational details bog down a story or are too personal. One of the examples Lopate provides is of a student who wrote about her marriage falling apart but didn't tell readers the reason why: her discovery that her husband was gay. "It was certainly her right to protect him," Lopate notes, "but the result was a muffled, baffling narrative."

Don't baffle readers. Obvious as this may seem, neglecting to convey what's at stake for you in a first-person story dilutes its emotional impact. More

Box 4.1 Eight ideas based on hurricane Donna research

1 How do meteorologists track hurricanes?

How has it changed since 1960, and what's been the impact? Given that some contemporary commentators have compared Donna to Hurricane Sandy in 2012, what's changed during the decades between the two?

2 Was Donna a landmark for hurricane tracking? ★★

The first weather satellite (TIROS) was launched in the spring of 1960, just a few months before Donna. This new way of documenting hurricane formation, as well as use of radar, is credited with producing much more accurate predictions by the U.S. Weather Service for Donna, which probably gave people more advance warning and time for preparations.

3 What's it like being a meteorologist now vs. in 1960? ★★

This could also examine what it means to be a meteorologist (a working scientist) vs. a weather tracker on TV news and other misconceptions.

4 Who becomes a meteorologist and why are they drawn to it? ★★

I can connect my own early love for meteorology to a profile of a contemporary meteorologist or several capsule profiles.

5 Does NOAA fact check or update reports from previous years?

If so, how and why? Many documents listing local weather predictions are now easily available online and part of the public record.

6 How are big storms portrayed in literature and myth?

An account of Donna hitting Long Island appears in John Steinbeck's Travels with Charley: *"Houses built in the benign spring and early summer took waves in their second-story windows"; Steinbeck also described imagining a tree crashing down on the camper truck (it would "crush her like a bug") he ended up taking on his famous cross-country trip.*

7 How often are first memories true? ★★

What do cognitive scientists and other experts say about the validity of first memories? And what are the most common things people first remember? The age of two seems very young to remember anything, so I wonder how unusual that is and when most people start remembering.

8 What does the latest research say about mental illness and memory? ★★

Is misremembering family events more extreme among the mentally ill? I can connect research findings to anecdotal experience with my mother.

important, it's a form of misdirection, unintentional as that may be. The *situational details* underpinning your point of view are not the same as orienting facts like age, gender, or ethnicity, although the basics can help explain it. Didion opens "In the Islands" with the date—1969—and by the second paragraph, she's stated her family situation at that time: "We are here on this island in the middle of the Pacific in lieu of filing for divorce."

Most of us take our own situations for granted, forgetting that readers don't know us and won't be able to intuit them. In my initial memory draft, I failed to mention my mother's lifelong struggle with mental illness or that her extended family on the east coast was a volatile mix of Sicilian and Irish American. While readers might not notice the missing parents in that draft, I didn't provide enough hints for this gap to register as odd (except to my therapist). Only after I began revising did I realize my mother's bipolar disease plays a role in the story—and how much I don't like talking about her illness.

It's also true that cultural barriers hold back many writers. In my experience as a teacher, students of color are often hesitant to explain their situations, especially at the start of a writing project. That's the case even though being Black in America, for instance, likely impacts much of their lives. I'm sympathetic and encouraging, of course, but their work is being judged by a white woman. White judgment has long been tied to a political reality that silences people of color. If I ignored political reality or my position of privilege in writing this book, I would end up misdirecting readers, too.

During the civil rights movement, James Baldwin wrote sharply and personally about race, but doing so wasn't an easy decision for him. Contrast this with Didion in 1960s Los Angeles (or Hawaii). She faced many emotional and health problems, yet she was a young white woman married to John Gregory Dunne, another successful white writer. Didion reports that a friend said one Hollywood house they rented at the time was in a "senseless-killing neighborhood," but they weren't living in Watts or Compton. In her essay "The White Album," Didion makes a point of saying the *Los Angeles Times* named her a "Woman of the Year" in 1968 (along with Nancy Reagan).

Cultural barriers persist, chipping away at writers from inside and out. It makes sense to withhold information that will ostracize you, but in doing so, you may also internalize taboos that keep you from speaking up. Baldwin didn't hold back about being Black and growing up in Harlem, but in his most celebrated essays he didn't reveal he was gay. Didion only implied she was white. The more "objective" reporting she did for magazines assumed a white point of view, even if her topic was the Black Panthers.

Naming your biases is why self-reporting helps define what it means to be human at a particular time and place. Ethnicity conveys personal origins, as do details about your family. Even so, being white, employed, educated at a private college, famous, or otherwise successful may well give you permission to write that others don't feel. The key is to be as intentional as possible about what you're *not* saying.

Beyond not baffling readers, keep this first-person rule in mind: *Hiding who you are and what you feel isn't a simple style choice.* It's about fear of exposure, something most of us wrestle with every day. Certain conversational tics are tipoffs that a speaker is avoiding an emotional hot button. For instance, people frequently shift out of the first-person voice when talking about themselves. In a 2016 *Vanity Fair* profile, here's how Benedict Cumberbatch describes his response to a traumatic 2004 carjacking at gunpoint in South Africa, after he and some friends were driving back from scuba diving:

> I wanted to swim in the sea that I saw the next morning. If you feel you're going to die, you don't think you're going to have all those sensations again—a cold beer, a cigarette, the feel of sun on your skin. All those hit you as firsts again. It is, in a way, a new beginning.

Cumberbatch's image as an actor is based on his cerebral, British detachment. And yet, I'd counter that a POV shift like this is a kneejerk form of self-protection. Imagine his words recast: *I felt as if I were going to die, that I wouldn't get to have all these sensations again—a cold beer, a cigarette, the feel of sun on my skin.* The difference in emotional impact of "sun on my skin" is palpable.

There are good reasons for shifting point of view, and authors like me do it all the time. In this book, I'm giving "you" lots of advice, addressing you as a teacher or mentor would. But a POV shift can also be a defense against what you don't want to say. In student papers or other nonfiction pieces I'm editing, I routinely see authors leap out of the first-person voice as if they've been burned. They move into "you" or "we" platitudes just at the point when they need to stick to their own experiences.

Self-awareness is a mental muscle that gets stronger with practice. You don't have to be in therapy, but receiving feedback from trusted readers is one of the best ways to uncover what you haven't said—and need to say. Writing workshops provide peer feedback on story ideas and first drafts. Journalists get help from editors. And I'll keep pushing you to question yourself throughout the reporting and writing process (Box 4.2).

Box 4.2 Question yourself

- Which facts have I remembered wrong?
  - What personal details are missing?
  - When do I shift from "I" to "you"?
  - Do I include too many snarky asides?
  - Is my emotional response unclear?
- Does my emotional response seem out of proportion?
  - What doesn't make sense?

That's because *the best feature ideas make writers uncomfortable*—another rule for self-reporters. Many nonfiction writers pursue a topic because of strong feelings, but their motivations may not be conscious at the start. Other chapters in *First-Person Journalism* detail strategies for mixing personal material with research. Chapter 5 connects the dots between point of view and your active "I" stance. But the self-awareness you develop by investigating yourself sparks the whole enterprise.

Voice Lesson 5

1 **Cumberbatches:** Ask a trusted reader—a friend, a classmate, your spouse—to look over your memory draft and to flag "Cumberbatches" based on the questions in Box 4.2. These self-protective tics are clues that you may be holding back.

2 **"You" shifting:** Take a first-person piece you've already written, and mark every place where you shift from the "I" voice to "you" or "we." In your notebook, rewrite those lines using the first-person voice. Do the sense and emotional impact of the lines change?

Admitting what you'll never know

An unexamined "I" may mimic intimacy, but it doesn't shed light. Blog posts and social-media updates tend to be littered with distracting side comments, be they snarky (she's *such* an asshole) or self-deprecating (well, that's just little ol' me being stupid). In the hands of a funny writer like Lindy West, such self-reflexiveness can disarm readers, helping to get across who the writer is. In "Lady Kluck" from her 2016 collection *Shrill*, for example, West describes growing up with no images of "funny, capable, strong, good fat girls" like her. Then she tosses in an ironic aside:

> [F]at women were sexless mothers, pathetic punch lines, or gruesome villains. Don't believe me? It's cool—I wrote it down.

She proceeds to list hilariously bad "female role models," including Maid Marian's big-breasted chicken nurse Lady Kluck in the 1973 Disney movie *Robin Hood*.

As I noted in the previous chapter, though, too many writers undercut themselves with irony or generic platitudes, as if afraid to admit what they don't know. The main goal of first-person journalism is to look *outward* in order to communicate your personal response to an audience. But if you don't look inward first, your inner Sherlock will leave the building. If you aren't honest with yourself, you won't be honest with readers.

In practice, reporters often end up with piles of research and interview transcripts that don't clarify the facts. David Carr put it this way: "Everyone likes a good story, especially the one who is telling it, and the historical facts are generally sullied in the process." Yet as my cousin Tom observed in "tales become as we like to remember them"—and as Carr did in his memoir—there's also value to admitting uncertainty. Truth can still be gleaned from something that may never be verifiable.

Many nonfiction writers try to skip over what they can't verify, but one of the most useful aspects of a first-person voice is that you're free to say, "I don't know, and I may never know." You don't always have to play expert. Instead, admitting uncertainty—especially *why* you're uncertain—helps establish a clear point of view. It also empowers readers to question their own beliefs by demonstrating how it's done.

Didion exemplifies the first-person journalist who admits to uncertainty as a narrative strategy. In her 1970 notes from a trip through the American South, for example, she reflects on the last time she'd been there as a child in the early 1940s. Her father had been stationed in Durham, North Carolina, during the war. The family traveled from California to join him, not a happy time in her recollection. Didion writes:

> Thirty years later I am certain that my father must also have been with us on weekends, but I can only suggest that his presence in the small house, his tension and his aggressive privacy and his preference for shooting craps over eating peach ice cream, must have seemed to me so potentially disruptive as to efface all memory of weekends.

Part of what works in Didion's account are the specifics she does pin down— where her father was stationed, the time period, the "small house," "his preference for shooting craps over eating peach ice cream." She selected the right details to tell readers in order to convey the emotional reasons for why she can't remember those weekends.

Expressing uncertainty does require enough factual detail to convince readers you've tried to find out what's missing. Many beginning writers say things that amount to "I don't know if this is true, but I think it is, so I'm going to tell you anyway"—a verbal shrug. Here's one more key rule: *"I don't know" doesn't excuse lazy reporting or thinking.* Introducing doubt is not the same as being wrong or airbrushing away facts.

If you have done your research, the next step is to interpret what it means for readers. In Didion's classic "In Bed" from *The White Album*, she doesn't present an encyclopedic review of all migraine research. She selected a few significant facts to make her main point. By relying instead on vivid personal anecdotes about her own struggle with migraines, she underscores that they're a real medical condition, not just an emotional one, countering much of the male conventional wisdom at the time.

A personal essay or journalistic feature is not a Ph.D. thesis. In revising my memory exercise, I didn't include every quote from my cousins or bit of research I'd jotted down about hurricanes. I made choices as a writer, and my original draft became "Hurricane Warnings," the short essay that appears at the end of this chapter (and which was published in the 2019 anthology *Into Sanity*). I added a new opening section about my mother—my real focus—rather than the hurricane. I establish my adult point of view at the start. And I acknowledge uncertainty about many of the facts I do include, emphasizing the fragile nature of memory in families who struggle with mental illness.

Being skeptical about your own experience isn't an attitude you assume to sound smart or to ward off criticism. Skeptics aren't necessarily cynics, unrelatable jerks, or emotionless robots. They're self-reporters with the courage to go public about their doubts. If you don't question your memories and biases, you may never question what other people tell you or the conventional wisdom about what "everyone knows."

We're molded by the world around us. It's hard to separate a personal story from the social circumstances that have shaped your perception of who you are and what it means. It's even harder to question what the people around you believe. The next chapter focuses on different narrative stances in first-person features, because deciding on your stance helps frame stories that may challenge readers' ideas about the truth. It also determines just how much you need to reveal about yourself to convince them.

Memory essay: Write about an early memory

1 **What you don't know:** Practice admitting what you don't know: In your notebook, draft three sentences to explain why the facts are slippery in your memory draft. (In at least one sentence, connect your inability to pin down the facts with what you feel.)

2 **Fact chart:** Which facts do you need? Make a chart that lists necessary orienting and situational details ("Yes") on one side and unnecessary ones ("No") on the other.

3 **Your essay:** Rewrite your memory draft as a brief personal essay—no more than 1,000 words, if possible—adding any of the confirmed facts you've decided to include. Think about how pinning down certain facts (or acknowledging those you don't know) may change the narrative or your own perspective on what you're remembering.

Sample story
Hurricane Warnings

My mother had a terrible memory. Sometimes, I thought her misremembering was an aggressive act, the way she'd misinterpret family stories. In 2013, her last year, when we were told she had Alzheimer's, the diagnosis felt sadly anticlimactic. Other disasters had already done their damage: a broken spine that made her wheelchair-bound, arthritis that cramped her artist's hands, mental illness.

One of the last memories I asked her about, at least five years before her death, was the way she used to hit me and my brother with a hair brush when we were little. Her first response was a shrug. *I had to, because one time you kids wouldn't go to sleep. I put you down for a nap, but you just kept getting up. You were so active.*

As I recall, my elderly parents both laughed when she said this.

I was driving. We were in a rental car (too small, my father noted) during one of my regular visits to the Bay Area. I'd taken them out to dinner—to Max's Diner, a favorite of theirs, at the top of Crow Canyon Road—and now we were heading home. My parents loved the ride as much as the food. We wound through the northern Californian hills of my childhood, past horse farms and live oaks, far from upstate New York where my Italian American mother had grown up.

But when I then asked if they really thought it was okay to hit a child, I saw her misremembering in action. *What! You think that's wrong? Okay, maybe it didn't happen. I don't remember, Martha, please.*

• • •

In September 1960, I don't remember the adults saying *Donna* or *hurricane.* I was two years old, and I wouldn't have known these words. But based on everything I've since read, the adults around me must have been scared. They would have followed the news reports about Hurricane Donna for days as the "storm of the century" battered its way up the east coast from Florida and the Carolinas.

At the time, we were staying at my aunt and uncle's house in Albany, New York. I don't think my father was there, but my mother and seven-month-old brother must have been with me.

It's the first thing I remember, that storm. The morning after Donna blew through, I stood at Aunt Audrey's front door. The screen was open; the sunlight made me squint. I probably saw downed trees and power lines, maybe a broken TV antenna and swampy lawns. I think I wore footie pajamas. Somebody held me back—my mother? an older cousin?—I don't know who, yet I retain the feeling of wriggling, of wanting to break free, of irritation and thrilling wildness.

The most exciting part turns out to be in dispute, however. For years, I was sure I saw the next-door neighbor's roof blow off. The adults may have pointed it out or talked about other roofs down south. It's possible I saw *The Wizard of Oz* when it was broadcast on CBS in 1959, although I would have been only a year old. With Donna, I was a toddler, unable to fathom an abstraction such as a hurricane being in different places over time—so reality surely mixed with fantasy.

My later research indicates that wind speeds weren't very high by the time Donna reached Albany; the National Weather Service reported gusts of 50 mph at most. My mother didn't remember anything about a roof or the storm. Years ago, before my aunt had passed away, I asked her about it, too. In consultation with my uncle, Aunt Audrey thought a nearby roof might have blown off but wasn't sure if it was next door.

Still, I can't write off this first memory as just hearsay or pure fantasy. Recently, I emailed other family members to ask what they recall. Three of my cousins, the children of my aunt and uncle in Albany, confirmed that a nearby roof had blown off (or part of one) on the house across the street. My cousin Tom hadn't yet been born in 1960, but he and his three siblings "did hear the stories."

The roof of that particular house was flat, Tom says, "which is very unusual in our area primarily because of the snow, so if the wind caught it right, it could take off like a wing and get airborne." He was told it blew over his house and remembers playing with the remaining debris in the backyard when he was little, using it to build forts.

So, it did happen—or I heard about it happening—even if my cousins admit their own memories are fuzzy. (Tom says he was always told it was a tornado.) It's unlikely I saw the roof blow off, but that's what I remember: a roof spinning, circulating like the storm itself.

• • •

It's a strange first memory: a big storm, standing in an open doorway, wanting to escape, almost no sense of any other person present. It feels unfair, as if I never asked to remember it—but *unfair*? Can a memory really be unfair? How odd that sounds, how childlike.

The truth that's emerged is sloppy, yet I'm surprised by the grip it has on me. I can't let it go. It's as if I've just realized in my late fifties that I'm not the boss of memory, no matter how much I want to be.

I could invoke Tolstoy's famous opening by noting that all unhappy families remember things in different ways. But when mental illness is part of the family, retrieving and confirming memories is more like a battle with zombies. The memories die but keep coming back to life in unexpected, misbegotten shapes. It's like casting a fishing line into a pool and reeling up a pile of burning leaves. Or a neighbor's roof.

It's hard to trust anything you've heard. After all the fits and starts in my adult career, that's probably why I ended up a journalist.

My mother wasn't diagnosed with bipolar disorder until the 1970s, but I felt ashamed long before that. That's the unfair part; I never had any control over her moods or what they did to me. I'll admit now that I wish I'd imagined the whole thing about the roof, because the reality points to what I'd rather forget: the dark weather in my own family.

I suspect my mother was frantic as Donna approached, not because I remember it—the absence of both my parents and brother in my recollection is a telling void—but because as I grew older, I knew what it was like to live with her. She had a shifty spark behind her eyes, as if too much light were trapped behind a cloud; spittle would pool at the corners of her mouth. In September 1960, she was only 25, with a baby and a two-year-old, and a hurricane would've been like pouring oil onto flames. Aunt Audrey was the stable one.

But still, well into adulthood, I saw that neighbor's roof twirling in the clouds like Dorothy's house in a tornado. The giddy gut-feeling of standing in my aunt's doorway, lit up by the returning sun and fear and a great big world of possibilities, sticks this memory to many later memories, to my love of clouds and atmospheric disturbances. Maybe even at the age of two, I saw myself riding that roof into the sky, alone.

Sources

The Night of the Gun by David Carr (Simon & Schuster, 2008), p. 11, pp. 25–26.
NOAA hurricane table: "What is the complete list of continental U.S. landfalling hurricanes?," Hurricane Research Division, National Oceanic and Atmospheric Administration (NOAA) website. www.aoml.noaa.gov/hrd/tcfaq/E23.html

"Hurricane Donna 1960" from "Hurricanes in History" page, Hurricane Research Division, National Oceanic and Atmospheric Administration website. www.nhc.noaa.gov/outreach/history/

"Hurricane Donna, 1960," from photo gallery and caption ("Winds of 100 mph were recorded on eastern Long Island while New York City was also hit with powerful gusts, as pictured here") *New York Daily News*, September 1960.

"Hurricane Donna, September 2–3, 1960: Preliminary Report with the Advisories and Bulletins Issued," U.S. Weather Bureau (Department of Commerce), 1960.

"Television: The Oz Bowl Game," *Time*, January 15, 1965. www.content.time.com/time/subscriber/article/0,33009,941895,00.html

"Storm Data, September 1960," U.S. Weather Bureau, 1960.

Tom Hutson, personal correspondence with author, March 14, 2017.

To Show and to Tell by Phillip Lopate (Simon & Schuster, 2013), pp. 17, 80.

"In the Islands," "The White Album," and "In Bed" from *The White Album* by Joan Didion (Farrar, Straus and Giroux, 1979), pp. 133–134.

"The Henry James of Harlem: James Baldwin's Struggles" by Colm Tóibín, *Guardian*, September 14, 2001. www.theguardian.com/books/2001/sep/14/jamesbaldwin

"Cover Story: The Mind-Bending Benedict Cumberbatch" by Michael Schulman, *Vanity Fair*, October 4, 2016. www.vanityfair.com/hollywood/2016/10/benedict-cumberbatch-cover-story

"Lady Kluck" from *Shrill* by Lindy West (Hachette, 2016).

South and West: From a Notebook by Joan Didion (Knopf, 2017).

5 Establishing your stance

How close am I to the story?

In his 2003 book *The Adversary: A True Story of Monstrous Deception*, Emmanuel Carrère recounts the chilling tale of Jean-Claude Romand. For more than twenty years, from the 1970s to the early 1990s, Romand pretended to be someone he wasn't: a doctor and researcher at the World Health Organization. He had no medical license and didn't practice medicine in the French provincial towns near Geneva that were his home base. Instead of driving over the Swiss border every day to work at WHO headquarters, as everyone assumed, Romand passed the time in solitary walks or reading in cafes and parking lots. But eventually, his former mistress and other people started asking questions— until 1993, when he shot to death his wife, two small children, and elderly parents, apparently because he couldn't bear for his fraud to be exposed.

Carrère revisited some of Romand's lonely haunts, and in *The Adversary*, the author describes one small casino parking lot near the border in personal terms (English translation):

> It's the clearest memory I've kept of my first visit to the landscape of his life. There were only two other cars, unoccupied. It was windy. I reread the letter he'd sent me with directions, I looked at the water, looked up at the gray sky to follow the flight of birds whose name I didn't know—I can't identify birds or trees and I find that sad. . . . [As a writer] I know what it's like to spend all one's days unobserved: the hours passed staring at the ceiling, the fear of no longer existing.

The Adversary is far from a sympathetic view of Jean-Claude Romand, but it wouldn't get under the skin as it does without such self-reflection by Carrère. His short book alternates with seeming ease among first-person descriptions, third-person summaries of the murderer's life story, the point of view of one of Romand's best friends, and Carrère's correspondence with Romand himself.

Yet by this much-lauded French author's account, he struggled with how to tell the story. By the time of the 1995 trial, which Carrère attended, Romand had confessed to the murders; the focus was on sentencing. (France has no death penalty, and in 2019, Romand was released after 26 years in prison.) The

DOI: 10.4324/9781003132189-7

question of why a man would do such a thing hung over the courtroom. The judge herself asked Romand, "but *why?*," getting back the equivalent of a shrug.

The Adversary went on to become a fictionalized movie of the same name (*L'adversaire*). Carrère, also a prize-winning novelist, settled on how to convey a disturbing self-deceiver who constantly reinvents himself. But once the author decided to inject his own point of view into his nonfiction narrative, it determined his *stance*.

Stance is the first-person element we'll focus on in this chapter, and it refers to how a writer positions their "I" voice in a story. Are you close to the events that happened or a more distant observer? Have you figured out the right emotional tone, and—most important—can you direct readers to what really matters? Stance is related to self-reporting, the element highlighted in the last chapter, and establishing your stance relies on the same crucial tool for first-person journalists: self-awareness. You need to assess how much to say about yourself, as well as your observational perch on the events you're describing. This process aspect of stance underscores the importance of *No first drafts*—and another first-person rule:

> *Your emotional motivation is not the same as the story.*

Strong emotion certainly has a place in first-person journalism, but reporting with enough distance on your own experience is usually the bigger challenge. In this chapter, we'll start with how point of view relates to positioning your "I." We'll look at what that means in practice, touching on an example of my own in which the feelings motivating me to write needed reining in. Then we'll cover five different stances and story types for first-person feature writers.

From POV to first-person stance

In a lively debate with friends, most of us take into account the point of view of each talker. Readers, in turn, often want to know the point of view of an opinion writer if a provocative topic is being discussed. But for writers themselves, there's also a craft definition for point of view that involves the perspective and limitations on what can be known by the narrator telling the story. Here, we're closer to the first-person element of stance.

At the most simplistic level, narrative point of view is about pronouns (and not just because gender pronouns require more flexibility than editors used to allow). Obviously, you don't just decide on a few pronouns and move on, but pronoun choice does signify the limits of what can be known by the voice telling the story. So, when writing from the *first-person point of view*, you use "I," telling a story from your own perspective or a fictional character's "I" perspective. The world described to readers is limited by what that narrator knows.

With the *second-person point of view*, you employ "you," either in the standard form of talking to readers—as I'm doing in this sentence—or as a way to get emotional distance on a personal experience. That leap can be intentional for literary writers, heightening the feeling of disassociation for "I." (*You walk into the bar, unsure whether to order another drink.*)

When writing in the *third-person voice*, your narrator avoids using "I." You make factual statements without tacking on first-person qualifiers such as "I think" or "I saw." In fiction and creative nonfiction, third-person stories may be limited to a single character's perspective or jump between several characters. Third-person narrators can also assume an *omniscient point of view*, observing events and people from above, like a god, with no limits on what it's possible to know.

Authorial omniscience has long been common in third-person journalism, topical nonfiction books, true crime stories, expert treatises, even Wikipedia entries. It's sometimes referred to as the "neutral voice," one in which objectivity, balance, fairness, or consensus is the stated goal. But if you scratch below the surface of this goal, you'll find that writing omnisciently *is* a stance, one authors can don for good or ill. It assumes that factual information should come from expert sources and not be expressed in personal terms.

Opinions are all too often proclaimed from an omniscient point of view or at least an impersonal one. As a consequence, the generic voice of the expert is now easy to fake. In contrast, omniscience is tough to pull off in first-person features. The first-person voice signals the presence of an individual writer or speaker, not a god who knows all.

Establishing who is doing the observing and how that perspective may be limited is basic to first-person journalism. Once you link personal attitude with observational position, you're defining your stance as a first-person journalist— and your stance will frame how you present both facts and your own biases. With stance, you not only choose a narrative position; you decide on what kind of reporting to do and how much to say about yourself.

Journalists are rarely experts, so the stance they take is based on how they interpret what other people tell them. Here's where narrative POV isn't enough to explain stance. In a single feature, a writer can shift between using "I" to tell a personal anecdote—to the third-person voice to provide historical background or quotes from experts—to "you" in offering suggestions—and back to "I" or "we" for expressions of belief. Meanwhile, that writer's overall stance may be coolly observant and analytical or intimately personal and vulnerable.

Consider how Carrère ended up changing his point of view *and* stance when writing *The Adversary*. In a 2006 essay, "Capote, Romand, and Me," he elaborates on why it was so difficult for him to turn years of research and notes into this page-turning narrative. I've come across few other accounts that delve so precisely and honestly into why a nonfiction author might struggle with establishing a first-person stance. Carrère writes that he kept turning to Truman Capote's classic "nonfiction novel" *In Cold Blood* for inspiration, assuming he'd follow Capote's "deliberately impersonal approach" to tell Jean-Claude Romand's story:

> I think that I never consciously asked myself whether I should write in the first person. I cross-referenced the points of view, ceaselessly asked myself which version I should tell, from what angle, and simply never considered my own. And if I didn't think about it, I suppose it's because I was afraid of it.

Over the decades, other journalists have questioned Capote's reporting approach when he went to Kansas in 1959 to find out why two strangers brutally killed the Clutter family on their farm. But Carrère homes in on the omniscient narrative stance of *In Cold Blood* and why it's problematic for this work of nonfiction. It's well known that Capote befriended the murderers while they were in jail, even promising to help them, until they were executed.

Carrère finds himself in a similarly vexed position as both outside witness and someone with access to a murderer's thoughts through his interviews and letters. The author describes being so confused that he gave up on the book. Then, as a form of mental housekeeping, he decided to write a personal report that he didn't intend to publish, and that's when Carrère came up with the opening of *The Adversary*:

> On the Saturday morning of January 9, 1993, while Jean-Claude Romand was killing his wife and children, I was with mine in a parent-teacher meeting attended by Gabriel, our eldest son.

In order to write the book, he needed to position himself as an observer with biases (including a wife and family of his own) right from the start, which no longer felt duplicitous in the way *In Cold Blood* does. Michelle McNamara's *I'll Be Gone in the Dark*, another true crime book I noted in Chapter 3, also opens with first-person observations about her own obsessiveness. As Carrère concludes in his essay (the italics are mine): "In saying yes to the first person, *in occupying my place and none other* . . . I had found the first sentence, and the rest came—I won't say easily, but in one go, naturally."

Voice Lesson 1

1   **Your response:** What do you think of the omniscient voice in nonfiction? Do you agree with Emmanuel Carrère's view of Truman Capote and *In Cold Blood*? In your process notebook, jot down your expectations of an omniscient narrator. (If possible, read "Capote, Romand, and Me," which is part of *97,196 Words*, the 2019 English translation of an essay collection by Carrère.)
2   **Bonus response paper:** If you've read *In Cold Blood* or *The Adversary*, write a response paper comparing and contrasting these books.

Determining your emotional distance

The first-person stance you take, then, involves awareness of your position as an observer. You can sit in the figurative clouds, documenting what other humans do miles below. Or you can join the other humans, reporting from a close personal perspective, maybe even as a participant in the action. Or you can do it all. Defining your stance starts with establishing your observational perch—how close to or distant your "I" is to the story being told.

A first-person stance isn't necessarily intimate, however, even if many aspiring writers assume it is. Regardless of how close first-person journalists are to the story, they are reporters. They combine specific observations with analysis. When we say a writer has a strong voice or style, their voice comes through the details they include and their take on the world rather than sheer emotionality. At the same time, good feature writers always convey their stance, whether they're describing an event in their own lives or have researched something and are explaining it from a third-person perspective. To paraphrase Carrère, they occupy their place and no other.

My emphasis on self-reporting and stance underscores one of the biggest differences between first-person journalism and other forms of personal nonfiction: *the active "I."* Postmodern and constructivist critics may argue that any first-person voice is unreliable. Literary nonfiction writers often play around with self-presentation to emphasize that all truth involves creative reconstruction. The idea that self-reporters are always observing—and should make their position as an observer clear—can be off-putting to writers whose goal is to immerse readers in a narrative as if it were a short story or to disguise the "I" behind other pronouns.

Occasionally, it makes sense for a literary nonfiction writer to split off their "I," as Carmen Machado does in her 2019 memoir *In the Dream House.* Her "I" observes her past self as "you" to convey the disassociation and personal disintegration caused by an abusive relationship. Yet truthful as a literary hybrid like that can be, I've seen (and, as an editor, rejected) too many stories in which a writer describes their own actions as if they happened to somebody else—for no good reason except that it's trendy. A hypothetical example: *She watches the sky, alone in her misery, avoided by every stranger passing by.* Who is this person? Why do we care?

Switch to the first-person voice and feel the difference: *I watch the sky, alone in my misery, avoided by every stranger passing by.* This statement now comes from a particular, vulnerable person. I'd also rephrase it again to increase credibility: *I watch the sky, alone in my misery,* as if *avoided by every passing stranger.* This writer is actively interpreting their own experience; they're not presenting themselves as the passive object of an omniscient narrator.

At the other extreme, many bloggers and personal essayists consider expressing the full depth of such misery to be the most credible account. Writing from a first-person perspective can feel like a breath of fresh air, and straight-shooting talk about intimate emotional experiences does have gut impact. It's an active "I" voice, all right, the kind that's often called authentic. Yet talking about what you feel isn't necessarily more truthful.

That's why framing stance in terms of emotion is misleading for first-person journalism. The stance you choose will fall somewhere on an emotional spectrum of personal expression (Box 5.1). First-person authors like Carrère and McNamara can be passionate, curious to know everything there is to find out about grisly crimes that distress them, yet when they write the story, they curb emotional displays or TMI that doesn't serve readers.

I define my stance in this book as personally authoritative—close enough to convey how passionate I am about first-person journalism yet distant enough to assess the topic beyond my own experience. My tone is warm, yet teacherly, and I include

---

Box 5.1 Emotional spectrum

intellectual distance   personally authoritative   intimate close-up

---

personal anecdotes about being an editor and a writing instructor to underscore my credibility. My perspective is not that of a memoirist; *First-Person Journalism* is not just about me or the events surrounding my life. While I address readers in the first-person voice, I analyze the work of other writers, present an overall framework, and offer advice. As you'll see in the next section, I even observe my own writing process with the distance required to interpret what can go wrong.

The active "I," more than anything, is about an active mind and heart responding to life. Beginning feature writers are often advised to think about explaining a topic to their grandmother or a friend who knows nothing about it. That's great advice for first-person journalists, too. Instead of assuming that the meaning of your story will emerge—that readers will be patient enough (or smart enough) to figure it out—put your "I" in charge, directing readers to what matters most.

Voice Lesson 2

1   ***Third-person:*** Write a paragraph describing yourself from the *third-person POV.*

2   ***First-person:*** Write a second paragraph describing yourself from the *first-person POV.* This time, include at least one unexpected personal detail, making your self-description as quirky as possible. (Avoid, at all costs, writing a dry biographical note or a standard "About Me" blurb.)

3   ***Your take:*** Do you prefer one self-description over the other? Why? In your notebook, discuss the differences in perspective and how you might combine them.

Personal example: Reining in myself

Let's put the spotlight on a time I wrestled with finding the right emotional perch. Back in early 2014, just after my father had died, I began drafting an opinion piece about writers as entrepreneurs. I assumed it would be a snap to write. The piece was meant for my column in *Talking Writing*—and "The Trouble With Being an Entrepreneur" did appear in the fall issue that year. Before it was published, however, I ended up doing a surprising number of rewrites.

I'm an inveterate reviser and fiddler, but the changes I needed to make involved a more fundamental problem than cuts and reorganization: I was too angry. It took the help of another editor for me to realize my stance didn't match the topic. Take the opening from my first draft:

> Here's how brainwashed I've been by the pleasures of digital media. Until recently, I blamed certain authors for expecting to be taken care of by publishers. *Whiners! Buck up—get out there and hustle. Don't wait for the literary elite to give you a fancy Big Author Life on a platter, because that was always a fantasy, anyway. Join the 21st century, where we can all create our own destinies.*

There's a hook, if you believe a slap in the face is energizing. But phrases like "a fancy Big Author Life on a platter" indicate my unexamined resentment about literary publishing at the time. There was a deeper impetus for my feelings, too. In the draft's second paragraph, I tried to explain that my father's recent death had put me into a tailspin: "I've been on the kind of goofy, awful midlife ride that's had me wailing *No!!!* with every hairpin turn."

I wasn't being dishonest. Yet the emotional language ramped up too fast, sounding melodramatic. In a later paragraph of that draft, I even call my anger a "clarifying thing," turning the feeling that motivated me to write into the explanation. It determined the action—like that "goofy, awful midlife ride" barely under control—rather than a more observant "I" directing readers in a genuinely clarifying sequence of ideas. I didn't yet have enough distance to use my first-person perspective to get readers questioning the larger issue: whether business thinking has coopted the writing profession. That was my goal, but the outcome? *Poor Martha, she's pissed.*

Fortunately, I didn't publish the original version I'd titled "I'm Sick of Being an Entrepreneur." When my editor at *Talking Writing* reviewed a subsequent draft—a revision of the overwrought original—she said it still felt like a gallop among a zillion ideas without a chance to catch her breath. Not only had I included extraneous material from business writers about entrepreneurialism, I kept allowing my feelings to stampede along like a spooked horse.

For this reason, a first-person stance isn't always emotionally intense *or* detached. To extend the horse metaphor, it doesn't have to gallop at one speed. Think of stance as the active "I" taking the reins and directing readers, allowing them to catch their breaths before speeding up again. A personal "I" can drive the story—until you pull back to explain the historical context—all in the same feature, as long as you manage the pace for readers.

Heeding my editor's advice, I finally took the reins of that horse. The published version of "The Trouble With Being an Entrepreneur" opens with far less rancor than my original draft, providing enough personal detail to ground what's to come:

> Until recently, I enjoyed calling myself an entrepreneur. Publishing on my own terms felt liberating. It also seemed realistic. In 2007, when my son went to kindergarten and I headed back into magazine journalism, I discovered that I had to figure out digital media or change professions. So, I started blogging. By 2010, I'd cofounded an online magazine.

In this opening, I've laid out my circumstances at the time: mother of a kindergartener, heading back into my profession, discovering I had to change to catch up. Before criticizing the whole idea of entrepreneurship, I admit I was seduced by it, too—and I don't hide behind my outrage.

Voice Lesson 3

1   *First-person:* In a paragraph, describe the room you're sitting in from the *first-person POV*.
2   *Third-person:* Switch to the *third-person POV* to write a new paragraph describing the room.
3   *Your revised take:* How do the two descriptions differ? Do you prefer one over the other? Why? Decide on your *first-person stance*, then rewrite the room description. Feel free to incorporate details from any of your previous self-descriptions, including the quirky one.

Addressing readers: Five stances

In practice, first-person journalists often combine stances in a single feature or essay: analyzing statistics with intellectual distance, giving friendly advice, witnessing events as outside observers, telling their own story, or interpreting how individual experience reflects the universal. Carrère mixes stances throughout *The Adversary*, sometimes telling the story as a third-person witness, sometimes offering personal observations. Mixing stances is part of first-person journalism, something Chapter 10 examines regarding story structure.

But in this section, we'll define five stances separately in order to pin down how first-person journalists address readers in different kinds of features (Box 5.2). While it may be tempting to place these stances on the emotional spectrum in Box 5.1, moving from intellectual distance to intimate close-up, this list of five isn't one-directional. It operates more like a circle, with "analyzer" and "interpreter" coming together in personal essays.

Analyzer: This stance most closely conforms to traditional feature writing in journalism. After researching a current public event, person, or hot topic, the reporter presents the most relevant facts and often advances an argument based on the evidence. Topical features fall into sub-categories such as profiles, explainers, and trend stories. Lighter subjects (a profile of a pop star, a fashion trend) generally include vivid details and anecdotes meant to entertain, not to make an intellectual point. Yet these details are still laid out for readers in a logical sequence. And when topical features are written from a first-person perspective, as an increasing number now are, they don't suddenly turn into a nonlinear stew of feeling.

Box 5.2 Five first-person stances

1 *Analyzer*—topical feature or opinion piece

2 *Adviser*—how-to article or self-help

3 *Witness*—directly observed report of events

4 *Storyteller*—personal narrative

5 *Interpreter*—personal essay

Even in third-person features, the analyzer's voice can be informal and warm. What matters is the quality of the evidence supporting a provocative argument. Opinion writing may seem to be the most emotional of feature categories, but it relies on analysis, something we'll explore in more detail in Chapter 8. Otherwise, such pieces are rants, not journalism.

Take the unexamined feelings in my first draft of the "Entrepreneur" piece. By the final version, my "I" expresses the argument in personal ways, yet there's a logic to how I lay out the ideas, backed by enough evidence—a sample of typical writer's advice; my direct observations of trends in digital media—to move my experience beyond the personal. Compare this third-person paragraph late in the final piece with my original handwringing:

> It's easy to be seduced into thinking that writers, artists, and entrepreneurs are kindred spirits. Like writers and artists, entrepreneurs must be dreamers, ignited by ideas, willing to put in "sweat equity" and perhaps work for nothing for years because they believe in their products. Maybe that makes them sexy rebels—James Dean "thinking different" on an Apple billboard. But it doesn't make them artists. Entrepreneurs look for market openings: what will sell and become popular, what customers want. The goal is payoff on all that sweat.

Adviser: The classic how-to article is a magazine staple and ubiquitous on many digital platforms, encompassing earnest recipe posts, "ask the expert" columns, FAQs, and snarky listicles. People do want information about everything from how to knit a sweater to "21 Ways to Make Your Dog Happy for Life" (a 2012 listicle from *The Dogington Post*). On the flip side, this feature type is one of the most formulaic, especially when the writer assumes expert omniscience or a lock-step "first, you do this, then you do that" tone. All too often, advice is eye-glazing.

Most people don't like being told what to do, especially by know-it-all journalists or professorial academics. That's why a first-person perspective has long been common in how-to features in lifestyle magazines. I've made up the following paragraph to illustrate a familiar approach:

> *I was so disappointed at first that I almost gave up. After all, I'm a fifth-grade teacher with two toddlers of my own. I've got enough on my plate without becoming*

a technical whiz at [fill in the blank], including the unwashed plates my spouse leaves all over the kitchen. But I'm stubborn, too, and I kept trying and failing, until I got it right—and if I can do it, so can you.

It's still a formula. It opens with an anecdote about when this fictional teacher failed at doing something. In the standard feature, three or four tips for how to do "fill in the blank" would follow. But as an adviser, this "I" is a regular person, maybe a trusted friend, not an expert.

Witness: For classic "you are there" features, journalists directly observe news events as they unfold, particularly dire situations like natural catastrophes or military actions. Their "I" voice may pop up only a few times in such a feature to indicate the circumstances of reporting. More often, though, they do more than document what's happening. While a first-person account as a witness usually means observing other people as an outsider, it's not necessarily an emotionally distant stance. Reporters interpret what they observe and their own reaction to horrors. It can have the moral authority of testimony, something the world needs to hear.

Philip Gourevitch, in his award-winning book *We Wish to Inform You That Tomorrow We Will Be Killed With Our Families*, describes going to Rwanda in the mid-1990s, reporting many harrowing stories of those severely affected by the genocide of Tutsis in 1994. (In a 2009 *New Yorker* piece "The Life After," he also follows up 15 years later.) In Gourevitch's opening chapter, he echoes Joan Didion: "I'm telling you this here, at the outset, because this is a book about how people imagine themselves and one another—a book about how we imagine our world." The Rwandan government at the time, he notes, did something previously unimaginable by directing the majority Hutus to kill anyone who was a Tutsi. Gourevitch adds:

> I wanted to know how Rwandans understood what had happened in their country, and how they were getting on in the aftermath. The word "genocide" and the images of the nameless and numberless dead left too much to the imagination.

The witness stance can also involve direct participation in events. In "I Went Home to Texas to Cover the Virus. Then My Family Got It," Edgar Sandoval's 2020 *New York Times* feature about a coronavirus outbreak in the Rio Grande Valley, this reporter says near his opening that "I never expected that I would be part of this story." He volunteered to go to the Texas-Mexico border because many members of his family lived near McAllen, the largest town in the area. "I knew that the warm, close-knit family culture I had grown up with in the Valley would make social distancing a challenge," Sandoval notes. But the situation became personal much faster than he assumed. As he was boarding the plane in New York, one of his sisters sent a text message in Spanish: "Brother, it looks like all of the Sandovales have Covid."

Sandoval went on to report on other local families, to talk with public officials, and to include statistics. He details how the virus spread from one person to another by documenting his family members' movements. But the later sections about his mother's illness have the most impact. As she barely hangs on in the hospital, Sandoval writes of himself:

> I fought the urge to reach for her and say something profound. Should I say I love you? Was it time for a heartfelt farewell? What if this was the last time I would see her alive?

By the end of his feature, she has started to recover, but in allowing his own fear and vulnerability into the account, Sandoval is not only a witness. He's telling his own story.

Storyteller: In many ways, all journalists are storytellers, recounting events as they observe them happening or piecing together the details based on information from sources. Good storytellers create gripping narratives with lots of action and a dramatic arc. One traditional journalistic feature category is the "tick-tock" narrative, which vividly recounts the chronology of a major news event. Often based on the reporting of several staff journalists, these third-person stories can read like an action novel. Here's a fictional example:

> *When Bruce Whitington walked into the laboratory at 5 a.m., the guys were still laughing at a joke about the shabby toilets, wondering if the boss would ever spring for more than two-ply. Then the first bomb went off.*

If such stories are told in the first-person voice, however, the focus of the story is more likely to be something that happened in the writer's own life. In first-person journalism, the storyteller stance applies to personal narratives that come closest to memoir. What distinguishes such narratives as journalism is the reason for a personal focus and the depth of reporting.

Alex Tizon's "My Family's Slave" is a powerful example of personal storytelling by a well-known journalist. Published in 2017 in the *Atlantic* after his untimely death, it lays bare Tizon's struggle to come to terms with his own cognitive dissonance about the woman he knew as Lola (an affectionate term for "grandmother" in Tagalog). In fact, Lola was a domestic servant who immigrated with Tizon's family from the Philippines to the United States with no choice in the matter. The blurb for his story puts it this way: "She lived with us for 56 years. She raised me and my siblings without pay. I was 11, a typical American kid, before I realized who she was." In his opening section, Tizon baldly frames his need to unburden himself:

> To our American neighbors, we were model immigrants, a poster family. They told us so. My father had a law degree, my mother was on her way to becoming a doctor, and my siblings and I got good grades and always said "please" and "thank you." We never talked about Lola. Our secret went to the core of who we were and, at least for us kids, who we wanted to be.
>
> After my mother died of leukemia, in 1999, Lola came to live with me in a small town north of Seattle. I had a family, a career, a house in the suburbs—the American dream. And then I had a slave.

In this long narrative feature, one that sparked a global discussion about contemporary slavery and domestic servitude, Tizon wove between two storylines: he pieced together Lola's experience and recounted his own journey back to the Philippines to return her ashes to her village. He researched Lola's background; he examined the veracity of family stories and his own misperceptions as a child. And he didn't spare himself in making this secret public, even though Tizon and his family did their best to treat Lola as a beloved grandmother once she moved in with him. In his concluding scene in the Philippines, he's a self-aware storyteller:

> I hadn't come sooner to deliver Lola's ashes in part because I wasn't sure anyone here cared that much about her. I hadn't expected this kind of grief. . . . The old people—one of them blind, several with no teeth—were all crying and not holding anything back. It lasted about 10 minutes. I was so fascinated that I barely noticed the tears running down my own face.

Interpreter: Interpretation is also part of all journalistic feature writing. Opinion and how-to writers interpret what they know for readers. Alex Tizon was an interpreter of his own experience in "My Family's Slave"—so are Gourevitch, Sandoval, and Carrère. Yet Tizon's stance was determined by his narrative storytelling, and in lighter features, a writer may barely scratch the surface of conventional ideas. In personal essays, self-reflection defines the writer's stance, which can seem intimate, even vulnerable. Other interpreters take the long view.

Omniscient narrators make pronouncements about what's true and what isn't, sometimes using the royal we or the preacher's voice: *We are all sinners, doomed to repeat our past mistakes.* Personal essayists also make pronouncements, but their "I" connects the dots between individual experience and the larger world. In his 1953 essay "Stranger in the Village," James Baldwin opened with first-person recollections of his time as the only Black man in a remote Swiss village—"If I sat in the sun for more than five minutes some daring creature was certain to come along and gingerly put his fingers on my hair, as though he were afraid of an electric shock"—and closed with sweeping statements about the legacy of racism in America:

> I am not, really, a stranger any longer for any American alive. One of the things that distinguishes Americans from other people is that no other people has ever been so deeply involved in the lives of black men, and vice versa. . . . It is precisely this black-white experience which may prove of indispensable value to us in the world today. This world is white no longer, and it will never be white again.

Baldwin was famously a preacher in his teens, and his god's-eye sections have the cadence and elevated language of a minister. In "Stranger in the Village," he positioned himself as an outside observer, adding a twist on what it means to be a stranger. Deep emotion underlay his rhetoric, but it's held in check by a distanced, less combative stance that was probably meant to appeal to *Harper's* educated white readers in the early 1950s.

Regardless, his authority as an interpreter is on full display in "Stranger in the Village," an essay that continues to resonate many decades later. He directs readers from small Swiss children laughing at him to the cathedral of Chartres and aphorisms that are now famous—"People who shut their eyes to reality simply invite their own destruction"—transcending his personal circumstances in the span of only a few pages.

Voice Lesson 4

1 **Your stance:** Take one of your own pieces of writing and identify the stance—does it fit the kind of story it is? What if you took on another stance? Reflect on this in your notebook.
2 **Response paper:** Read James Baldwin's "Stranger in the Village" and Teju Cole's "Black Body: Rereading James Baldwin's 'Stranger in the Village,'" a 2014 personal feature in the *New Yorker*. Then write a response paper about Cole's "Black Body." Compare how Cole establishes his first-person stance with Baldwin—how do they differ and why?

Rethinking voice: Active response

In the closing pages of *The Adversary*, Emmanuel Carrère relates that Jean-Claude Romand was befriended in prison by two Catholic volunteers who, despite factual evidence to the contrary, believed Romand was always meant to find a religious vocation. (When he was released in 2019, he entered a monastery.) In speaking with these friends, Carrère "found their affection—so straightforward, so natural—both admirable and almost monstrous." His own view of Romand is troubled, and it helps readers interpret the man's self-deception:

> I no longer saw any mystery in his long imposture, only a pathetic mixture of blindness, cowardice, and distress. . . . He is not putting on an act, of that I'm sure, but isn't the liar inside him putting one over on him?

It's an unnerving insight: Romand's "liar inside," fooling himself into believing he's good. But Carrère's observations imply we're all tempted by self-deception, and in this, his own first-person voice is both vulnerable and controlled. He admits uncertainty yet comes to a conclusion.

The spare quality of his voice—its transparency—reminds me of George Orwell's famous maxim: "Good prose is like a windowpane." In his 1946 essay "Why I Write," Orwell also argued "that one can write nothing readable unless one constantly struggles to efface one's own personality." Ironically, Orwell (aka Eric Blair) wrote under a pseudonym, and he infused his own journalism with personal bite and high moral dudgeon. But I've always embraced his emphasis on clarity with no "humbug." I would only add this: sometimes there's value in seeing the writer's struggle through the windowpane, too.

In this book, I'm calling on you to use the active "I" voice and to speak straightforwardly and truthfully. But in many discussions of great authors, the writer's voice is evoked as something absolute, unattainable unless you're born with it. By this reasoning, voice flows from genius or the Muse descends at midnight to anoint the chosen. If you don't have it, you never will. Or voice is conflated with style, even the choice of pronouns.

No and no and no—and I'll refrain from expressing my irritation with a colorful expletive. That's a style choice, by the way. The words you use may be studded with f-bombs or flowery verbiage—or the preacher's "we"—but language style is only a surface indicator of who you are and too often disguises what you think and feel. For first-person journalists, becoming self-aware of your stance and the limits to what you know *is* the way to a strong voice.

So, question your own kneejerk reactions while also passionately engaging with the world. This is what I mean by active response. Don't stuff a story with fancy language or melodrama or your cleverness just to impress an audience. Fabrication and self-deception easily become habitual. Instead, respond to *everything* you encounter. The rust on your car door. The swirl of opalescent light on a puddle after it rains. Observe—respond—observe. A distinctive voice emerges through your commitment to a topic and the rich, real-life details you notice, not the way you polish words. As Carrère might say, you occupy your place and no other.

Review: Your personal take on a media work

1   **True questions:** Select an essay, a book, a movie, a podcast, or another work of art you'd like to review from a first-person perspective. Read (or look at) the piece you've selected. As a warm-up in your notebook, respond to the following four true questions:

 • *What will make my personal voice believable?*
 • *What will make my first-person review accurate?*
 • *What will readers expect when they read this review?*
 • *How do I know what I know?*

2   **Your stance:** In your notebook, list at least five things you like (pros) and five things you don't (cons) about the work you've selected to review. Reflect on your overall attitude, then decide on your stance: will you be an analyzer, a storyteller, or an interpreter? Most first-person reviews involve some combination of those roles. Consider the way Teju Cole positioned himself in reviewing Baldwin's "Stranger in the Village."

3   **Your take:** Write a first-person review (between 800 and 1,200 words).

Sources

The Adversary: A True Story of Monstrous Deception by Emmanuel Carrère, translated by Linda Coverdale (Metropolitan Books, 2000; French edition by P.O.L. éditeur, 2000), pp. 1, 82, 191.

"Notorious French 'Doctor' Who Killed Family Released to Abbey," *France 24*, June 28, 2019. www.france24.com/en/20190628-notorious-french-doctor-who-killed-family-released-abbey

"Capote, Romand, and Me" by Emmanuel Carrère in *97,196 Words*, translated by John Lambert (Farrar, Straus and Giroux, 2019; originally published in French by P.O.L. éditeur, 2016), pp. 108, 109.

"Emmanuel Carrère's Disconcertingly Personal and Utterly Gripping Prose" (review of *97,196 Words*) by Robert Gottlieb, *New York Times Book Review*, December 12, 2019. www.nytimes.com/2019/12/12/books/review/97196-words-emmanuel-carrere.html

"Dream House as an Exercise in Point of View" in *In the Dream House: A Memoir* by Carmen Maria Machado (Graywolf Press, 2019), p. 14.

"The Trouble With Being an Entrepreneur" by Martha Nichols, *Talking Writing*, Fall 2014. www.talkingwriting.com/trouble-being-entrepreneur

"21 Ways to Make Your Dog Happy for Life" by Ron Miller, *The Dogington Post*, September 4, 2012. www.dogingtonpost.com/ways-make-your-dog-happy-for-life/

We Wish to Inform You That Tomorrow We Will Be Killed With Our Families: Stories From Rwanda by Philip Gourevitch (Farrar, Straus and Giroux, 1998), pp. 6–7 (Picador edition).

"The Life After" by Philip Gourevitch, *New Yorker*, April 27, 2009. www.newyorker.com/magazine/2009/05/04/the-life-after

"I Went Home to Texas to Cover the Virus. Then My Family Got It" by Edgar Sandoval, *New York Times*, July 14, 2020. www.nytimes.com/2020/07/14/us/coronavirus-texas-rio-grande-valley-border.html

"My Family's Slave" by Alex Tizon, *Atlantic*, June 2017. www.theatlantic.com/magazine/archive/2017/06/lolas-story/524490/

"Stranger in the Village" in *Notes of a Native Son* by James Baldwin (Beacon Press, 1955; originally appeared in *Harper's* in October 1953), pp. 166, 179 in 2012 paperback edition.

"Black Body: Rereading James Baldwin's 'Stranger in the Village'" by Teju Cole, *New Yorker*, August 19, 2014. www.newyorker.com/books/page-turner/black-body-re-reading-james-baldwins-stranger-village

"Why I Write" by George Orwell, Orwell Foundation website (originally published in *Gangrel*, Summer 1946). www.orwellfoundation.com/the-orwell-foundation/orwell/essays-and-other-works/why-i-write/

Part III

Reporting beyond the self

Moral authority doesn't amount to binary notions of right and wrong. A first-person feature that's both authoritative and authentic requires emotional openness to both sides, even when others rush to judgment.

DOI: 10.4324/9781003132189-8

6 Observing real life

How do I describe people and places?

I've always thought of myself as a visual person, although I suspect my family and friends would laugh if they heard this. I'm *so* analytical. I love to pick apart intellectual arguments and come up with frameworks. I love to luxuriate in words. Yet words are most meaningful to me when they evoke reality. We don't all share the same eyes or ears or hands, but we do live in a world of particular places, things, and people. I can imagine whole alternate worlds, but none compels me as much as the real one I observe every day.

In Part Three of *First-Person Journalism*, this chapter and the next two dig into the *who-what-where-when* facts that underpin reporting craft—but with a first-person twist. Chapter 7 focuses on identifying the right mix of credible sources and attribution of those sources from your "I" perspective. Chapter 8 explores the use of counterpoints in reported stories and opinion writing, when writers nod to those who disagree to strengthen their own arguments.

And here, in Chapter 6, we'll highlight the first-person element of *observation*, which is at the heart of what it means to be a journalist. Creative writers would say observation is at the heart of what they do, too. Yet in first-person journalism, learning to pay attention to details isn't just a means to an aesthetic end. Describing what we see and hear (and take in with our other senses) serves journalism's ethical purpose: to document and inform readers.

Journalistic description relies both on direct reporting—observing events for yourself—and on doing the research necessary to unearth context for readers. Working journalists develop good observational skills, and they know the main storytelling formulas. They can turn out assignments fast, hooking readers with specific details to describe a scene.

But underscoring how those details are being selected and conveyed by a first-person observer can get readers to pay attention in new ways. Here's just one example of the interplay between close observation and surprising details: the opening paragraphs of Julie Phillips's 2016 *New Yorker* profile "The Fantastic Ursula K. Le Guin."

Published before Le Guin's death in 2018, it doesn't lead with the author's storied success as a science-fiction and fantasy writer. Instead, Phillips describes one of Le Guin's "bouts of political anger" over the Malheur Wildlife Refuge in eastern Oregon, near the author's ranch. Just after New Year's Day in 2016,

DOI: 10.4324/9781003132189-9

an antigovernment militia occupied the refuge, including Ammon and Ryan Bundy, brothers who were often media spokespeople. In an email to Phillips, Le Guin called them "hairy gunslinging fake cowboys." But Phillips closes her opening paragraph with a humorous twist, paraphrasing more from that email: Le Guin "had been mildly cheered up, she added, by following a Twitter feed with the hashtag #BundyEroticFanFic."

In this 6,000-word-plus feature, a lot is conveyed in the opening paragraph about the quirky personality of a celebrated writer in her late eighties. Phillips follows up with more context—Le Guin's family roots in eastern Oregon, her longtime marriage to husband Charles. But by the fifth paragraph, Phillips offers another angle based on first-person observation:

> When I met Le Guin at her house in Portland this summer, she was in a happier mood. Coming out onto the back porch, where I was sitting with Charles in the late-afternoon sun, to offer us a bourbon-and-ice, she was positively cheerful, her deeply lined, expressive face bright under a cap of short white hair, her low, warm woodwind voice rising into an easy laugh. The bourbon is part of the couple's evening ritual: when they don't have company, they have a drink before dinner and take turns reading to each other. On the hillside below us, two scrub jays traded remarks through the trees.

This paragraph offers a complete *capsule description*—a few sentences that evoke a person or place with vivid specificity: bourbon-and-ice, a "cap of short white hair" and "woodwind voice," Le Guin and her husband's ritual of reading to each other. It extends our perception of Le Guin beyond her tendency toward "tirades" and her status as a writer. Yet the most surprising—and telling—detail comes at the end of the paragraph: "two scrub jays traded remarks through the trees." While including this detail may seem to be a random decision on Julie Phillips's part, those jays do a lot of writerly work in bringing the scene to life.

When I asked Phillips why she included those jays, her first response by email was: "It's funny. . . . I often forget to look around when I'm in a new place or I'm interviewing someone. And yet of course those kinds of things are often essential to the story." But with the jays, Phillips went on to say she'd become interested herself in identifying common California birds:

> So, during the conversation some Birding 101 part of my brain was going, *Ooh, scrub jays!* Then I used it in the piece because I was trying to convey the Westernness of her environment, drawing on my own sense of what was typically Western.

In this chapter, we'll discuss different kinds of details, the value of observing from a first-person perspective, and strategies for notetaking and description. But throughout, I'll emphasize capsule description—culling down what you observe to a few *telling details*—not because this makes the world easier to understand but because it highlights surprising connections.

Relevance versus vagueness

In casual conversation, people often gush on about how *wonderful* or *awesome* something is, offering very few details beyond "my vacation to Rome" or "that movie with what's-her-name." In conversation or a casual text, the expressed emotion behind generic descriptors can carry some of the meaning, especially in the way an experience affected the speaker. But in written form, such adjectives amount to verbal clutter. Readers' eyes skip over them, quickly glazing if there's a whole run of *it was so awesome, you can't imagine how beautiful it was!!!*

Vagueness is the enemy of truth, beauty, and good writing. This shouldn't be shocking news to journalists or anyone who has taken a writing class. The value of specific details is proclaimed by every writer I've heard interviewed and every writing guide I've read. It amounts to bedrock for those of us who teach writing. But in my experience, railing against "vagueness" can be vague, too, given that so many students still turn in drafts full of vague summaries.

Ironically, this often happens when they first attempt to describe their own families or where they grew up. What do they know better than these people and places? Yet it turns out that familiarity is not the same as the ability to observe yourself or others. Writing students may not trust their own eyes or believe that the specifics will matter to anyone else. They haven't yet learned to navigate the messy shore between what they feel and the content of their own stories.

The flip side of generic description is a verbal diarrhea of details that only interest the individual writer or speaker. We've all been there—the Facebook post that goes on and on about eating macaroni and cheese—the colleague who pins you against a wall with every detail about her childhood stamp collection. Such details aren't necessarily TMI, by the way. Any of them could be a hook in the hands of a practiced feature writer. But part of that practice comes in knowing why readers (or listeners) should care about macaroni and cheese or stamps. Here's another rule, one that underscores the nature of reporting in general:

> *Specific details matter more than vague generalities, as long as the details are relevant.*

Relevance is a cardinal virtue of journalistic writing. It's also another abstract principle that can get lost in the heat of observing and reporting. In newsrooms, the relevance and focus of an assigned story are often determined by editors. But my goal in *First-Person Journalism* is to get you, as writer and reporter, actively involved in telling your own stories. That means you not only need to operate more like an editor; you need to question yourself to figure out which *who-what-where-when* details are necessary to make sense of a story.

Box 6.1 Details and the reader

• Use **specific** names and dates.
Vagueness is the enemy of good writing.

• Use **vivid** descriptive words.
Avoid generic glosses like "wonderful" or "amazing."

• Use **relevant**—and unique—details.
Every audience can be hooked, as long as it matters to them.

Such self-reporting requires observing yourself with more distance than many aspiring first-person journalists know how to do. And yet, once you've developed the skill, it can be a relief, validating that what you observe about the real world *is* worth describing (Box 6.1).

Because this chapter is all about avoiding abstractions, let's get specific about how journalists include basic details, starting with two hypothetical descriptions of a fire:

> **No:** *A bad fire happened.*
> **Yes:** *A four-alarm fire happened last Saturday near midnight at a fifty-unit apartment building on Rosemont Street.*

I've underlined the details in the second version to demonstrate how a generic reference turns into a reported event. In just one sentence, there's a *what* (a four-alarm fire), a *when* (last Saturday near midnight), and two *where's* (a fifty-unit apartment building, Rosemont Street).

There's nothing personal or evocative about local news writing like this, but the reporter supplies the basics that moor the description in reality—and that's the point. For readers in the community where Rosemont Street is, a four-alarm fire is highly relevant; they want to know what happened, who was involved, if the fire is out, and if it's safe to go there. Prosaic writing can be boring for many reasons, but making it meaningful is not simply about cutting down the number of words readers have to plow through or adding stylistic twists. Sometimes you simply need to add more information to breathe life into a real event.

At the least, journalists add location and time tags to establish where and when something was observed. I've heard literary writers deride these as "tombstones" that undercut the lyrical flow of a memory or an emotionally charged experience. I've rarely found, however, that noting the actual location or time period of an event undercuts anything in a story, especially if these details answer questions most readers would ask. Consider a second hypothetical example:

> **No:** *I love music. The group was awesome.*
> **Yes:** *I love hip-hop and jazz. When I heard 5 Galz at the Concord Arena last night, their beats made me sit up and shout.*

Again, the second version packs in many specifics in describing an event: three *what*'s (hip-hop, jazz, beats), a *who* (5 Galz), a *where* (Concord Arena), and a *when* (last night). Most important for first-person reporting, it includes the observer's perspective on the action. With a close first-person stance, this writer describes their own reaction to the concert ("made me sit up and shout") rather than describing the impact on other people in the audience.

If this were a real news feature, an editor might ask whether the reporter's personal reaction is relevant for documenting a cultural event. That depends on the nature of the assignment, the audience for a feature, or the publishing venue. But regardless, the details not only help pin down the context, they indicate the writer's point of view and possible biases.

Although tossing in quirky details from a personal perspective might not seem lofty enough to hook a reader, the quirky specifics are what make a scene feel real. Think of those scrub jays in the description of Ursula Le Guin on her porch. Observing people in a particular place yields the richness of what it means to be alive. For all nonfiction writers, that's step one, and the exercises in this chapter are designed to get you observing the world like a journalist.

Voice Lesson 1

1   ***Observing:*** Here's a sample sentence: *I looked out the window.* Now look out an actual window. Spend a minute or so observing the scene, even if all you see are a few cars or trees.

2   ***Notetaking:*** In your process notebook, list as many details as you can about the scene from your window. Begin with the basics, such as what town or neighborhood you're in and the time of day. Then note more specific things that you see, hear, or otherwise sense.

3   ***Describing:*** Write a brief description of what you saw out the window (one or two paragraphs). You begin with *I looked out the window,* including the location and time tags. Then add at least one more sentence to your description to bring the scene to life.

Three kinds of details

Once you begin reporting an event or describing a new place, the details you observe will inevitably pile up, both chaff and wheat—or like a big field of hay that's been mowed but not yet bundled into stacks of meaning. We don't just hold up cameras or cell phones to record every second of our lives or anybody else's life. When we do record the world around us, we always make choices about what to take a picture of, which images or video clips to post on social media, who we call if something bad has happened, whose voice we want to hear.

In Chapters 4 and 5, I emphasized the value of establishing your perspective on a story by including certain basic details. With *orienting details,* you get across your approximate age, social position, nationality, ethnicity, or whatever else is relevant to the story. *Situational details* fill in the context for your story, such as the fact that you may have moved to another country or that you've just had your first child. And *telling details* convey your own point of view in surprising ways, creating a verbal snapshot in only a few words (see Box 6.2).

Box 6.2 Details, details

Orienting Details
Reporting basics: who? what? when? where?

Situational Details
Context and backstory: why is this happening now?

Telling Details
POV: who is observing and why are they surprised?

Once you've begun doing the initial research and writing about an observed event, it's helpful to categorize the different types of details you've noted, making separate lists for each type. Let's take a closer look at the three types, using published examples to illustrate.

Orienting details: Most of us are familiar with the *who-what-where* of news features, in which the most relevant details appear at the top of what's known as the inverted pyramid with a dateline. Orienting details are often in the headline itself, such as "Three Months, Two Continents, and Four Stints in Quarantine" by Amy Qin, published in the *New York Times* in May 2020. But Qin's feature is a first-person account of her experience as a reporter, and so the details in her opening also establish her "I" voice:

> Before the pandemic, my friends called me "the empress," a joking reference to my last name. But these days, they have begun referring to me by another, slightly less esteemed royal moniker: I am now the Quarantine Queen.
> That's because in the last three months, I have completed four rounds of quarantine in four cities, on both sides of the Pacific Ocean.
> Like many others, I passed the time by dialing into Zoom calls and bingeing on reality television. But along the way, I also rode the wave of the coronavirus pandemic. Each city where I idled—San Diego, Beijing, Los Angeles and Taipei—offered a window into the different ways in which governments were grappling with the virus.

In just over a hundred words, we know *when* this took place beyond the dateline ("the last three months," "coronavirus pandemic"), *where* she traveled ("San Diego, Beijing, Los Angeles and Taipei"), and *who* is doing the reporting (she points to her Chinese heritage in her lead with a reference to the founding emperor of the Qin dynasty). We also get a sense of Qin's "I" voice in her wry description of herself as the "Quarantine Queen" in the opening paragraph.

Situational details: Qin's first-person story is a relatively lightweight tale about her frenetic schedule. But it would mean little if she hadn't detailed her situation as a journalist who hopscotched continents during the 2020 pandemic, separated from her fiancé. And longer feature stories or personal essays require more context about why a writer is observing a given scene.

Take another 2020 first-person feature about the impact of the pandemic, this one by Elizabeth Kolbert of the *New Yorker:* "How Iceland Beat the Coronavirus." In the second scene, Kolbert introduces the context for an unlikely reporting situation: "I had initially planned to go to Iceland in March, for a story unconnected to the coronavirus. Suddenly, the trip was called off. The European Union was barring Americans from entering. . . ." She then details the maneuvers she went through to refocus her story and to get permission to enter Iceland.

Within a few paragraphs, she establishes her own situation. But this veteran feature writer also goes on to convey the situation of others she encounters on the flight to Reykjavík:

> Icelandair had, by this time, suspended service from the United States, except for sporadic flights out of Boston. The day I left, a Saturday, the international terminal at Logan was as solemn and silent as a mausoleum. Not a single ticket desk was open. On the plane, I counted fourteen seats occupied, out of nearly two hundred. I spoke briefly with a woman seated a few rows in front of me. She was going to visit her fiancé, an Icelandic soccer player, and was unhappy that they would be spending the first two weeks of her stay in separate apartments.
>
> The in-flight magazine, which apparently hadn't been replaced for several months, was filled with pictures of vacationers in the snow. It read like an illuminated manuscript—a relic from another era. One of the crew members told me that he and almost all of his colleagues, including the pilots, had been given three months' notice; they were working only occasional flights. Despite the generalized gloom, it was thrilling to be going somewhere; for the previous eight weeks, the farthest I'd travelled was to the liquor store.

Kolbert reports what the crew members and woman she talked to think of their own situations. But more important, she uses her personal perspective of what other people tell her to reveal more about the unusual circumstances for everyone ("I counted fourteen seats occupied, out of nearly two hundred"). And she encapsulates what it felt like in a few telling details: all those unoccupied plane seats, an airport that seems "as solemn and silent as a mausoleum"; vacationers from an out-of-date magazine that "read like an illuminated manuscript."

Telling details: So, here's a not-so-secret secret: good feature writers often blend all three types of details in their observations. A comparison to an illuminated manuscript, for instance, doesn't convey much to readers without knowing the context for why Elizabeth Kolbert of the *New Yorker* is observing photos of people frolicking in the snow. And yet, it's the telling details—the happy Icelandic vacationers, the mausoleum airport—that stick with readers.

The following capsule description is from Austin Murphy's 2018 *Atlantic* feature "I Used to Write for *Sports Illustrated*. Now I Deliver Packages for Amazon." The title already conveys the situation for this middle-aged journalist, one who'd been laid off from his prestigious magazine job. As Murphy frames it early on in his feature:

> This proved problematic when my wife and I decided to refinance our home. Although Gina, an attorney, earns plenty, we needed a bit more income to persuade lenders to work with us. It quickly became clear that for us to qualify, I would need more than occasional gigs as a freelance writer; I would need a steady job with a W-2. Thus did I find myself, after replying to an indeed.com posting for Amazon delivery drivers, emerging from an office-park lavatory a few miles from my house, feigning nonchalance as I handed a cup of urine to the attendant and bid him good day.

Murphy provides context with situational specifics: his wife is an attorney, they want to refinance their house, they're a relatively privileged couple. We even get his wife's name. But the surprising detail he opts to put at the end of the paragraph is the thing readers likely take away: "feigning nonchalance as I handed a cup of urine to the attendant."

In a paragraph-long capsule like this, the telling detail often comes at the end. The surprising jays "trading remarks" in Julie Phillips's capsule description of Ursula Le Guin were at the end of that paragraph, too. This is a stylistic choice on the part of experienced writers, one meant to increase the impact of a description and to catch readers off-guard so that they want to find out what happens next. But putting a telling detail at the end also demonstrates why selecting the right image or quote can encapsulate the whole story. Indeed, Murphy follows up that capsule description with what is arguably the *nut graf* (or theme paragraph) of his piece:

> Little did I know, while delivering that drug-test sample, that this most basic of human needs—relieving oneself—would emerge as one of the more pressing challenges faced by all "delivery associates," especially those of us crowding 60. An honest recounting of this job must include my sometimes frantic searches for a place to answer nature's call.

Framing the story's theme in this way is another form of capsule description. Murphy connects handing over a urine test (a telling detail) to a key story thread: not only his search for a bathroom once he gets the job but the trouble all contract drivers have finding one. Murphy's first-person feature is humorous; it's not an investigation into bad work conditions. And yet, he gets across the challenges, especially when he describes what some of his non-white coworkers faced. One Black driver told him he wore every form of Amazon-branded merchandise on his person to convince homeowners he wasn't a "porch pirate" thief (let alone needed to use their bathroom).

Voice Lesson 2

1   *Observing:* For your description of the window scene in Voice Lesson 1, highlight (or underline) all the details you've included in it.
2   *Notetaking:* Categorize those details in three different lists: *orienting, situational,* or *telling.*
3   *Describing:* Have you included all three detail types? Why or why not? In your notebook, reflect on whether you need to add more of certain types of details to bring this scene to life.

Conveying the feel of a place

Many first drafts by students handle place details as if they're no more than background wallpaper. If readers are lucky, there's a location tag (the name of the city or neighborhood). The place is a "garage" or a "farm" with "trees." The story describes people or events, as if the location has no impact on what's being observed. To use a sports cliché Austin Murphy might have once employed, that's a rookie mistake.

Describing the feel of a place in more personal ways greatly affects how readers engage with a story. Yes, the focus of a third-person news feature is topical; the format demands no more than a location tag or dateline reference to a place. But even in a short news feature, telling details about the place where something happened can be evocative for readers. Observational details are informative beyond just the facts. One of the strengths of first-person journalism is that it involves an individual response to a scene. Consider the place details in Murphy's story:

> Will I be in the hills above El Cerrito with astounding views of the bay, but narrow roads, difficult parking, and lots of steps? Or will my itinerary take me to gritty Richmond, which, despite its profusion of pit bulls, I'm starting to prefer to the oppressive traffic of Berkeley, where I deliver to the brightest young people in the state, some of whom may wonder, if they give me even a passing thought: What hard luck has befallen this man, who appears to be my father's age but is performing this menial task?

Murphy's description of different delivery routes in the East Bay is certainly relevant to his story about being an Amazon delivery driver. But his personal perspective conveys a lot about the economic class differences among El Cerrito ("astounding views of the bay"), Richmond ("gritty" with a "profusion of pitbulls"), and Berkeley ("oppressive traffic," "brightest young people in the state"). He also connects his own middle-aged situation to what those bright young people might think of him.

As an exercise in my courses, I ask students to look at a photograph of the iconic Katz's Delicatessen in New York City and to describe the busy scene inside. Based on the information available with the photo, the basics are easy to pin down: the name of the place and its location—that is, the *where*. The *who* of all the people shown in the restaurant isn't identified, but because there's visual documentation, you can describe them and *what* they're doing. The photographer's notes on the image I've used say it was taken in 2007—so that's the *when*. (Feel free to locate this photo online or to Google around and find another image of Katz's interior.)

The basics aren't what give the scene life, however. If you were standing in Katz's, you could take in other sensory details beyond what it looks like—such as what it sounds like, smells like, feels like in terms of the temperature, the busyness, the overall emotional tone. These all have the potential to be telling details. They're the things that stand out and make a description feel vivid. Even based on looking at a photo, you might notice other details that go beyond the basics, such as all the photographs on the walls, the different ages of patrons, how full most of the tables are, the big fluorescent lights. Here's my capsule description:

You Want Loud?

Katz's Delicatessen looks loud even in this photograph, swirling with sweatshirt colors and caps, the packed tables under twin fluorescent lights multiplied by all the pictures crammed on the wall—people and more people, past and present. Some patrons might remember World War II. Others were born after 9/11.

I refer to Katz's by name, but the details I include have more to do with the feel of the place—or in this case, the feel of the photograph. If this were part of a feature story about Katz's, I'd focus the description more, making sure the details I chose were relevant. I might mention that, according to the Katz's website, it was founded in 1888 in the Lower East Side near its current location and that it started selling pastrami subscriptions in 2018. I might say more about what such delis have represented to Jewish immigrants over the decades and how the inflections of Yiddish have influenced the way New Yorkers talk.

I might also position myself as the observer, making clear why I'm writing about Katz's. I'm not Jewish, and I didn't grow up in New York City; I've never eaten at Katz's. But based on my current vantage point in 2021, the crowds in the photo sadden me. After a year of coronavirus worries, enjoying a sandwich in a crowded deli is no longer something I take for granted.

Voice Lesson 3

1   *Observing:* Spend five minutes observing a crowded restaurant or looking at a photograph of a crowded restaurant. (There are many busy restaurant

scenes available online, including a whole gallery of images of Katz's Delicatessen.) If you're observing a restaurant in real time, be sure to take a photo or brief video of the scene so you can refer to it later.

2   **Notetaking:** In your notebook, list all the sensory details you notice about the scene, including the lighting and the energy of the people there. List basic orienting details, too, and situational details that provide context for your observation of the scene.

3   **Describing:** Write a capsule description of the restaurant from your own point of view (no more than 100 words). Base the description on your observation notes and, if you observed a restaurant in real time, any photos or video recordings you took.

Reporting what people do and say

As you'll see from the writing assignment at the end of this chapter, particular places can be an excellent focus for a neighborhood story. Places also convey a lot about how and why events happen there and what people do in them. That's because people animate places, especially urban places, which is why description of one relies so much on the other.

Describing people starts with observing them carefully, a practice that goes beyond identifying their eye or hair color. What are they wearing? Which part of their outfit stands out or is surprising? How do they move their hands when they talk? Do they tend to smile or to frown? Are they openly expressive or closed down? Are their voices loud or soft? Do they speak quickly, almost tripping over their words in excitement to express themselves? Do they pause, looking upward, thinking through what they're going to say next?

That's just a start on the sort of questions a feature reporter might ask themselves in noting down a subject's appearance. You'll come up with others based on the actual people you observe in a natural setting or talk to as part of an interview. If you're people-watching to help describe a place, then you'll likely observe how crowded it is, what the people are doing there, how much they're interacting with each other. In documenting and describing a natural setting, your focus will be on physical details. You may overhear people talking, jotting down snippets of informal conversation without identifying who the speakers are beyond their actions and appearance.

But once you decide to talk to someone at the scene, you're interviewing them, and a different set of observations comes into play. Transcribing and conveying what real people say is very much a part of the reporter's craft. It's also the part many non-reporters find daunting, especially after watching all those movies of reporters thrusting mics in people's faces. But most of us aren't trying to interview the president or a CEO, and once you get in the habit of noting down what people are saying, it can be fun. We spend a lot of our lives talking, either in real time or virtually, and often quotes move the action in a story forward.

First things first: at the beginning of any interview—whether speaking with someone on the phone, in person, or virtually via Skype or Zoom—ask permission to record (or video) it. Then you have a document, and you can check it later. Once subjects adjust to the fact that they're being recorded, this also helps establish a more conversational rhythm. *First-Person Journalism* is not a guide to journalistic protocol, but I will emphasize that for anyone you might quote or name in a story, you should document what they say. You'll need to refer to recordings or your notes later not only to jog your memory but to verify the wording of direct quotes. And recording without subterfuge helps ensure that your subjects know their words are on the record.

Yet observations of body language or interaction style matter as much as recording what somebody says, especially if the person you're talking with will be the focus of your story. In my own reporting, I've often found myself retreating to a hallway or bathroom right after interviewing someone, noting down everything I observed about the person, the room where we talked, and the way that person moved around the room. I also note my own reactions to some of what was said or even the slant of light coming through the windows. Few or none of those details may end up in a final feature, but they do help me conjure the feeling of a conversation.

One of the interview tips offered in Box 6.3 is to go somewhere with your subject. Take a walk in the park with them, visit their favorite bookstore or local café, walk around the office where they work. The point is to watch them in action—to see how they behave around their employees, for instance, or who they greet when they're walking around their neighborhood.

Box 6.3 Interview tips

Ask and confirm the basics with your subject:
name, age, occupation, where they live

But also ask unexpected, open questions:
What are you binge watching now?
What food do you really hate?
What's the worst argument you've ever had with someone?
If you could change your profession, what would you be?
What scares you most?

If possible, go somewhere with your subject:
a café, a park, their place of work, their home

In my hallway notes, I also highlight spoken words that stand out, sometimes circling key phrases and connecting them to observations of what the person was doing as they said them. Even if I'm recording everything and snapping photos, I take notes as I'm talking with someone, because the words I take down catch my attention and may well end up as the direct quotes I include in the final feature.

More important, this hybrid approach to notetaking and recording is part of self-reporting for a first-person journalist. The process of notetaking helps me define the way I make meaning of what was said from my particular point of view.

Every journalist has their own methods for recording and taking notes, but I can well imagine Elizabeth Kolbert's inner grin as she framed this quote from her official Icelandic host Kári Stephánsson, head of deCODE Genetics: "As soon as I got into his Porsche, he asked me where I was from. I said western Massachusetts. 'Massachusetts is probably the most boring place on earth,' he declared."

Julie Phillips also told me by email that details "can start the story, too." She described doing an interview with a writer at his house that at first didn't click:

> He had his standard life story that he'd told to every interviewer, and that I already knew from reading previous interviews. I kept asking questions but couldn't get him to change course. When he went to make tea, I saw he had a lot of photographs and postcards on one wall of his living room. I asked him to tell me about who they were and why they were important to him. His stories around those pictures ended up becoming the heart of my profile.

Voice Lesson 4

1   *Observing:* Practice interviewing by recording a 10- to 15-minute Q&A with a family member or friend. Make sure you can see them while they're talking, whether you're conducting the interview in person or virtually. Also, ask at least two open-ended, unexpected questions.

2   *Notetaking:* During and after the interview, jot down in your notebook what they're wearing, their body language and other appearance details, the setting for the interview, and so on.

3   *Describing:* Write a capsule profile of your interview subject from your own point of view (no more than 150 words). Base the profile on your notes and your recording. Include at least two direct quotes from your interviewee in this capsule description.

Direct reporting of events

Beyond describing what places look like and what people say, many features also pose questions—and these questions revolve around hot topics or events. Describing events calls for both the ability to observe people in action and to summarize what happened.

Direct reporting begins with the *who-what-where-when* basics news reporters pin down in covering a national or local disaster (recall that fictional fire on Rosemont Street). Feature stories also target the *how* and *why* consequences of events, and there, a writer's perspective shapes how action is described to readers. We'll look more closely at sequences and timing in Chapter 9, but in essence, a story involves action and its outcome.

Box 6.4 outlines *what-who-where-when* for "Something Happens." In reality, most stories include more than one "something." An event and its outcome trigger another event, another outcome, and so on. It's the writer's job to decide on the beginning and end of a story, based on the reporting assignment and what's known at the time.

Still, in an event description, it can help to break it down into discrete actions. The more you can distinguish between specific actions and outcomes, the better you'll get at describing what happened. In the case of a major news story, this may even become a narrative tick-tock, as in "11 Journalists on Covering the Capitol Seige: 'This Could Get Ugly,'" a *New York Times* feature that appeared a few days after rioters broke into the U.S. Capitol on January 6, 2021, disrupting certification by Congress of the Electoral College votes for President Joseph Biden.

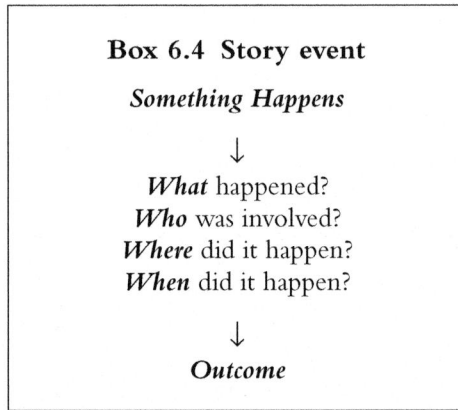

Box 6.4 Story event

Something Happens

↓

What happened?
Who was involved?
Where did it happen?
When did it happen?

↓

Outcome

The resulting feature, compiled by Katie Robertson and Tiffany Hsu, weaves among first-person anecdotes by journalists on the scene, arranged in sections under time headings, such as "noon," and "2 p.m." Under the first "Morning" section, April Ryan, correspondent for *TheGrio*, described herself "working the phones, not really expecting anything big, thinking it was just going to be a lot of posturing." Meanwhile, Marcus DiPaola, a freelancer with a big TikTok following, said, "I knew it was going to be a complete mess ahead of time."

Relying on first-person accounts by these journalists indicates not only differences in perspective but also how confusing (and scary) the unfolding action was. By noon, Chad Pergram of Fox News recalled being dropped off by his wife: "[R]ight as I got out of the car, you could feel the tension, because there were protesters everywhere." Kadia Goba of *Axios* was more direct, describing what she witnessed as well as why she felt threatened:

> When I walked up the usual entranceway, Capitol Police told me I had to walk with the protesters. I was super pissed off about that. I walked through the crowd—and I'm a woman of color, so it was intimidating, to be honest with you.

It's not always possible to witness breaking news, and this historic event was not the norm for a Washington correspondent. News reporters called to a crime or disaster scene usually jump in after it's begun. Direct reporting can get short shrift in favor of remote interviews or relying on police reports and press releases. Many news organizations have limited resources and can't send out a reporter to cover, say, every school committee meeting or protest march.

Yet gathering eyewitness accounts after the fact is a legitimate part of piecing together an event, as is looking at videos or photos of a scene. The "11 Journalists" feature does that, spotlighting what happened with the use of dramatic time headings. Other feature writers may visit a scene only long after the fact or recall what happened years later. Regardless, I can't stress enough the value of being there—or at least walking on the actual dirt where an event once took place—especially if you're researching a story personally meaningful to you. Police reports, for instance, only present one side of a logged incident. Events influence people and their actions, just as unconscious biases impact the details that end up on the public record.

Note that action in a story doesn't only refer to car chases or a mob storming the U.S. Capitol. Action in features is also generated by disagreements over the facts or arguments about ideas. The *what* of "Something Happens" might be somebody starting a fistfight, a famous author relating her side of an argument, or an intellectual disagreement about research claims. Storytelling action refers to anything a person, creature, or other entity does that has an outcome.

Keep in mind *action* → *outcome* as a formula to help direct your observations. You can verify the *who-where-when* basics later to help pin down what you've witnessed. The same formula applies to watching a video of an event or a live broadcast. Describing live events requires lots of notetaking of the "first this, then that" variety, but your goal is to pull out telling details or action. As we'll see in the following chapters about attribution, counterpoints, and time travel, the whole point of summarizing action for readers is to give it meaning (Box 6.5).

Otherwise, it's just a car chase.

Box 6.5 Story meaning

Something Happens
what • who • where • when
↓
Outcome
↓
Meaning
How did it happen?
How do you know?
Why did it happen?
Why does it matter?

Voice Lesson 5

1   *Observing:* Watch a brief video clip from congressional testimony or a press conference with a public figure. For example, I've asked students to watch a *PBS NewsHour* video of Mark Zuckerberg and Alexandria Ocasio-Cortez at a U.S. House of Representatives hearing that took place on October 23, 2019. You can find this video online or use another comparable clip.

2   *Notetaking:* As you watch the video, write down as many direct quotes that stand out as possible. Also jot down what the people involved are wearing, their body language and other appearance details, the setting for the event you're observing, and so on.

3   *Describing:* Write a capsule description of the event that includes at least one direct quote and one paraphrase of a quote (100 to 200 words). Be sure to include a few telling details that convey what you, the writer, think of what you've observed.

Hint: Make this anecdote your own, even if it describes a well-known news event. Base your description on what you observe in the video clip, not what anyone else has written.

The art of capsule description

In writing classes, it's common to exhort students to "show, don't tell." That means you should let your descriptions and action do the explaining for you. But like all truisms, this one isn't always true—and it can lead writers astray, especially in stories that are designed to be read online where immediacy is key. A good telling detail, in just a few words or sentences, carries a lot of information beyond the thing described. Think of the way photo captions flag key details to supplement an image. When you put the right details together, you come up with capsule descriptions that convey the whole topic or its emotional resonance.

Anecdotes, or mini-stories, are another form of capsule description—such as Elizabeth Kolbert describing the meeting with her arrogant Icelandic host or the accounts at different points in time of those journalists during the Capitol riot. Anecdotes include both descriptive detail and action summaries. In a first-person feature, they may depict seemingly small incidents, but the telling details—or telling action—illuminate the feature's focus.

Lawrence Wright's "The Plague Year," a 2021 tour de force in the *New Yorker,* chronicles the coronavirus crisis in the United States the previous year through both well-known events and telling details. It's a forty-page narrative of the "mistakes and struggles behind an American tragedy," unfolding in tick-tock fashion. But it also tells the story through capsule descriptions of an array of places and people around the country. For instance, here's a capsule of a Black anesthesiologist at the University of Virginia's hospital in Charlottesville:

> When Dr. Ebony Hilton enters a room, patients see wide-set, lively eyes above her surgical mask. Her hair and body are hidden by a bonnet and a gown. Her accent marks her as a Southerner. She calls herself a "country girl," which is at odds with her assured manner. When the call comes to intubate a COVID patient, "it's already a situation where somebody is dying," she told me.

Wright's sections combine anecdotes about, say, Matthew Pottinger—a deputy national-security adviser who issued unheeded warnings early on—or Deborah Birx, the U.S. global AIDS coordinator who reluctantly joined the White House Coronavirus Task Force, only to leave under a cloud because, as one administration official noted, "They hate her." Wright, an award-winning investigative journalist as well as the author of a 2020 novel about a fictional pandemic (*The End of October*), rarely injects his first-person perspective into the long *New Yorker* article. But when he does, those passages encapsulate the emotional impact for everyone:

> On September 9th, our grandchild Gioia was born. She is the dearest creature. We stare into each other's eyes in wonder. Even in this intimate moment, though, the menace of contagion is present: we are more likely to infect the people we love than anyone else. Deborah Birx has recalled that, in 1918, her grandmother, aged eleven, brought the flu home from school to her mother, who died of it. "I can tell you, my grandmother lived with that for eighty-eight years," she said.

For me, artful capsule descriptions and anecdotes are the equivalents of fractals. In mathematical terms, fractal patterns get smaller every time they're repeated in a shape, as in the branches of a tree or the inner swirls of a nautilus shell. In the same way, anecdotes not only function on their own as stories within a story but also convey the larger whole. Humans tend to repeat the same things, even if social patterns are rarely simple or easy to understand. The fractal analogy isn't exact for real-world outcomes, but as nonfiction storytellers, much of what we're doing is wrestling a pattern from our observations.

First-person journalists let readers know that the pattern they observe is individually defined. The irony is that unique, specific details often seem more trustworthy than abstract glosses by acknowledged experts. In the next chapter, we'll switch to what may appear to be the solid realm of facts and sources. But as this book repeatedly underscores, facts can be molded to fit many agendas. Summarizing, selecting, and interpreting what you—a particular observer—see is the backbone of first-person feature writing as well as literary art.

In the final paragraph of her Le Guin profile, Julie Phillips closes with another capsule description, based on visiting the aging author on the Oregon coast:

> The next morning, Le Guin stood in the front yard of her house at the edge of the world, feeding a family of crows. The sun was out, and a block away the surf beat gently on the broad beach, where the town meets the waters of the North Pacific. Here the land seemed undone by the unknown distances of the ocean, and Le Guin seemed to be standing where the forces met, gazing beyond her garden to some farther shore.

This anecdote conjures an image of Le Guin facing death itself. It even circles around to birds again, although the black crows she feeds are no longer talkative jays.

Once you begin pinning down specific details—observing a neighborhood event, accurately recording the words of real people—you'll find there's plenty of mystery left. Choosing the right details doesn't necessarily explain anything more than noting what two scrub jays did. Yet those details may surprise readers into intimations of mortality, moments of being, or meditations of their own about the world we all share.

Local profile: Write about a neighborhood place

1   **Observing:** Visit a public place in your neighborhood—such as a church, library, or café—and observe it for at least half an hour. Note down everything you see, hear, or otherwise take in with your senses. In your notebook, list as many specific descriptive details as you can. If you overhear any conversations, write down quotes that strike you. (Alternatively, look for video documentation of a place in your neighborhood and describe what you observe in the video.)

2   **Interviewing:** If possible, interview at least one stranger in the place you're observing, asking what they think of it and getting down their contact details. You might want to interview such sources again by phone to fact check their names and other details. Alternatively, you can interview friends or family about the place—or call a local official or business proprietor after your visit to ask what they think and to do some fact checking.

3   **Researching:** Before writing your profile, research the history of the place you observed—when it first opened to the public, for example, and what people thought at the time. Also, verify orienting details and other factual information gleaned about dates and names from interviewees. Background research is a good way to correct any misperceptions you have about a local place.

4   **Describing:** Write a short first-person profile of the place you observed (between 800 and 1,200 words), including at least one interview quote and some background information. Be sure to add enough orienting and situational details to let readers know who you are.

Sources

"The Fantastic Ursula K. Le Guin" by Julie Phillips, *New Yorker*, October 16, 2016. www.newyorker.com/magazine/2016/10/17/the-fantastic-ursula-k-le-guin

Julie Phillips, personal email communication with author, October 22, 2020.

"Three Months, Two Continents, and Four Stints in Quarantine" by Amy Qin, *New York Times*, May 13, 2020. www.nytimes.com/2020/05/13/world/asia/coronavirus-quarantine.html

"How Iceland Beat the Coronavirus" by Elizabeth Kolbert, *New Yorker*, June 1, 2020. www.newyorker.com/magazine/2020/06/08/how-iceland-beat-the-coronavirus\

"I Used to Write for *Sports Illustrated*. Now I Deliver Packages for Amazon" by Austin Murphy, *Atlantic*, December 25, 2018. www.theatlantic.com/ideas/archive/2018/12/what-its-like-to-deliver-packages-for-amazon/578986/

Katz's Delicatessan website. www.katzsdelicatessen.com/

"Katz's Deli" photograph by peasap (Paul Sapiano), 2007, accessed on Flickr; Creative Commons license (CC BY 2.0). www.flickr.com/photos/peasap/1913499041

"11 Journalists on Covering the Capitol Seige: 'This Could Get Ugly'" by Katie Robertson and Tiffany Hsu, *New York Times*, January 9, 2021. www.nytimes.com/2021/01/09/business/media/journalists-capitol-mob.html

"Ocasio-Cortez Questioned Zuckerberg About False Political Ads. Facebook Is Now Defending Its Policy" (video and transcript), *PBS NewsHour*, October 24, 2019. www.pbs.org/newshour/politics/watch-ocasio-cortez-questioned-zuckerberg-about-false-political-ads-facebook-is-now-defending-its-policy

"The Plague Year" by Lawrence Wright, *New Yorker*, January 4 and 11, 2021, pp. 44, 56 (print edition). www.newyorker.com/magazine/2021/01/04/the-plague-year

7 Attributing sources

Where do my facts come from?

Before I ended up in magazine journalism, I thought of attribution in a different way than a journalist does. In college, my senior thesis in social psychology involved attribution theory, which focuses on how we regular people (aka "naïve psychologists") understand the behavior of others. According to the theory—which first gained cachet in the 1950s and 1960s with the publication of Fritz Heider's *The Psychology of Interpersonal Relations*—we attribute why somebody else does something to "situational" or "dispositional" causes. We decide whether a man in a hoodie, say, is sleeping on a park bench at 7 a.m. because he just worked a graveyard shift at the hospital (the situation) or he's a lazy, homeless drunk (his disposition).

Our ideas about personality or the circumstances that might cause a person to do something don't lay out neatly in real life, of course, especially when we're assessing strangers. Humans don't always make rational choices about the intentions of others; nor do they observe behavior with the distance of psychologists. My college thesis hypothesized gender differences in attribution, as well as attribution errors—what we'd now think of as cognitive biases.

Years later, once I became a magazine editor, I fell in love with the way feature writers synthesize information for readers. No more slow parsing of academic research! No more waiting for statistically significant results to add up to a conclusion! And yet, as an editor I also grew skeptical of the conclusions many writers seemed to leap to. I learned the craft of verifying and fact checking information on the job, but I still find myself posing the same question readers often ask: *How does this writer know that's true?*

In news reporting, you can check specific facts and corroborate details to verify that something happened. But when it comes to interpreting "something," journalists and sources often have different points of view. That's why *attribution*—telling readers where your information comes from—matters. This may sound simple, but attribution confuses even experienced reporters, and for first-person feature writers, it also involves conveying how you're interpreting information and why you trust it. Some typical questions I've heard: *How much attribution is enough? Sure, I tell readers who said a quote or whether statistics are based on research—but how many details do I need to give about the source? If I'm writing for a respected news site, won't readers assume the facts I present are correct?*

DOI: 10.4324/9781003132189-10

These are all good questions, by the way. Readers who have faith in the press will believe the facts they read on major news sites, but others won't. For instance, if I'm reading the *New York Times*, *Guardian*, or stories from other major news organizations, I assume unattributed facts are based on solid reporting. I agree with the "Associated Press Statement of News Values and Principles," which emphasizes that when facts in a news story "could reasonably be disputed," they need attribution. The trouble comes in determining which facts are disputed.

In this book, I've highlighted *attribution* as a key element instead of fact check-ing because readers often dispute factual claims made by first-person writers. Assumptions about third-person neutrality don't apply. *First-Person Journalism* doesn't get into the nuances of news gathering, but first-person feature writers need to do fact checking, too, if only to determine how reliable their sources are. In digital media, attribution of factual claims has become increasingly important for traditional reporters as well. Effective attribution forces all non-fiction writers to wrestle with how credible their information is—be it based on personal experience, direct reporting, documentary footage, a website, or what somebody else says.

Unfortunately, many personal nonfiction writers have a hard time grasping why attribution is necessary or even the concept of attribution. For more than a decade, I've seen attribution problems in hundreds of student articles or the literary work I've edited.

Except wait a minute—I just made an authoritative claim. You could cite me as an expert in writing instruction (I did cofound a digital magazine), but anecdotal evidence is not the same as a controlled study or scholarly research. Why do you believe what I say?

My point is not for you to question me. It's to underscore that claims based on personal experience depend on the perception of readers and their belief in your credibility. Anecdotal evidence often is all journalists have at their dis-posal, but acknowledging the limitations of reporting can build more trust than categorically stating something is true. At the very least, tell readers how you collected your anecdotes. Such attribution provides context.

This chapter covers the basics of attributing sources and what constitutes a credible source for a feature writer. I also emphasize why positioning yourself as a first-person observer and interpreter of information can get readers to trust you as an expert source. Is a first-person account of a topic more subjective? Yes. But a first-person perspective also helps writers inform readers more transpar-ently about where their facts come from.

What is attribution?

Fact-checking practices can seem arcane to the uninitiated, but there's a pro-tocol for it at traditional magazines and news sites. More to the point, most readers understand its purpose. Contrast this with attribution. The Media Insight Project, sponsored by the American Press Institute and the AP-NORC

Center, has conducted research on the public's knowledge about journalism. Its 2018 study "Americans and the News Media" reports that, of the 2,000-plus non-journalists surveyed, "More than 4 in 10 do not know what the term 'attribution' means, and close to 3 in 10 do not know the difference between an 'editorial' and a 'news story.'"

Expertise about an unfolding news story is based on reporting done by many different writers and vetted by editors. At major news organizations, the accumulation of information constantly goes on in the background, but too often, readers and viewers get little explanation for how the facts have been checked and verified or who is doing it. They just see the headlines.

Enter attribution. In another 2014 "strategy study" on the American Press Institute site—"Build Credibility Through Transparency"—Craig Silverman defines its value like so:

> One of the oldest and most hallowed forms of transparency in journalism is attribution. You link what was said to the person who said it. You cite your sources. You provide a roadmap that leads back to all the people you spoke to, the documents you read, the other articles and research that helped form your work.

Silverman goes on to discuss the importance of what he calls "ethical curation" of other news sources in a given piece and the role of hyperlinking to provide readers with additional information. As an example of curation, he quotes from the *NPR Ethics Handbook*:

> When in doubt, err on the side of attributing. . . . Every NPR reporter and editor should be able to immediately identify the source of any facts in our stories—and why we consider them credible. And every reader or listener should know where we got our information from. "Media reports" or "sources say" is not good enough. Be specific.

Just how much context you provide when you attribute a source like this relies on judgment about what readers need to know. Silverman attributed the quote to the NPR handbook and linked through to the website; the insertion of an attributed hyperlink is now a well-accepted tool in providing more transparency about sources. For my purposes, however, I'll add that the quote is part of a special section in the NPR handbook on attribution under this guideline: *Attribute everything.* More context helps underscore my main point.

I could have also mentioned that Craig Silverman is currently a *BuzzFeed* editor; has been called "the Fake News Watchdog"; edited the *Verification Handbook*; and wrote *Regret the Error*, a long-running blog on the Poynter Institute journalism site. I'm doing so now, yet there's more: the "fake news watchdog" label comes from a 2017 *Politico* profile; Tom Rosenstiel, former executive director of the American Press Institute, cowrote *The Elements of*

Journalism. Rosenstiel also founded and directed the Project for Excellence in Journalism. Whether readers need to know so many details can be one of the biggest practical challenges of *attribute everything*.

There's a balance to be struck between too much information and not enough. In journalistic features, not enough is never the goal. Yet feature articles are addressed to general audiences, and in my humble opinion, most of us don't want an eye-glazing catalog of *First, I contacted my source on LinkedIn, which lists him as getting a doctorate in criminology at the University of Pennsylvania in 1981. He said he's "freelance" now (later checking shows he's lived with his mother since 1983 and filed for SSI), but he knew about an archive in her attic. Then I called his mother, who agreed to let me "fiddle around in there all you want, just don't leave a mess." Then I swept up all the dust I'd raised. . . .*

Instead, a first-person reporter's credibility often rests on the context they provide about the bias of their sources. Take the additional information I provided about Silverman and Rosenstiel. For this book-length guide of mine, the details signal their credibility as experts, and citing them enhances my credibility as a writer who's done her research. Context about who they are also highlights their biases as longtime journalists and advocates for the press. In a book, I have space to include more context about sources.

In a short article, it's tempting to drop all that attribution context. If the facts have been checked and claims about what happened corroborated, editors may well cut what they deem unnecessary background in an effort to keep readers from falling asleep. Readability is a worthy goal, too, and standards for how much attribution to include are based on an individual magazine or news site's assessment of what their audiences expect.

But for better or worse, the digital transformation of media *has* changed how much readers trust the facts they're told. Here's my own variation on NPR's guideline:

Attribute everything you can with context, even if it seems like too much.

It's easy to dismiss those who distrust traditional news sites as ignorant or pig-headed. Except, attribution theorist that I am, I know how much my own judgments are fueled by a need to explain "bad" behavior with inherent personality characteristics rather than social circumstances. In other words, I'm a believer—in research protocols, in science, in college educations, in good reporting. So are most reporters and editors. The hitch is that journalism believers can no longer assume readers have the same faith in reporting practices that we do.

Attributing how you know what you know means you, the reporter, are always confronted with cognitive dissonance. That's not a comfortable position for most nonfiction writers, who want to present themselves as experts, be they academic researchers or on the scene with a shoulder camera. But it means you not only nod to the sources behind your expert façade; you also have to figure out which ones to attribute. Most important, you need to make sure your own biases aren't influencing decisions about which claims are wrong.

Voice Lesson 1

1   **You're the expert:** Now it's your turn. In your process notebook, list three things you're good at or feel you know a lot about. (Examples: training as a professional chef, a particular medical condition, growing up with a mentally ill family member, a sport or hobby.)
2   **Topic description:** For one item on your list, write a brief paragraph to explain what it is and why people need to learn more about your topic.
3   **Opinion check:** In your topic description, did you make any sweeping claims or statements of belief? Why or why not? In your notebook, reflect on how you might add evidence by attributing some of what you know beyond your own expertise or personal opinions.

Sources in first-person features

What makes any of us credible observers and reporters? Why *should* readers believe us? We're human, we misinterpret things all the time, and most of us desperately want to resolve complexity. Our fallibility doesn't justify bad journalism, but it does mean we need to keep contemplating where we went wrong, what we've left out, and our information sources.

There's already reasonable confusion about what constitutes a reliable source for facts. Non-journalists (when surveyed by the Media Insight Project or other researchers) tend to think of sources as people who are interviewed by reporters, whether on the record or off, anonymous or not. But sources can also be books and articles, video clips, public social-media posts, or your own observations. In journalistic terms, a source is anything or anyone that provides information about the topic of a story, yet that definition is broad and poorly understood by readers. As the Media Insight Project noted in its 2018 study, "The bottom line: The public is ready for a relationship with more understanding and trust, if news media can take the right steps to earn it."

So, let's take a step or two toward understanding sources. We can start by distinguishing *outside sources* (Box 7.1) from *personal sources* that include family, friends, and a reporter's own expertise. Both outside and personal sources contribute to the factual basis of a first-person story. But even in a personal narrative, bringing in a few reliable outside sources will expand the story beyond your individual experience, potentially connecting with a larger community of readers. More important, attributing outside sources acknowledges that expertise rests on the shoulders of others, as it almost always does in journalistic features.

Journalists traditionally look to statistics, research findings, or outside expertise for factual information. Readers may be convinced by different kinds of evidence—for some, personal stories are the most trustworthy sources—but determining how much to attribute to outside sources requires research before you make a decision. The reporting that feature writers do involves locating the right experts and learning about a topic in order to interpret it for readers. You need to know enough to ask good questions as well as to trust your gut.

Credible as any outside source seems, it will present information framed by institutional biases, even for regulated "gov" websites. The U.S. Bureau of Labor Statistics, for instance, doesn't consider childcare or eldercare to be work in a formal sense unless it is paid. In this, it adheres to mainstream economics, which focuses on those in the labor force to calculate productivity and other indicators that set fiscal policy. But as feminist economists have argued for decades, that bias makes the labor of family caregiving invisible. The 2020 coronavirus pandemic spotlighted how much actual work family caregiving involves if public schools and daycare centers are closed. In a 2020 opinion feature, Gus Wezerek and Kristen Ghodsee open by flatly stating, "If American women earned minimum wage for the unpaid work they do around the house and caring for relatives, they would have made $1.5 trillion last year."

Box 7.1 Outside sources

government agencies
academics and other experts
major trade organizations
think tanks and foundations
news organizations

Journalists have long wrestled with how to balance different sources to provide an accurate interpretation. In the family caregiving example, I cited two reliable sources with different agendas to make my point. I've attributed a well-known government agency with a website that can be easily checked; I selected an interactive feature by a *New York Times* reporter (Wezerek) and a University of Pennsylvania professor (Ghodsee). If you don't agree, you might dismiss Wezerek and Ghodsee as part of the media elite. They present fancy visuals and statistics but no personal account of their biases. But because I don't hide my own feminist leanings, I hope it's clear why *I* chose them. If I'd included a personal anecdote from the time I had to cut back on paid work to raise my son and help out with aging parents, you might be more convinced.

The two big differences between first-person journalism and standard feature reporting come down to (1) how writers convey anecdotes based on personal sources and (2) an increased use of what Silverman and others call curated sources—that is, work published by other writers. Opinion pieces are often a reaction to what somebody else said or wrote, and on digital sites they tend to attract more traffic than news reports. Beyond the business logic, however, when features delve into contentious cultural topics, there's bound to be bias on all sides.

That brings us to another step for identifying sources in first-person features. Ask yourself, "Where do *all* my facts come from?" (see Box 7.2). The three basic categories for sourcing facts are interviews, documents, and direct observation.

But because first-person journalism mixes personal and outside sources, I've expanded the categories to five: personal experience; direct observation; interviews with other people; published outside sources; and documentation of past events via archives, photos, recordings, or video.

Note that Wikipedia, Encyclopedia Britannica, or other general-information sites are not part of my list of sources. Websites and apps allow you to pin down basics such as the distance between two cities (Google Maps) or the weather on a certain date in 1981 (NOAA). By all means, check for names and dates, and keep track of general information from encyclopedia sites in your notebook. But in interpreting a complicated topic for readers, attributing what you know to Wikipedia is not a convincing way to portray yourself as an expert.

Box 7.2 Sources for first-person features
Where do all my facts come from?

personal experience
first-person anecdotes and expertise

direct observation
description of other people, places, events

interviews
real-life or expert quotes

books, articles, research studies
key statistics, historical context, quotes

documentation of events
photos, video, trial transcripts, emails, social media

Beyond the need to establish expertise with specific attribution, there are other reasons to be wary of crowdsourced encyclopedias. Here, I want to distinguish fact checking in general from feature reporting and attribution. Wikipedia can be a good starting place for finding primary sources—most entries include reference citations and links to promising reporting leads—but it isn't a source itself for attribution. Wikipedia "editors" (writers) are anonymous; the entries don't include a byline, so it's unclear who put the information together.

But the more serious problem with relying on Wikipedia or other such sites is that they often replicate discrimination against those who have been left out of traditional media. Digital entries are compiled based on what's been published and what is available for linking on the web. Yet there are many other sources, past and present, that don't appear in the digital record. They may not have been penned by academics with positions at universities or by widely published journalists; they may have been published before 1990 and haven't been digitized. They may have been written by people of color, women, nongovernment-sanctioned journalists, or anyone else who's been cut off from official publishing venues.

In the 2020 entry "Wikipedia: Verifiability, Not Truth," the site lays out its own standards, stating: "Any material added to Wikipedia must have been published previously by a reliable source. Editors may not add content solely because they believe it is true, nor delete content they believe to be untrue." It's an admirable approach to verifying what's on the public record, but it also points up gaps in that record. Wikipedia itself urges caution:

> Users should be aware that not all articles are of encyclopedic quality from the start: they may contain false or debatable information. Indeed, many articles start their lives as displaying a single viewpoint; and, after a long process of discussion, debate, and argumentation, they gradually take on a neutral point of view reached through consensus.

While this attitude toward evolving knowledge is not unlike claims about news reporting being the first draft of history, emphasizing "consensus" and "neutrality" amounts to an overall bias about information sources. The neutral voice of Wikipedia can and has disguised bias, not to mention perpetrated some well-known fakeries.

The rise of opinionating in digital media means we're bombarded by sweeping claims that are treated as unquestionable. It's a major reason why so many writers think attribution is unnecessary. Indeed, I just made another claim. Maybe you believe me because you agree. Maybe it's because you're convinced I'm an expert—and that's a start. But I hope you consider me trustworthy because I've attributed outside sources about journalism in earlier sections of this chapter. As with so many topics that involve expertise, little advice is new.

Voice Lesson 2

1   **You're the expert:** Choose one of the "expert" topics you listed in Voice Lesson 1.
2   **Identify sources:** Come up with at least five sources for your expert topic—if possible, one or more for each of the five categories in Box 7.2.
3   **Fact check:** In your notebook, answer the following questions for each source you've found:

   • *Does the information come from a legitimate organization?*
   • *Why do I think the source is reliable?*
   • *How can I identify the source's biases?*
   • *Can I check specific claims or numbers with other outside sources?*

Attribution tags and linking

Effective attribution isn't simply a matter of throwing in links or "science tells us." If you're an expert yourself, a biographical note at the end may suffice to establish your credibility. Often, however, your expertise or that of the experts you quote requires context. First-person journalism is an excellent strategy for undercutting the distrust so many readers and viewers feel. The "I" voice helps take the sting out of authorities talking down to them, and as a writer, your stance is not that of an omniscient expert. Instead, good first-person reporters acknowledge what their outside sources are, indicate their own attitude, and often draw on life experience.

Box 7.3 Attribution strategies

- quote tags ("she said," "according to Dr. Smith")
- paraphrasing tags ("she thinks," "he points out")
- generic tags ("scientists say")
- implied sources (after initial attribution)
- personal experience ("I saw," I know")
- self-reflexive references to reporting and research

Attribution in expository features in general relies on different text tags (see Box 7.3). Sometimes a *generic attribution tag* like "experts say" is enough for readers, especially in DIY listicles or how-to features on websites. But many sites combine *specific attribution tags*—"Maria said" or "According to the U.S. Bureau of Labor Statistics"—with links to sources.

Consider the following hypothetical example. It's not from an actual article of mine, but I do attribute a real outside source as of this writing. We'll begin with an unattributed statement:

> *Millennials love their smartphones.*

It certainly feels true, and it's stated authoritatively. It's the kind of thing that "everyone knows." But how does everyone know this—and why should we believe it? Here's my first revision:

> *Millennials love their smartphones. According to a <u>2019 Pew Research Center study</u>, almost all participants younger than 38 said they use the internet. About 20 percent described themselves as "smartphone-only internet users."*

I've now added an attribution tag and a link (underlined) to a research study ("Millennials Stand out for Their Technology Use, but Older Generations Also Embrace Digital Life"). I've also selected and paraphrased key numbers, as well as included a brief quote from the study report.

Readers can always go to that report for full details, but in this hypothetical assignment, my task is to explain the gist for a general audience. A short quote signals my understanding of the specifics without inducing eye glaze. Still missing, however, is more context for why this information might connect with my intended audience. Another revision:

It's not surprising that millennials love their smartphones. According to a <u>2019 Pew Research Center study</u>, almost all participants younger than 38 said they use the internet. About 20 percent described themselves as "smartphone-only internet users." But these days, even your grandmother is catching up.

By revising the opening statement and adding another sentence as a conclusion, it's become a mini-story with a beginning, middle, and end. It's also directed at a millennial audience. My attitude is clear, even though the paragraph isn't written from the first-person point of view. If I continued writing this topical feature, I'd probably add a similar combination of key numbers and a short quote to support the statement about "your grandmother is catching up."

Digital feature articles often mix links, commentary, and generic attribution tags (such as "recent research by media experts") with a specific tag to a representative study. This mix of generic and specific attribution with links is a good overall approach for conveying that you know what you're talking about. Providing *no* attribution or links to outside sources is a red flag. Yet linking to every intriguing study you've ever come across can undermine the focus of a short feature, scattering attention and sending readers bouncing off in all directions.

The amount of text attribution and linking depends on your audience (the general public? middle-school kids? fellow experts?) as well as your focus. There are other pointers to an outside source's credibility, too. In my example, the Pew Research Center is a well-respected source for research on media and other trends in the United States. But what if I, the user, happened to stumble on this study by Googling around and had never heard of the Pew Research Center? It's got an authoritative name, but many a false front for lobbyists and nefarious self-promoters might describe themselves as a "nonpartisan fact tank," as Pew does on its website.

Trust in experts can no longer be taken for granted. That's why considering the perspective of your audience makes such a difference in convincing them, not just insisting on your own expertise. Digital media makes it easy to link to "studies" that don't prove anything in a statistically valid way or have been sponsored by corporate marketers. In *Web Literacy for Student Fact-Checkers*, Michael Caulfield recommends a search via Google Scholar to establish how many times a study or author has been cited by other researchers. In addition, he emphasizes checking into who founded or continues to run a website you're not familiar with.

While it's tempting to link to a source without attributing it in the text itself—*Martha, do I HAVE to clutter up my beautiful prose with boring stuff like "according to blah-blah-blah"?*—there are drawbacks to the just-fling-in-a-link method. Linking to sources on websites is based on the notion that readers who care will follow the breadcrumbs, while the incurious apparently believe what they're told. Regardless, readers are supposed to connect the dots for themselves. But if a link to an older site is a broken, as they often are, a lack of attribution in the text means readers are left with no pointers to the source, as if the facts themselves have evaporated.

Note that a first-person approach can allay some concerns about missing attribution. In the next example, taken from a 2015 feature in *Wired* by Christian Jarrett—"All You Need to Know About the 'Learning Styles' Myth, in Two Minutes"—the short bio at the end of the article lays out the authority of this "cognitive neuroscientist turned science writer" to speak on the topic. But Jarrett's use of his first-person voice to tell a story *and* attribute sources is what convinces me, starting with the lead: "On a sunny hike along a Madeiran levada a couple of years ago, I got chatting to a retired school teacher and I told him about the brain myths book I was writing."

The link on "book" takes readers to Jarrett's *Great Myths of the Brain* on Amazon, his most cited work to date on Google Scholar. That establishes him as an expert immediately, and there's no confusion about attribution for the link. More than that, opening with a first-person anecdote allows him to frame his main point—being a visual or verbal thinker doesn't really determine how well you learn a task—in an approachable manner. He contradicts the conventional wisdom without proclaiming his expertise from on high. As of this writing, some of the generic links to outside sources in the second paragraph of his *Wired* feature are broken, but in a first-person piece we have a better sense of why they were important enough to cite.

Voice Lesson 3

1   **You're the expert:** For the expert topic you chose in the last voice lesson, describe your expertise for readers in the first-person voice. Feel free to write a paragraph or more in your notebook—then try editing it down for readers.
2   **Attribution context:** For each of the five-plus sources you came up with in Voice Lesson 2, write at least one sentence describing it, including as much attribution context as possible.
3   **Link check:** In your notebook, describe how you might include a link to published sources that are online. Reflect on whether you need to attribute such sources specifically in the text or can just use a generic tag like "research studies."
4   **Bonus response:** What mix of links with specific and/or generic attribution do you find most convincing? In a response paper, compare Christian Jarrett's *Wired* article with another feature he's written about the "learning styles myth" (such as for the British Psychological Society's *Research Digest*). How would you define the different audiences for these features?

Danger! Avoid voice hijacks

As nonfiction writers, we make choices all the time about quoting, sources, and our perspective on the information we take in. Much of what we know as journalists comes from other sources—what people tell us about their lives, how they describe what caused an accident, why they believe the earth is flat or will soon be engulfed by the Singularity. You can find a source to confirm almost anything, even attribute it to "Dr. X, President of the Singularity Club," but that doesn't mean it's true (see Box 7.4). For that reason, think carefully about how to frame direct quotes or claims made by other people you include in a feature, especially if those quotes could hijack your own point of view.

Presenting a truthful account of a complex topic is determined by more than attribution tags. It also depends on your voice and wording as a writer—which in turn depends, again, on the audience for what you're explaining. While I'm no fan of jargon, I recognize its usefulness as shorthand for those already familiar with a topic. Indeed, terms like "attribution" and "verification" are journalism jargon.

Box 7.4 Why attribution matters

- Not all sources for information are credible.
- What people tell you isn't necessarily true.
- Neither are their stories or "facts."
- Even the most credible experts have biases.
- Motivations for behavior are hard to judge.

But whenever prose slides into too much jargon, it's in danger of becoming a *voice hijack*. Writers sound like the expert they're parroting rather than themselves. For instance:

> *Why do I love first-person journalism? It's a hybrid, one backed by research on general writing skills instruction (GWSI). As editor Joseph Petraglia notes in his introduction to* Reconceiving Writing, Rethinking Writing Instruction, *"the vulnerability of GWSI is hardly a secret among writing professionals and its intellectual fragility has been felt for years and manifested in several ways." Such fragility also manifests in journalism discussions and the uncertain and shifting practices instructors employ in journalism classes or on the job.*

This hypothetical example of mine includes attribution to an actual source, but my voice ends up hijacked by the academic wording of the direct quote. Consider a revision:

> *Why do I love first-person journalism? It's a hybrid, one that undercuts a flat recitation of facts in news features or the endless parade of boring essays churned out in composition classes. As editor Joseph Petraglia notes in his provocative 1995 introduction to* Reconceiving Writing, Rethinking Writing Instruction, *the "intellectual fragility" of general writing skills instruction "is hardly a secret among writing professionals." Here's another open secret: Despite the digital march of progress, many veteran reporters still flinch at the thought of using "I."*

The word count of both versions is almost the same, but in the second version my active "I" voice directs readers. By cutting down the quote and paraphrasing, I both nod to an expert to make my case and avoid being hijacked by a longer quote from an academic.

In far too many mediocre digital features, writers channel the claims of sources without fact checking or distinguishing between "what experts say" and their own interpretation. I see hijacks so often when grading student drafts that they prompt me to check the original wording from the source to see if a dull paraphrase has been plagiarized. They almost never are, but it still amazes me: the way a writer's engaging voice disappears when a boring expert shows up.

A voice hijack can also crop up with any person interviewed, even if they aren't spouting obscure jargon. The writer interviews a local celebrity, for instance, and then relates a story their subject told them as a straightforward narrative anecdote, as if it's the verbatim truth—with no cues for readers such as "she told me her grandmother walked twenty miles to school every day" or "he laughed when I asked about the time he was arrested for shoplifting." Readers also benefit when writers indicate whether a quote came from email correspondence, a phone call, or an in-person interview. What people say in conversation differs from what they compose in writing.

You'll note that both my examples of attribution in the previous paragraph involve "I" or "me." You should avoid voice hijacks in third-person features, too, and it still requires good paraphrasing. But a first-person perspective helps with *complex attribution*: when you need to get across the difference between what you, the reporter, know versus what somebody else tells you. This is especially important in profiles, when a subject will tell the story of their life in what's often a polished version that doesn't hold up to journalistic scrutiny.

Take Tonya Harding, the Olympic figure skater who will forever be identified with the 1994 clumsy attack on competitor Nancy Kerrigan by thuggish cohorts of Harding's ex-husband. In early 2018, in conjunction with the release of the movie *I, Tonya*, a long profile of Harding by Taffy Brodesser-Akner appeared in the *New York Times*. Even the title—"Tonya Harding Would Like Her Apology Now"—demonstrates how skillfully Brodesser-Akner channels Harding's voice through paraphrasing yet distinguishes her own point of view. In fact, the writer's perspective is often at odds with what Harding says. For instance:

> Lord knows she's tried to be understood. Over the years, "E! True Hollywood Story" came along. "Entertainment Tonight" came along. Oprah came along. But the focus was so much about what happened in 1994; it was never about before or after, and if you want to understand her at all, you have to understand her childhood and her early adulthood. They all told her that they would let her explain, and each time she felt like she didn't really get her message across, because each time, it came down to: Well, did you do it, or didn't you? Did you know more than you said? Did you actually plan the attack? Are you sorry?

By the end of this long profile, one in which Harding comes off as both charismatic and deluded, the writer weighs in more directly, like so: "Here's the thing: A lot of what she said wasn't true. She contradicted herself endlessly. But she reminded me of other people I've known who have survived trauma and abuse, and who tell their stories again and again to explain what had happened to them but also to process it themselves." Whether or not you care about the specifics of Harding's life, Brodesser-Akner has humanized her subject far more profoundly than if she just provided the ex-skater with a platform to mouth off.

Voice Lesson 4

1   **You're the interviewer:** Interview a friend, family member, or colleague for 15 minutes. In particular, ask them to tell you about whether they liked their childhood or the story of how they became who they are today. (Alternatively, look for a video of a celebrity interview and take notes on their self-description of how they became successful or other stories they tell.)
2   **Key anecdotes:** Select at least two stories your interviewee (or the celebrity source) told about themselves and write them out in exactly the words they use as direct quotes.
3   **Complex attribution:** Paraphrase these direct quotes, adding attribution that indicates the source "told you" (or "told Oprah Winfrey") this story.
4   **Interview capsule description:** Write a summary of the interview (100 to 200 words) based on your observation of the interviewee, including both direct and paraphrased quotes. Be sure to distinguish your active "I" voice from that of your source, noting how truthful they're being.

The curse of knowledge

Let's return to my college thesis about attribution errors. The results of my experimental protocols were intriguing, if mixed. In one series, I asked many fellow Reed College students to observe a video of either a man or a woman in their early twenties spilling a cup of coffee. Feminist that I was, I predicted most observers of the woman would attribute the coffee accident to her clumsy disposition rather than to the situation (all the books and papers piled on the table where she was working). In fact, my results showed the opposite, probably because the guy spilling coffee, a friend of mine, was a better actor and much bigger personality than she was.

Other data I collected did line up with attribution theory, however. I surveyed students at a public high school in Portland, Oregon, about how they would interpret the behavior of themselves, their best friends, acquaintances, or strangers in different situations. A significant number said they and their friends would react a certain way because of the situation. Meanwhile, they tended to attribute the actions of acquaintances or strangers to inherent personality traits. In other words, the closer we are to someone, the more likely we are to assume they know what we do. We'll say a given situation made us nervous—*I jumped when you touched me because the street is dark*—not *I'm a nervous person*.

There are exceptions, certainly, but few of us explain our own behavior by saying we're greedy, evil, or any other unflattering label. Extend such attribution labels to strangers who don't look like you or identify as a different gender, and you'll see how biases play out in society. You'll also spot my early interest in the way we unconsciously judge others, something that continues to fascinate me and now informs *First-Person Journalism*.

Most reporters have become familiar with confirmation bias—emphasizing observations and quotes from sources that match the writer's preconceived notions about an event—and they're right to be wary of it. But no matter how neutral journalists attempt to be, there are other unconscious biases at play, one of the biggest being the curse of knowledge. We assume readers know what we do—about the American political system, say, or that a given source is a famous expert in their field—when it's far more likely they don't share our understanding of it.

The curse of knowledge has been studied in a number of disciplines, especially economics. In his 2014 writing guide *The Sense of Style*, cognitive psychologist Steven Pinker discusses how it impacts not only the way researchers frame questions but also how they write about what they know or have learned. He devotes a whole chapter to the curse of knowledge, noting that it is "insidious because it conceals not only the contents of our thoughts from us but their very form." The curse of knowledge underscores why cultivating self-awareness and questioning what you know matters so much for first-person journalists.

Just as I examined students in my psychology experiments, we can make empirical observations of other people and their behavior. Eventually the anecdotes add up, and we make statements of belief about why "most people" do what they do. Yet when it comes to the reasons for human behavior, resorting to physical laws doesn't explain it. As Pinker concludes in his chapter on the curse of knowledge, overcoming such biases "may be the one bit of writerly advice that comes closest to being sound moral advice: always try to lift yourself out of your parochial mindset and find out how other people think and feel."

I connect questioning where your facts come from to the "intellectual principles of a science of reporting" that Bill Kovach and Tom Rosenstiel argue for in *The Elements of Journalism*. Their nod to science involves testing hypotheses, possibly disproving what you first assumed. In their chapter on "Journalism of Verification," Kovach and Rosenstiel list these guidelines:

1. Never add anything that was not there.
2. Never deceive the audience.
3. Be as transparent as possible about your methods and motives.
4. Rely on your own original reporting.
5. Exercise humility.

Whether you're a reporter who assumes it's possible to remain objective or a Wikipedia editor with too much faith in the neutral voice, humility is in order. We can attempt to be scientists, but much of journalistic practice remains subjective, based on what is observed in "original reporting" or the reporting of others. Attributing sources by providing context about their expertise—or your own expertise—isn't the only tool for building trust or providing useful advice. Neither are links to additional factual information. The feature-writing challenge is to come up with the right mix of facts from credible sources along with interpretation of those facts. If you're honest about who you are as an observer, what you know, and what your biases are, you'll go a long way toward convincing readers, too—as we'll discuss in the next chapter.

Box 7.5 Classic how-to article

Lead—open with a story about yourself that illustrates the topic.
Nut graf—state the topic/technique/problem and why it matters.
Evidence—quote at least one credible expert.
Tips—tell readers how with at least three tips or steps.
Payoff—leave readers on a positive note—with an uplifting story.

How-to piece: Explain with three tips

1   **Your expert tips:** Choose one of the expert topics you've been working on in earlier voice lessons. In your notebook, list and summarize three tips for doing it.
2   **Your advice:** Write a short how-to piece (between 500 and 800 words) with these tips. See the how-to formula in Box 7.5. Open with a personal anecdote—perhaps how you initially failed at this activity and what you learned in the process. Then add a theme paragraph (nut graf) before your three tips—and use a heading to distinguish each tip section. If you intend to post or publish this on a digital site, consider adding photographs, videos, or other multimedia formatting.
3   **Source list:** In writing any feature, it's good practice to keep a complete list as you compile research and talk to people. In your notebook, organize your sources under the five categories in Box 7.2, including the URLs for where you found them, as well as full names and contact information for anyone interviewed. Attach the source list at the end of your how-to piece.

Reminder: Don't just stick in links—attribute every fact or claim you take from someone else. Based on your source list at the end, an editor might pare away the attribution later, but in journalistic outlets, they'll want to know where *all* your facts come from.

Sources

The Psychology of Interpersonal Relations by Fritz Heider (Lawrence Erlbaum Associates, 1958).

"Current Issues in Attribution Theory and Research" by John H. Harvey and Gifford Weary, *Annual Review of Psychology*, 1984, 35(1), pp. 427–459. www.researchgate.net/publication/200003646_Current_Issues_in_Attribution_Theory_and_Research

"Associated Press Statement of News Values and Principles" (under "Attribution"), *The AP Stylebook* and Associated Press website. www.ap.org/about/news-values-and-principles/downloads/ap-news-values-and-principles.pdf

"Americans and the News Media: What They Do—and Don't—Understand About Each Other" by the Media Insight Project (American Press Institute and AP-NORC Center for Public Affairs Research), June 11, 2018. www.mediainsight.org/Pages/Americans-and-the-News-Media-What-they-do-and-don%27t—understand-about-each-other.aspx

"Practice Ethical Curation and Attribution" by Craig Silverman, Chapter 4 of "The Best Ways for Publishers to Build Credibility Through Transparency," American Press Institute website, September 24, 2014. www.americanpressinstitute.org/publications/reports/strategy-studies/ethical-curation-attribution/

"Special Section: Attribution" in *NPR Ethics Handbook*, NPR website. www.npr.org/about-npr/688424402/special-section-attribution

"Craig Silverman: The Fake News Watchdog" (Number 21 of "The Politico 50"), *Politico Magazine*, 2017. www.politico.com/interactives/2017/politico50/craig-silverman/

"Tom Rosenstiel," American Press Institute website. www.americanpressinstitute.org/author/trosenstiel/

"Labor Force Characteristics," U.S. Bureau of Labor Statistics website. www.bls.gov/cps/lfcharacteristics.htm#nlf

"Women's Unpaid Labor Is Worth $10,900,000,000,000" by Gus Wezerek and Kristen R. Ghodsee, *New York Times*, March 5, 2020. www.nytimes.com/interactive/2020/03/04/opinion/women-unpaid-labor.html

"Wikipedia: Verifiability, Not Truth," essay on Wikipedia website. www.en.wikipedia.org/wiki/Wikipedia:Verifiability,_not_truth

"Research" under "Wikipedia: About," statement on Wikipedia website. www.en.wikipedia.org/wiki/Wikipedia:Verifiability,_not_truth

"What Should We Do About Wikipedia?" by Martha Nichols and Lorraine Berry, *Talking Writing*, May 20, 2013. www.talkingwriting.com/what-should-we-do-about-wikipedia

"Millennials Stand out for Their Technology Use, but Older Generations Also Embrace Digital Life" by Emily A. Vogels, Pew Research Center, September 9, 2019. www.pewresearch.org/fact-tank/2019/09/09/us-generations-technology-use/

"About the Pew Research Center," Pew Research Center website. www.pewresearch.org/about/

Web Literacy for Student Fact-Checkers by Michael A. Caulfield (Pressbooks, 2017; updated in 2021; Creative Commons). www.webliteracy.pressbooks.com/

"All You Need to Know About the 'Learning Styles' Myth, in Two Minutes" by Christian Jarrett, *Wired*, January 5, 2015. www.wired.com/2015/01/need-know-learning-styles-myth-two-minutes/

"Introduction: General Writing Skills Instruction and Its Discontents" in *Reconceiving Writing, Rethinking Writing Instruction*, edited by Joseph Petraglia (Lawrence Earlbaum, 1995; Routledge edition, 2009), p. xii.

"Tonya Harding Would Like Her Apology Now" by Taffy Brodesser-Akner, *New York Times*, January 10, 2018. www.nytimes.com/2018/01/10/movies/tonya-harding-i-tonya-nancy-kerrigan-scandal.html

The Sense of Style: The Thinking Person's Guide to Writing in the 21st Century by Steven Pinker (Viking/Penguin, 2014), pp. 67, 76.

The Elements of Journalism: What Newspeople Should Know and the Public Should Expect by Bill Kovach and Tom Rosenstiel (Three Rivers Press, 2001/2007), p. 89.

8   Convincing readers

What's my argument and who disagrees?

In 2005, in the exurban flatlands west of Melbourne and Geelong, a sad-sack dad, recently separated from his wife, took their three young sons to a mall on Father's Day. That evening, driving back to the town where they lived, he drove his old Commodore off a highway bridge into a deep farm pond. All three boys, between ten and two years old, drowned. But the dad got out of the sinking car and lived—and from that point on, whether Robert Farquharson had blacked out on the bridge, as he claimed, or deliberately turned the wheel gripped Australia.

As Helen Garner writes in her opening of *This House of Grief*, her 2014 book-length chronicle of the Farquharson case and its murder trial and appeal, the woes of this "hard-working bloke" could be summarized in a mournful country tune about heartbreak and a man losing his self-respect. Until the sweet little boys died, when it became a media feeding frenzy. Her first response on hearing the news, Garner recalls, was "Oh Lord, let this be an accident." But once the first trial started in the summer of 2007, "everyone had a view."

Garner, an iconic Australian novelist and essayist, joined the press covering the trial, producing an account that illustrates the many ways public perception of an event can be swayed. Her first-person "I" voice informs readers about day-to-day events at the trials, with good reporting and terrific capsule description. But more important, she depicts her own emotional up and downs as an observer, becoming a stand-in for readers. She grapples with whose version of events to believe and whether Farquharson is guilty—or, in a far more nuanced take than in a standard news story, to what degree he's responsible for his actions.

Up to this chapter, Part Three of *First-Person Journalism* on reporting approaches has emphasized direct observation and factual evidence. Here, we'll give the same attention to the emotional record, especially when there's a division of opinion. We'll address the first-person element of *counterpoints*, highlighting sources that disagree with a writer's argument.

Counterpointing also deepens the interpretation of facts in third-person features. But for first-person journalists, it enhances the trustworthiness of an "I" voice, undercutting false claims of objectivity. Expertise matters, but in the case of most public disagreements, you'll find experts to support either side. When feature writers include counterpoints, they let readers know that there

DOI: 10.4324/9781003132189-11

are different perspectives. For instance, early on in *This House of Grief*, Garner writes:

> On the Monday of the trial's third week, waiting and gossiping with the media people outside the court in weak spring sunlight, we calculated that the following day would be the second anniversary of the children's deaths. Imagining Farquharson's dread as the date approached, I allowed myself the luxury of the word *pitiful*. One of the print journalists, a court veteran whose work I had long respected, spun round and bit my head off.
>
> "Pity?" she cried. "How can you say he's pitiful when he's done the worst, the most terrible thing? Murdered his own children, who trusted and loved him? Three of them! Premeditated! And to get back at his wife! The utmost betrayal! Why is *that* pitiful?"

In Garner's portrayal, the veteran reporter clearly has strong feelings about the defendant. They may be based on years of observing other defendants plead their innocence in the dock or hidebound cynicism, but they indicate a bias. While this is one author's account of what somebody else said, it involves journalists, those bastions of balanced reporting.

A trial presenting crime-scene evidence of dead children would be grueling for anyone to sit through. Garner, as a first-person journalist, documents the emotional toll quite believably, if subjectively. She combines a novelist's skill in describing the characters she observes at the trials—Farquharson, his ex-wife, the lawyers, witnesses, experts—with reams of specific detail based on the transcripts she and other reporters received at the end of each day.

Traditional journalism advocates for facts, and I'm thankful for that. Yet most reporters know gut feelings are informative as well. Facts can be disputed, as Garner illustrates, lawyers providing pro and con stories to fit the same details. That's particularly true when strong emotions are at play, as they were at the Farquharson trials. And with no eyewitnesses, experts base their claims on everything from skid marks to medical knowledge to their own agendas.

This House of Grief not only recounts an event that galvanized Australia but also provides a self-aware personal narrative. Garner needed analytical distance to explain a respected colleague's response of "Why is *that* pitiful?" Analysis may be an old-fashioned aptitude, but it's the foundation of critical thinking, which never goes out of style for journalists. The following first-person rule highlights the value of thinking through an emotional argument:

> *Tell stories that not only move readers but also make sense of why people disagree.*

In this chapter, I emphasize transparency about your own agenda for arguing a point of view. Much as journalists may present themselves as objective experts or witnesses, they're also persuaders and advocates. These stances are obvious in opinion pieces by columnists or in personal essays, but even traditional news organizations are persuaders beyond the editorial page. They make choices about which news stories to headline and which to ignore.

The powers of persuasion can be used to engage readers, lie to them, or both at the same time. There's no doubt some first-person techniques enhance product marketing and media influence through the guise of personal authenticity. So, keep in mind the ethical purpose of journalism—to inform and document—especially if you find yourself ranting in public.

The curse of unconscious feeling

Admit it: you get angry sometimes. People annoy you or enrage you. They disagree with you, which makes you want to convince them that *you're* right. Take it from this highly opinionated writer: getting in touch with what you believe in or fervently oppose often has real impact. But too much anger can also be a turn-off or muddy up the facts.

Box 8.1 Examine your feelings

Question . . .
your intellectual *and* emotional responses

Question . . .
your own assumptions about what's true

Question . . .
your own agenda

Question . . .
what you know
and how much readers need to know

Writing from a personal point of view can push you to express outrage in a way you might not do otherwise as a journalist. As we discussed in Chapter 7, there's the curse of knowledge—all the wrong assumptions writers make about what readers know. But for first-person journalists, there's also what I call the *curse of unconscious feeling*. That's the hidden emotions driving us to write—fear, shame, guilt, anger, grief, and more.

Given the traditional training of journalists, dredging up such feelings may seem like a tough haul. I won't pretend there's an instant "ah-ha!" here. Developing self-awareness is one of the four main mental tools for first-person journalism, and it's an ongoing practice. Remember that self-reporters turn a skeptical eye on their own motivations. Self-examination is crucial for good reporting in general, and it also helps keep first-person writers honest (Box 8.1).

At about the midpoint of *This House of Grief*, Garner recounts a conversation she had with other women in a Pilates class about the ongoing trial. "I told them about the fathers I had met who stated categorically that in Farquharson's position they would have gone to the bottom and drowned with their kids," Garner writes. "The four of us agreed in very low voices that this could only be a fantasy." That anecdote neatly encapsulates gender differences in assessing motives. But then she follows up by telling them about a time forty years before when she, a high school teacher, and one of her students faced a "savage dog":

> Next thing I knew, I was standing behind my student, clinging to her back, while the owner dragged the dog away. In a second of primal terror, of which I have no memory, I must have pushed the girl between me and the danger.

Garner exposes herself and the power of unconscious feeling in passages like this. Until we're faced with a life-or-death situation, we may have moral certitude but remain unaware of the way emotions take over. She also demonstrates, as a first-person journalist, how to explore the consequences in a published account. Her story will send chills of recognition through many readers. At the same time, it's a counterpoint to conventional ideas about guilt and innocence.

Persuasive writing of all kinds can have such emotional and real-world impact that your first task as a feature writer is to figure out what your goal is. Why you want to convince readers will focus your reporting and your writing approach (see Box 8.2). Marketing and journalism have long overlapped, especially in print magazines, and in digital media these lines have blurred more. You may think that's good, bad, or no big deal. That's your opinion. But justifiable outrage can mask personal motives, too. In the murky realm of emotion, what you consider advocacy might feel like propaganda to somebody else.

Box 8.2 What's your writing goal?

Journalism
to interpret news or cultural events

Marketing
to sell a product or service

Personal Branding
to sell myself as an expert or influencer

Outrage
to tell the world how angry I am

Advocacy
to help the world be a better place

Voice Lesson 1

1   *Your feelings:* Make a list of five things that make you angry. These don't have to be political events or to involve newsmakers, but come up with items that might be the subject of an opinion piece. (If you're stumped, look over your "hate list" from Chapter 3.)

2   *Self-examination:* Choose one item on your list and reflect on why it makes you so angry in your process notebook. If you've selected a current news event that enrages you, dig under the most obvious opinions written by others. Write brief responses to the questions posed in Box 8.2—and identify personal experiences or unconscious feelings that may be sparking your anger.

3   *Capsule description:* In a short paragraph, describe the item you chose and make a case for your anger. Nod to your own experience and any unconscious feelings that may be at play.

4   *Bonus response:* Do you agree with Helen Garner's assessment of what men say about saving their children in an emergency versus what women say? Why or why not? Write a response paper about the differing gender motivations she describes, based on your own experience.

Point-counterpoint

Many of my students and fellow journalists assume writing with an "I" is all about expressing personal opinions. That's why I don't start my first-person journalism classes with opinion writing. While it's easy to get angry at political or world events, analyzing the facts (or lack of facts) underpinning an opinion involves more work than venting emotion.

Beyond the curse of unconscious feelings, we all have hot buttons. The things we like or enjoy can be terrific story hooks, but our hot buttons involve stronger emotions, some quite negative or rooted in identity. So, traditional op-ed style turns down the temperature, employing a point-counterpoint formula that coolly analyzes pros and cons, assessing critics before punching them out (see Box 8.3). Paying attention to the people or organizations who disagree with you is not a sign of weakness; it's a debate strategy. Your opponents may seem ignorant or crazy, but as a journalist, you need to find out who they are and why they disagree.

In addition to the logic of point-counterpoint, nodding to those who disagree with you requires empathy. If strong negative emotions are provoked, there's bound to be opposition—especially when writers ask readers to change existing attitudes. Consider a counterpoint example from the introduction to this chapter: when I said "there's no doubt" first-person journalism techniques can be used to sell products, I'm nodding to potential critics. Their concerns are reasonable. Yet my main point is to argue for legitimate uses of first-person journalism. I could opt not to include the counterpoint, but it would weaken my argument, implying that I'm overlooking the obvious fact that personal stories can be used deceptively. It would also oversimplify my understanding of the competing impulses nonfiction writers face.

Box 8.3 Opinion writing formula

1   ***Opening hook*** (*snappy title + lead*)
2   ***Main point or argument*** (*nut graf*)
3   ***Evidence*** (*supporting facts, anecdotes*)
4   ***Counterpoint*** (*caveat, what critics say*)
5   ***Closing punch*** (*ending*)

Point-counterpoint is an effective first-person strategy beyond opinion pieces. When combined with good self-reporting, it gives readers entrée to how journalists sift through facts and come to conclusions. It also exposes a writer's stance and biases in a transparent way. In "Why an iPhone Could Actually Be Good for Your 3-Year-Old," a 2009 article in the *Boston Globe Magazine*, Neil Swidey makes a convincing case for something counterintuitive:

> I say this as someone who doesn't even like the iPhone. I have never wor-shipped at the altar of Jobs, and have, in fact, always preferred the dowdy PC. . . . But I can see how quickly our youngest daughter has become a pro with the device, despite being just 4 years old and unable to spell anything more than her name. She belongs to a new generation.

Personal as his point of view is, Swidey reports on and attributes research in this feature. The subject of his story is not how his particular family deals with iPhones. It's about a larger issue or trend, and he combines personal anecdotes with outside sources, including credible experts who are worth listening to as counterpoints. He writes that "for a reality check, I went to see Dr. Michael Rich," who at the time ran the Center on Media and Child Health at a Boston hospital. Rich talked about why he considered smartphones for toddlers wor-risome, but Swidey adds:

> [H]ere's what makes Rich's perspective so valuable. In a field where some children's advocates view all media as bad while industry-bought voices speak only gee-whiz-ese, Rich opts for nuance. He rejects the notion that parents try to seal off their child from all media.

First-person features of all kinds—data-driven trend stories, topical explain-ers, think pieces—are often labeled "opinion" simply because they use the first-person voice or make an argument. But the label matters less than under-standing what convinces readers: head *and* heart, fact *and* feeling, relevant statistics *and* personal testimony. In the structure of a feature itself, different ways of interpreting the world can operate as point-counterpoint. You can document your own feelings as a witness, then shift to a more analytical stance to relay a sequence of events, then move back to a personal anecdote, and so on. Here's another first-person rule:

> *Don't isolate facts from emotional consequences—connect them when reporting.*

Engaging stories are often akin to battles between opposing views. Magazine features have long hooked readers by challenging the conventional wisdom, as Swidey does with the parenting mantra that screen time is bad for kids. Point-counterpoint is a source of dramatic tension, something I'll address as part of the storytelling mix in Chapter 10. But counterpoints also play another role in journalistic features. While we may want to resolve conflicts in our own lives, examining the opposition is part of informing and educating the public.

For both reporting and storytelling reasons, identifying the *key oppositions* in your feature will direct the way you present your main argument (see Box 8.4), which brings us back to the mental tools of self-awareness and questioning. First-person journalists don't just express their opinions because they can or because everyone else is. They do so to make a point.

Box 8.4 Key oppositions

what I believe ← → people who disagree
conventional wisdom ← → contrarian POV
what everyone expects ← → surprising outcomes
what I remember ← → what actually happened
what I used to believe ← → what I now believe
what I imagine or wish ← → reality
what I know ← → what I'll never know

Counterpoint: Storytelling for public relations, marketing, social-media influence, and advocacy is often calculated to resemble a journalistic opinion piece, combining a few selected facts with personal stories, even emotional opposition. *And what's wrong with that, Martha?* an opponent might ask. *Why not tell a good story as well as promote myself? It's a twofer!*

Point: You can, as long as you make your agenda clear. Readers may embrace what you say because they agree with you. There's a place for straightforward marketing and personal branding, as well as advocacy journalism in which reporters are transparent about their biases. Yet the rise of sponsored content in digital media, some of which is deceptively formatted to look like a standard news article, puts many of us on our guard. Once readers find out you've been masking your real goal or faking what you feel, you've lost their trust.

Voice Lesson 2

1 ***What you believe:*** In your notebook, make a list of at least five words or phrases that are meaningful to you. Think of words that have emotional impact and are connected to your beliefs.

2 ***Your main point:*** Choose one of your list items and describe the *main point* (or argument) of an opinion piece you'd like to write. *Hint:* Focus your point in one brief phrase or sentence.

3 ***Point-counterpoint:*** Highlight the opposition. Create a point-counterpoint chart with at least three items under the opposing terms. For example, if your main point is *Bacon will make anyone feel better*, the point-counterpoint chart might look like this:

Bacon—yay!	*Bacon—nay!*
It's a favorite in most cultures.	It disgusts some people.
It's a comfort food in hard times.	It's bad for your health.
The salty-smoky flavor is unique.	The flavor can be replicated.

4 ***Capsule op-ed:*** In a short paragraph (no more than 100 words), use a point-counterpoint formula to write a brief opinion piece. Be sure to nod to at least one counterpoint.

Not all experts are the same

An omniscient stance or neutral third-person voice implies authority. There's more work involved in establishing your expertise as a first-person journalist, although in these digital times, personal stories go a long way toward convincing readers. Writing from your own point of view can meet many journalistic goals, including that of news analysis.

But first, let's address the practical matter of incorporating outside sources, following up on the previous chapter about attribution. Citing a good research study or quoting a credible expert is the standard approach to providing evidence for an argument. The trick is to attribute evidence from the right experts, not just any website that pops up at the top of a Google search. A student of mine once remarked wryly that not all experts are created equal. I'd add that not all self-proclaimed experts should be given the time of day. The ghostly voices of disguised influencers and marketers invade nonfiction writing, making claims that too many reporters don't question.

In Chapter 7, I mentioned a 2015 *Wired* article by Christian Jarrett, a neuroscience expert, about what he calls the "learning styles myth." In it, he challenges the popular idea that teachers need to accommodate different learning styles to improve student performance. Yet as of January 2021, when I Googled "different learning styles," I got a long scroll of online articles, including "4 Different Learning Styles You Should Know: The VARK Model" (University of

Kansas) and "The Seven Learning Styles—How Do You Learn?" (Inspire Education). These digital features advise teachers on how to help students with different learning styles (visual, auditory, reading/writing, kinesthetic), as if no would argue with this premise.

But if I filter an online search for "different learning styles" with Google Scholar, one of the top results is "Learning Styles: Concepts and Evidence," a 2008 literature review in *Psychological Science in the Public Interest*. As of this writing, it's been cited 2,834 times, an indication of its influence in the field. In the abstract, the authors point out that the conventional wisdom has spawned "a thriving industry devoted to publishing learning-styles tests and guidebooks for teachers" (one that continues more than a decade later, I would add). Yet they conclude:

> The contrast between the enormous popularity of the learning-styles approach within education and the lack of credible evidence for its utility is, in our opinion, striking and disturbing. If classification of students' learning styles has practical utility, it remains to be demonstrated.

The learning-styles myth is one of many examples of an entrepreneurial desire to sell products that tramples over factual evidence. Classes promoted by education sites and social enterprises may be well intended, but misinformation spreads in many ways. The purpose of journalism is to question such marketing claims, not to repeat them just because "experts say."

Here's a second practical matter in handling outside sources: *Don't be a mouthpiece*. In Chapter 7, I also introduced the danger of voice hijacks, which happen whenever a writer describes or explains a topic in somebody else's voice—be they a scientist, doctor, or critic. Even if you use direct quotes, voice hijacks can make it sound as if you're transcribing what somebody else tells you, which takes you into PR territory. Hijacks are a particular problem in how-to pieces, given that third-person digital content is often a masked form of marketing.

Voice hijacks are more glaring in first-person features, however. For example, a gripping personal anecdote abruptly shifts into academic diction or a ponderous quote from an expert. In other cases, the hijack is more subtle. Journalists are trained to be good observers, which means absorbing the world around them, taking in various cues subconsciously from people interviewed. Mimicking what we hear can come a little too naturally.

If you find yourself bedeviled by hijacks, try recasting every bit of expository information you've researched in your own words. It will clarify your understanding of a topic and indicate gaps in reporting. Whether you're writing an opinion piece or a topical feature, do enough reporting to understand who the main experts are, identifying their biases or any disguised goals. In some cases, there will be a general consensus, with experts saying similar things. But if they disagree, background research helps determine which side has the most factual weight. Only then can you credibly use a generic attribution tag like "scientists say."

Voice Lesson 3

1 ***Your main point:*** For your capsule op-ed from the last voice lesson, come up with at least three outside expert sources to support your argument. How credible are these experts? In your notebook, describe which ones seem most reliable. (If you've already attributed experts or factual information in your op-ed, explain why you trust those sources.)

2 ***Counterpoints:*** Do the same thing for at least one counterpoint in your op-ed.

3 ***Dueling experts:*** Revise your capsule op-ed by adding credible outside sources for your main point *and* credible counterpoints. This may change the tone and involve more attribution context for sources you're citing. Even so, try to limit the revised version to no more than 200 words. It's good practice for focusing an argument.

4 ***Bonus revision:*** Try this exercise with the how-to topic you wrote about in Chapter 7.

Establishing first-person authority

Evaluating what experts say is part of what makes you a credible reporter. It also helps establish your own expertise. Yet factual evidence alone rarely convinces readers, no matter how strategically you argue a point. First-person authority to speak the truth is based on professional qualifications, authentic life experience—and, preferably, a combination of both. Anyone can challenge an opinion, but authoritative first-person writers make clear what's at stake and why they believe what they do. That's the case in third-person analyses, too, but when your bylined story is voiced by "I," you're more exposed to criticism (Box 8.5).

The flip side to an analytical challenge is speaking passionately when a grave injustice has been done. While I don't start my classes with opinion pieces, I sometimes ask students to write an open letter as a first assignment. By this, I don't mean letters written as "we, the undersigned," in which hundreds of well-known writers or other celebrities protest, say, Amazon's 2014 dispute with Hachette over fees for e-books ("Letter to Amazon.com, Inc., Board of Directors,") or argue for impeaching Donald Trump in 2021 ("Historians and Constitutional Scholars' Statement on the Second Impeachment of President Donald Trump."). Such crowdsourced documents can have an impact, but I emphasize open letters by individual writers.

There are many famous examples, such as James Baldwin's "A Letter to My Nephew." His letter originally appeared in the December 1962 issue of the *Progressive* magazine in response to the hundredth anniversary of the Emancipation Proclamation's enactment on January 1, 1863. "Dear James," Baldwin opened, "I have begun this letter five times and torn it up five times. I keep seeing your face, which is also the face of your father and my brother." Within a few paragraphs, he moves from fond family memories to racism across the generations: "This innocent country set you down in a ghetto in which, in fact, it intended that you should perish."

Box 8.5 What gives you authority?

Acknowledge what the other side says.
Be forthright about what you believe.
Use *evidence* to oppose a counterpoint.
Make your case with facts + good examples . . .
. . . but say it in your own words.

First-person open letters are a hardy perennial, and they've proliferated recently as a more personal response than the classic op-ed. In 2016, Michael Luo's "An Open Letter to the Woman Who Told My Family to Go Back to China," directed at a white woman who yelled this at him in public on a Manhattan street, appeared on the print front page of the *New York Times*. In 2019, Ariel Felton paid homage to Baldwin with her own "A Letter to My Niece" in the *Progressive*. "Dear Thalia," she writes:

> We all used to wonder aloud what you'd be like as you got older. As a baby, you knew nothing of the definitions the world was going to press onto you later in life—black, female, Southern. Nobody was yet telling you who to be like, who not to end up like. The world had not yet told you who you were, who you could or should be. You just were.

Such open letters aren't the same as private correspondence, although they can be heartfelt and personal. They are public expressions of feeling that make specific points. Their first-person subjectivity underscores what a writer is advocating, but they also use personal anecdotes as evidence. Ta-Nehisi Coates's "Letter to My Son," which appeared on July 4, 2015, in the *Atlantic* (adapted from his award-winning book *Between the World and Me*), opens with "Last Sunday the host of a popular news show asked me what it meant to lose my body." The context for this public letter to his 15-year-old son was the deaths of Michael Brown, Eric Garner, and other Black boys at the hands of the police. Coates goes on to report his private feelings about his son for public reasons:

> [A]t the end of the segment, the host flashed a widely shared picture of a 12-year-old black boy tearfully hugging a white police officer. Then she asked me about "hope." And I knew then that I had failed. And I remembered that I had expected to fail. And I wondered again at the indistinct sadness welling up in me. Why exactly was I sad? I came out of the studio

and walked for a while. It was a calm late-November day. Families, believing themselves white, were out on the streets. Infants, raised to be white, were bundled in strollers. And I was sad for these people, much as I was sad for the host and sad for all the people out there watching and reveling in a specious hope. . . . I was sad for my country, but above all, in that moment, I was sad for you.

As we discussed in Part Two of *First-Person Journalism*, a strong writing voice doesn't amount to yelling the loudest. It's also not about performing your emotions for an approving audience. Empathy humanizes a story, but regardless, a strong voice is *your* voice. The strength lies in your individual perception of the world and your ability to focus on what's relevant.

Authenticity of this kind underpins all effective writing, especially writing that's intended to persuade. Readers are rarely convinced by TMI, but self-reflection about a writer's thinking process can be powerfully compelling. Rather than glossing over how you arrived at a conclusion, exposing your initial confusion can forge a bond with readers (Box 8.6). Like Coates, if you've established your first-person authority to speak—as Helen Garner does, too, in *This House of Grief*—challenging what the majority thinks is courageous.

Box 8.6 What makes you authentic?

Expose your own foibles first.

Acknowledge who you are.

Don't fake what you know.

Don't make sweeping claims . . .

. . . but don't pull your punches.

Criminal trials, in particular, come down to judgment of another human being by society. Guilt may seem clear based on the evidence presented by lawyers, but holding someone accountable is not the same as the objective truth about a defendant's intentions. In Robert Farquharson's case, he received a guilty verdict and three life sentences, appealed, got out on bail, lost again in 2010, and as of this writing remains in prison. To many, he is "simply evil," as Garner notes in her 2015 essay "The Darkness in Every One of Us."

In that essay, an edited version of a speech she gave at the Sydney Writers' Festival a year after *This House of Grief* came out, Garner describes how often she'd been asked to justify spending seven-plus years writing about a "monster" like Farquharson: "People seem more prepared to contemplate a book about a story as dark as this if the writer comes galloping out with all moral guns blazing." Then she adds:

If he *had* been a monster, I wouldn't have been interested in writing about him. The sorts of crimes that interest me are not the ones committed by psychopaths. I'm interested in apparently ordinary people who, under life's unbearable pressure, burst through the very fine membrane that separates our daylight selves from the secret darkness that lives in every one of us.

For Garner—and for me—moral authority doesn't amount to binary notions of right and wrong. A first-person feature that's both authoritative and authentic requires emotional openness to both sides, even when others rush to judgment. If you feel pushed to speak out, addressing your response to a particular person can clarify your stance and authority. Do you loathe or love them? What have they done, specifically, to make you feel that way? Can you see them as one flawed human being rather than a generalized Other? Can you encourage them to see you differently, too? Hard as these questions are to answer, they're your road to a more nuanced, truthful perspective on the world—and the sense you make of that world for readers.

Open letter: Address a public figure or topic

1   **True questions:** In your notebook, reflect on what you want your open letter to be about. Choose something that moves you, pro or con. Then as a warm-up, respond to the following four true questions. If you answered them previously, how do your responses here differ from those you wrote at the end of Part Two of *First-Person Journalism*?

  • *What will make my personal voice believable?*
  • *What makes my first-person view feel accurate?*
  • *What will readers expect when they read this open letter?*
  • *How do I know what I know?*

2   **Your addressee:** You can direct your letter to a public figure, celebrity, newsmaker, or family member, depending on your topic. Consider converting your capsule op-ed to an open letter, speaking to one person to help focus your argument and stance.

3   **Your letter:** Start with a first-person anecdote, then weave in key facts or quotes from others to support your personal testimony. Include counterpoints and avoid voice hijacks. Your open letter can be longer than an op-ed, but try to keep it at 1,000 words or less.

4   **Bonus responses:** Read one of the open letters mentioned in this chapter (by Baldwin, Luo, Felton, or Coates) and write your own response to that author. Alternatively, write an open letter to Helen Garner about her 2015 essay in the *Monthly*, "The Darkness in Every One of Us." (If you can't access it online, search for interviews with her about *This House of Grief.*)

Sources

This House of Grief by Helen Garner (Text Publishing, 2014), pp. 1–2, 5, 27, 133.

"Why an iPhone Could Actually Be Good for Your 3-Year-Old" by Neil Swidey, *Boston Globe Magazine*, November 1, 2009. www.archive.boston.com/bostonglobe/magazine/articles/2009/11/01/why_an_iphone_could_actually_be_good_for_your_3_year_old/

"4 Different Learning Styles You Should Know: The VARK Model," University of Kansas website, School of Education and Human Sciences. www.educationonline.ku.edu/community/4-different-learning-styles-to-know

"The Seven Learning Styles—How Do You Learn?," Inspire Education website (portal for online classes). www.inspireeducation.net.au/blog/the-seven-learning-styles/

"4 Types of Learning Styles: How to Accommodate a Diverse Group of Students" by Callie Malvik, Rasmussen College blog, August 17, 2020. www.rasmussen.edu/degrees/education/blog/types-of-learning-styles/

"Learning Styles: Concepts and Evidence" by Harold Pashler, Mark McDaniel, Doug Rohrer, and Robert Bjork, *Psychological Science in the Public Interest*, December 2008, 9(3), pp. 105–119 (accessed through Sage Journals). www.journals.sagepub.com/

"Letter to Amazon.com, Inc., Board of Directors," updated version by Authors United, September 2014. www.authorsunited.net/

"Over 900 Authors Sign Open Letter to Amazon," *Publisher's Weekly*, August 6, 2014. www.publishersweekly.com/pw/by-topic/digital/retailing/article/63591-over-900-authors-sign-open-letter-to-amazon.html

"Historians and Constitutional Scholars' Statement on the Second Impeachment of President Donald Trump" by Historians and Scholars for Legal Impeachment, *Medium*, January 11, 2021. www.legalscholarsonimpeachment.medium.com/historians-and-constitutional-scholars-statement-on-the-second-impeachment-of-president-donald-51a9a8dab61e

"Hundreds of Historians Join Call for Trump's Impeachment" by Jennifer Schuessler, *New York Times*, January 11, 2021. www.nytimes.com/2021/01/11/arts/historians-impeachment.html

"A Letter to My Nephew" by James Baldwin, *Progressive*, December 1, 1962. www.progressive.org/magazine/letter-nephew/

"An Open Letter to the Woman Who Told My Family to Go Back to China" by Michael Luo, *New York Times*, October 9, 2016. www.nytimes.com/2016/10/10/nyregion/to-the-woman-who-told-my-family-to-go-back-to-china.html

"A Letter to My Niece" by Ariel Felton, *Progressive*, February 1, 2019. www.progressive.org/magazine/a-letter-to-my-niece-felton/

"Letter to My Son" by Ta-Nehisi Coates, *Atlantic*, July 4, 2015. www.theatlantic.com/politics/archive/2015/07/tanehisi-coates-between-the-world-and-me/397619/

"The Darkness in Every One of Us" by Helen Garner, *Monthly*, July 2015. www.themonthly.com.au/issue/2015/july/1435672800/helen-garner/darkness-every-one-us#mtr

Part IV

Storytelling to make an impact

As truth-tellers, the best tool we have is to keep asking, "How do I know what I know?" This central philosophical question will push you to be accurate in reporting factual information. It will nudge you to admit what you don't know and to reflect on the consequences.

DOI: 10.4324/9781003132189-12

9 Moving through time

How have I and the world changed?

As I begin writing this chapter, it's the end of December 2020. I won't finish until 2021, and when you read this book, it will likely be many months or years later. Still, my advice exists in what's called the constant present. My active "I" voice speaks to you from the page or screen, using the present tense to denote that what I'm saying remains true over time beyond my immediate experience. However, if I recount a memory or past event, I'll pin down the date, establishing "before" and "after." In other words, I'll tell you a story.

For nonfiction storytellers, moving through time starts with a basic rule: *Don't confuse readers about when something happened.* But obvious as this may be, I often end up confused. Did Serafina find out about her uncle's drinking before or after she went to Harvard? What year did she start college? Who was the U.S. president then? Had the iPhone been invented yet?

Directing readers with your active "I" voice almost always involves orienting them in time, yet many stories told by well-respected writers, podcasters, or documentary filmmakers still seem chronologically vague to me. It's as if everything is happening in the perpetual now. That's a conscious choice for some artists, but most timing problems in nonfiction are unintentional. They may even reflect unconscious attitudes about what matters to readers.

There are common qualities in all good stories, whatever the genre, but when it comes to unnecessary vagueness, I'm biased in favor of journalism. I like datelines. I vastly prefer chronological clarity to having to check, say, Wikipedia to figure out the date for a public event. Too often, vagueness about dates or sources amounts to the same thing: the writer didn't do enough research to get the facts straight. Just as attribution context helps explain to readers how writers know what they know, timing cues can make sense of a story: when did it begin, how does it end, and what sequence of events led to those consequences?

Part Four of this book spotlights the building blocks of first-person feature storytelling. Among these blocks, the story arc of beginning-middle-end creates a solid foundation, just as reporting relies on effective observation, attribution, and counterpointing. The next chapter covers how writers mix factual information and personal anecdotes to engage readers; Chapter 11 emphasizes focusing a story idea for impact. But because the reporting practices of Part Three

DOI: 10.4324/9781003132189-13

often influence narrative techniques, this chapter opens with the element of *time travel*. Here, we'll examine storytelling approaches to convey the passage of time.

The ability to move through time as a writer is akin to the way we experience it internally. Memories from different periods overlap or conflate; few observers recall an event with documentary accuracy. (Just ask lawyers and their witnesses.) Good storytellers can cut among scenes that still feel as vivid as the day they took place. Feature writers move around with flashbacks to good effect. Essayists do a lot of time traveling.

Regardless, in *First-Person Journalism*, I ask nonfiction writers to position themselves explicitly in time when telling their own or somebody else's story (see Box 9.1). As we've discussed in previous chapters, the curse of knowledge affects how much attribution of sources is provided (or, more likely, not provided). The curse of knowledge leads to chronological confusion, too. Writers tend to forget that readers don't know when an event happened or need to be reminded. Quotes from famous people often appear with no timing cues. Inspirational words litter the web, yet rarely do they include dates or original sources, let alone historical context.

Box 9.1 Why talk about time?

We position ourselves in time.
past, present, future

Events move forward in time.
this happened, then this happened . . .

Action drives stories.
What happens next?? Tell me now!

Timing cues create story arcs.
beginning, middle, end

Features often focus on trends.
personal or cultural changes over time

Consider this quote by Albert Einstein: "Look deep, deep into nature, and then you will understand everything better." If you Google the quote, it pops up all over blogs, posters, or other products for sale. It's attributed to Einstein in compilations of nature quotes, but without the date and source. At *Talking Writing*, we wanted to base the title of our Spring 2013 issue, "Deep Into Nature," on this quote. But we didn't launch that issue until we'd established when and where Einstein had said it, which turned out to be harder than I expected.

With the help of staffers at Cal Tech's Einstein Papers Project and elsewhere, one of my research aides eventually tracked it down: the quote appears in this form in the 2005 *New Quotable Einstein*, in which editor Alice Calaprice attributes it to a 1951 letter he wrote to his stepdaughter Margot Einstein after the death of his sister. Einstein died in 1955, not long after. Knowing he wrote this toward the end of his life takes the words deeper than a green slogan.

Like attribution tags for sources, time tags are guideposts for readers. Timing cues provide more attribution context about outside sources. What event in time motivated a quote by the famous scientist? When did he come to America and what happened before? How long ago was that research published? Adverbs like "first," "next," "then," "later," and "last" also etch a sequence of actions—and what happens after each action—in time. Adverbial timing cues aren't glamorous, but they go a long way toward avoiding needless chronological confusion.

With nonfiction, how we capture the past accurately *and* meaningfully is the challenge. That's why we'll explore the need to pin down timing facts as well as narrative techniques to convey the past. We'll touch on three aspects of story timing: sequencing, chronology, and the "time machine" of self-reflection. Feature storytelling often involves documenting and interpreting change. In particular, trend stories, which are rich in historical background and reported research, examine why a change happens over time. Yet, as we'll see in the next section, timing cues help readers understand even a seemingly simple list of instructions.

Sequence: What comes first?

In the 1965 film *The Sound of Music*, Julie Andrews as Maria the governess famously teaches the von Trapp kids to sing. In "Do-Re-Mi," she tells them the obvious: start at the beginning. When you're explaining how to do something, the sequence matters, whether you're baking a pie, installing a new oven, or learning an octave. After all, everyone has had to forge their way through instructions. But here's a secret I know as a teacher and former technical writer: most readers don't read instructions, especially when the words aren't set to a memorable song.

Why is that? Instructions feel like work, and they tend to be poorly written. But the main problem is that they don't present a clear sequence from the reader's point of view—not the engineer's POV or the expert baker's POV, but the *reader's* point of view. When you're explaining an activity, a machine, or why an event happened, you need to start with the very first thing a novice needs to know. That's true for recipe posts as well as breaking news stories.

One way to pin down the sequence is in a list. As a process exercise, listing will nudge you, the writer, to figure out if you're missing any steps. For reporters who need to explain how something works or to narrate a public event, it's an excellent practice regardless of what ends up in the published story. And in a how-to article, once you've finalized a list, you can call out each step with a heading. At a glance, tip headings emphasize the order of operations.

Figuring out what comes first is the tough part. Even in a lockstep list, where you start has to do with assessing why a reader is interested in a topic. The funny thing is that even experts don't know as much as they think. Or a writer's way of explaining is so convoluted that experts can't follow the story, let alone beginners. This is where the curse of knowledge really is a curse. Imagine if Maria sang this explanation for making an apple pie: *Put some filling in the crust and bake it.* Hard to hear that set to a catchy tune.

The flip side would be if she sang about everything she's ever learned about pie-making, in no order, for an hour. After which, the sweetest kid would be flinging mud at her in that mountain meadow. If under-explaining is a problem, over-explaining is the curse of the pedagogue—the expert who doesn't remember what it's like when failure feels like a real possibility.

You can try to condense everything, but readers don't want to fail. Period. Coming up with an effective explanation requires you to understand not only all the steps but also to lead with the most important one to achieve success. Take my explanation for making an apple pie:

> *Two things matter in making a great apple pie: the crust and the apples. If you hate making pie crusts, you can buy decent frozen ones—don't waste time agonizing. But never use store-bought fruit filling. Take the time to peel and slice fresh apples (a mix of red and green is good). It's simple to mix the sliced apples with sugar, spices, and cornstarch. Then pour the filling into the bottom crust, top it with another crust—and bake.*

It's not a recipe—I don't list specific amounts or baking times—but I do say what an aspiring apple-pie baker should focus on, especially if they're worried about screwing it up. This kind of explanation is a story with a clear beginning, middle, and end.

Many readers don't like being told what to do, but I'd say what they truly hate is feeling inadequate. Call it the curse of unconscious feeling, but explanations that lack the human touch can lead to brain freeze, resentment, or despair. As a woman, I've had to fight internalized feelings of inadequacy around anything technical. If you extend that to other identity categories, you'll see why getting the facts right isn't enough to help beginners succeed. Sequencing the order of actions may seem like an analytical task, but determining what matters most to readers relies on empathy.

Your job as a first-person writer is to use your subjectivity—recalling what it *felt* like to be a novice—to get around the curse of knowledge. Keep your audience or potential audiences in mind: Will they share your cultural background and assumptions? Will they have access to the same technology and information you do? In my introduction to this chapter, the first rule I state is to not confuse readers. When the advice being offered is process-oriented and conceptual, the first step may seem so basic (*confusing readers is bad*) that it's hardly worth mentioning. Except it almost always is, especially if your stance is that of an adviser who has the reader's back.

Again, think of Maria, who reassures her musical novices that starting at the beginning is fine and may even be fun. The best first step for explaining a complicated process is often a nod to the emotional as well as intellectual demands of learning something new. Maria doesn't ask her young charges to start by singing the different choral parts for Handel's *Messiah*. And in learning how to move through time as a first-person journalist, I don't ask you to begin with a detailed timeline, for instance, of the 2020 coronavirus pandemic. Instead, as you'll see in the first voice lesson, I instruct you to list all the steps for making a pizza.

Explaining a complex sequence of events in a feature story ultimately requires enough research and reporting for you to understand how one thing led to another and why the starting point determined the outcome. Topical features about social trends or political consequences demand more than a list of baking steps. Yet the reporting and narrative techniques we use to convey information to readers still start with deciding where the story begins. In fact, that's why I've organized my presentation of material in this chapter in the order I have.

Voice Lesson 1

1   *Listing:* In your process notebook, list all the steps for making a pizza. *Hint:* Don't approach this as a professional chef. Feel free to consult recipes, if that's helpful, but consider how somebody who owns no special equipment beyond a toaster oven might do it. (As an alternative, you can list all the steps for eating a pizza or finding the best pizza in town.)
2   *What comes first:* If you've made pizzas before, think about what happened the first time. Did you make any mistakes? In your notebook, reflect on what you've learned and pin down the first thing a novice needs to know. If necessary, change the sequence of steps in your list to highlight that first thing. (If you've never made a pizza, try doing so now and see what you learn.)
3   *Explaining:* Write a paragraph that summarizes how to make a pizza, starting with the first thing novices need to know.
4   *Testing and revising:* Read your explanation to a friend or family member. Can they follow all the steps, or do they think something is missing? If they didn't understand everything in your explanation, revise the sequence based on their feedback.
5   *Bonus revision:* Try this exercise with the how-to topic you wrote about for Chapter 7. If you wrote a piece with tips, consider revising the order to come up with a better sequence.

Chronology: Orienting readers in time

Journalists may wonder why a nonfiction writer would ever stray from a strict chronology of events. That's a good question. I'd never argue that first-person journalists should massage the timing or change what actually happened to make a story more entertaining. But because real events often generate a sprawl of detail, presenting the most gripping (or relevant) action first may be a better storytelling strategy. Here, let me emphasize another rule:

Narrative chronology is not the same as the actual timeline of what happened.

Granted, there's no need to change the actual timeline just for the heck of it (or to appear arty or intellectual). Avoid needless confusion—always. Sometimes the chronological sequence is the whole point. Take the way tick-tock narratives stick to the timeline, sometimes moment-to-moment. They fill in details about a public event, such as the saga of the 2013 Boston Marathon bombing ("Timeline of Boston Marathon Bombing Events") or the 2020 explosion on the Beirut waterfront ("Beirut Blast Timeline: What We Know and What We Don't").

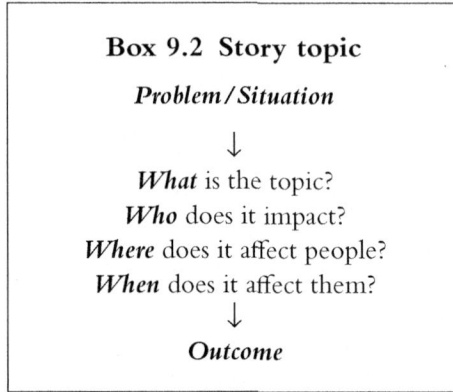

Box 9.2 Story topic

Problem / Situation

↓

What is the topic?
Who does it impact?
Where does it affect people?
When does it affect them?

↓

Outcome

But not everyone is obsessed by the moment-to-moment details. Readers often want to get to the gist much faster, even if the gist can't be accurately grasped through a headline. The feature storytelling task is to engage readers with more than a chronological sequence. In Chapter 6, I introduced *action →* *outcome* when observing and describing events. I'll extend that story setup now, framing the action as a problem to be solved (as in advice and opinion pieces) or a situation that changes over time (as in trend stories). When the action of a story involves a question or problem, a strict chronology may not satisfy readers (Box 9.2).

One popular storytelling format is to start in the middle of the action with a crisis or dilemma, before flashing back to when it started. The writer/narrator then moves forward chronologically to the crisis point and concludes the story by telling readers how it all turned out. Flashbacks are familiar from novels and movies. Yet feature writers and essayists weave in and out of chronological sequence, too. It's a good strategy for keeping readers with them beyond the initial blurb. It can also lead readers below the surface of what everyone knows.

Even first-person variations on the tick-tock can flash around to convey the limits of what was known at the time. Vivian Yee's "I Was Bloodied and Dazed. Beirut Strangers Treated Me Like a Friend," published not long after bombs ripped apart Beirut's port in August 2020, is a harrowing account of this *New York Times* correspondent fleeing the wreckage of her nearby apartment. She starts at the beginning of her experience: "I was just about to look at a video a friend had sent me on Tuesday afternoon—'the port seems to be burning,' she said—when my whole building shook." But at several points, Yee interjects what she learned after the fact:

> Later, someone would tell me that Beirutis of her generation, who had been raised during Lebanon's 15-year civil war, instinctively ran into their hallways as soon as they heard the first blast, to escape the glass they knew would break.

Flashing back and forth in time matches the decidedly unanalytical ways humans process information in the middle of, say, a disaster. That's why a first-person perspective can be such an excellent tool for making emotional sense of what happened. Indeed, the best reason to break the timeline is to help readers understand what the outcome means (Box 9.3).

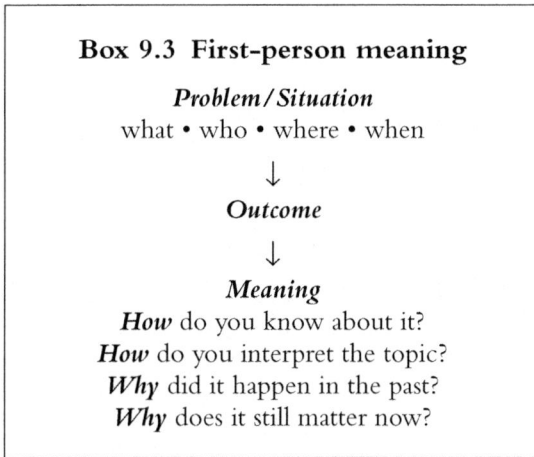

Box 9.3 First-person meaning

Problem / Situation
what • who • where • when

↓

Outcome

↓

Meaning
How do you know about it?
How do you interpret the topic?
Why did it happen in the past?
Why does it still matter now?

Beyond providing background insights, your active "I" voice can tell readers straight out when something happened—and that's a gift. Too many literary nonfiction writers ignore the value of this first-person rule: *Whenever you narrate an event, stamp it with a date or approximate time period.* Do not pass go before telling us the year or at least the decade you're writing about.

If you're a non-journalist, that blunt instruction may make you rebel. But if something happened to you, presumably you know when it did. For readers, it can seem oddly manipulative not to say so, as if it all took place in a cultural vacuum outside the real world of historical events. Alternatively, you may not remember exact dates and times, which will interest readers, too. The point is to explain what you know or don't know. If readers discover you've changed the actual timeline without telling them, fudging the chronology undermines your truthfulness.

Voice Lesson 2

1   ***"I blew it!" story:*** Describe a time you made a mistake, doing something that made you feel like slapping your hand against your forehead. Mistakes can have serious consequences, but for this story, keep it light and short (300 to 500 words).

2   ***Tick-tock version:*** Revise your "I blew it!" story as a tick-tock narrative in strict chronological sequence, complete with time/date headings. To help with the format, look at published examples, such as some of the news features cited in this chapter.

3   ***Flash around:*** Revise your story again, changing the narrative chronology. Try opening in the middle of making your mistake, when things were at their worst, then flash back to when it all started. Or weave in and out of the timeline to keep readers guessing or to provide more background information about your "I." *Hint:* Highlight all the time tags in this revision.

4   ***Bonus reflection:*** In your notebook, reflect on (a) whether and when you need timing cues; (b) which version of your story—in chronological sequence or not—you like best; and (c) how you're conveying the order of events if you don't use explicit time tags.

Time machine: Shifting between past and present selves

Writers do have the power to move around flexibly in time, which may seem at odds with my call for accuracy in narrative chronology. An essayist's recollections can be evoked so vividly it feels as if we've entered a time machine, whisking between past and present.

The trick is to let readers know that your contemporary "I" self is looking back at a past self, one who's changed since the event described. For instance, in my 2011 review "Don't Take Away My David Bowie," I move from past-tense memories of listening to the rock star as a teenager to present-tense analysis of a Bowie biography (Paul Trynka's 2011 *David Bowie: Starman*) to describing events in Bowie's life taken from the book. I open like so:

> Liking Bowie was my little secret. In high school, I was a brainy girl, the teachers' pet, but I went for guys who carried a whiff of danger. I was a geek who wanted to hang with the freaks—especially the ones who whispered in art class about the latest Bowie album, pronouncing it "Boowie," as if they possessed the key to cool.
>
> For me, camped on our green plaid couch in the early 1970s—flanked by my silent parents—watching David Bowie perform "Time" on TV was a transformative moment.

In two short paragraphs, there are many timing cues, the most obvious being a time tag—"the early 1970s"—and a reference to watching Bowie on TV, something on the public record. (I would have seen it on November 16, 1973, when the performances recorded in London a month earlier were first broadcast on NBC in the United States.) I also imply I was a teenager then by referring to high school and sitting with my parents.

But the biggest cue involves my stance: I establish in the opening that I'm recalling something based on memory. I describe my younger self not only in the past tense but also with the vernacular of the time. I lead with "my little secret," but my older "I" indicates that my attitude has changed. My fangirl love is no longer a secret: it's revealed in the title of the piece.

Keeping readers chronologically oriented is a core task for first-person journalists, because in real life, the action never stops. "The irony of writing about music you love is that it's like trying to trap smoke in a bottle," I point out in my review. I still believe this, yet I wrote those words more than a decade ago. The Bowie biography was completed years before that by the author. David Bowie himself died in 2016.

The fact of change doesn't negate the review I wrote. Beyond the specific book and Bowie, it's a first-person feature about the nature of memory and biography, and how pop music can shape life stories. I steer readers to bigger questions about storytelling:

> The best biographies craft the ungainly sprawl of life into a gripping narrative, one that illuminates a corner of human experience. Otherwise, they founder under a mass of trivia. . . . For a public figure, there's an obvious arc to the story: birth—struggling in obscurity—success!—disappointment—revelation and/or death. But simply sticking to the chronology is no guarantee of a page turner.

Think of your active "I" voice as a time traveler, then, curious and often surprised by the knowledge you recover. Such introspection is related to self-reporting as well as stance. Literary essays lend themselves best to this kind of time traveling, in which the active "I" looks back and reflects on changes in perspective over decades. Even then, witnessing past selves isn't easy. Some memories may simply be too painful to dwell on or to acknowledge. What you remember for readers is not the same as what you're internally haunted by, and it may not be possible to tell some stories from your past until you have enough distance on them.

In my own "Hurricane Warnings," detailed in Chapter 4, I portray my mother's mental illness as both a fact and something I shied away from. Yet the essay didn't take shape until I allowed myself to swoop around in time. In the final version, I open with a more recent scene (circa 2008) that depicts my aging parents actively revising events from my childhood. Then I jump back to 1960, my contemporary "I" digging into the facts behind one of my earliest memories: a major hurricane when I was two years old.

All of which leads to this timing rule for recalled memories or other reports on the past: *Establish how much time has passed between your active "I" and your younger self.* This is where creative nonfiction and memoir often diverge from journalism, putting readers right into a past scene as if it's from a novel. While I sometimes appreciate immersive literary works, I don't consider them to be nonfiction in the way that journalistic features or essays are.

In Joan Didion's "On Keeping a Notebook" from her 1968 essay collection *Slouching Towards Bethlehem*, she emphasizes the personal nature and fallibility of memories, which are often untranslatable to anyone else. And yet, "it all comes back," she wrote at the time:

> I think we are well advised to keep on nodding terms with the people we used to be whether we find them attractive company or not. Otherwise they turn up unannounced and surprise us, come hammering on the mind's door at 4 a.m. of a bad night and demand to know who deserted them, who betrayed them, who is going to make amends. We forget all too soon the things we thought we could never forget. We forget the loves and the betrayals alike, forget what we whispered and what we screamed, forget who we were.

Forgetting is a problem, but for first-person journalists, the bigger problem is deliberately avoiding who you once were or the mistakes you made. The process is constant, of course, because essayists keep traveling forward, taking verbal snapshots of themselves as they go. The "I" of Didion's essay was in her thirties; as of early 2021, she is 86, and some of her observations (especially about her daughter) sadly didn't play out as described in the late 1960s.

In recalling the past, strict factual accuracy sometimes matters less than emotional accuracy, especially if you're interpreting your own experience many years later. "*How it felt to me:* that is getting closer to the truth about a notebook," as Didion puts it. I'm not invoking "emotional truth" as an excuse for making things up. But being scrupulously honest about when and how you've misremembered has everything to do with being a self-reporter. In a 2021 *New Yorker* review of her work, Nathan Heller argues that what often mattered most to Didion was "figuring out how to use the first person across time."

Voice Lesson 3

1   *Response paper:* Read Joan Didion's "On Keeping a Notebook" (find it online or in *Slouching Towards Bethlehem*) and write a personal response to it. Do you agree or disagree? Be sure to say why and to connect it to the way you take notes or recall memories.

2   *Time traveling:* Write a short paragraph about a childhood event you remember from the point of view of your contemporary "I" voice looking back. Be sure to indicate how long ago the event happened. In your notebook, reflect on whether adding such timing and stance cues have changed the way you write about memories.

3   ***Bonus revision:*** Revise your "I blew it!" story (or your memory essay from Chapter 4), positioning your contemporary "I" voice in relation to the events you're recalling. How far back in time have you traveled—and has that affected the way you're telling the story?

Trends: Personal and cultural

In my review of the Bowie biography, I open and close with memories that are decades old. But in addition to recollections of what this pop idol meant to me, it's a topical review in which I analyze the book, the author Paul Trynka's approach, and Bowie's musical impact. In the concluding section, I link my memories to changes over time:

> Decades ago, I rode my bike around the suburban cul-de-sacs at dusk, listening to "Space Oddity." Maybe I had a transistor radio; maybe I just sang the words under my breath. Although I doubt this could be true, I remember being completely alone, the sky above me huge and glowing. I remember black birds disappearing into the clouds.
>
> When I think of Bowie now—or better yet, watch those old clips of "Time" or "Starman" on YouTube—it all comes rushing back, the heat, the noise, the shimmer. While writing this review, I've been charged up in a way I rarely feel as an adult.
>
> Journalists like Trynka do their best to write around famous subjects by viewing them through the eyes of others, and they can arrive at one form of truth. But the Bowie who emerges by *Starman's* epilogue seems disappointingly smaller than life—a cheaply arrayed star let down by his handlers, in hiding, waiting for another chance.
>
> That's not *my* Bowie. And it's not Trynka's, either, because he held back from giving us his own youthful connection to the music.
>
> Even his opening anecdote about the "Starman" moment that meant so much to British fans is presented impersonally: "Thursday evening, seven o'clock; decadence is about to arrive in five million living rooms." Trynka narrates from on high, with only an occasional "we" or "us" to hint that he might have been a kid agog at Ziggy, too.
>
> From my perspective, "Starman" was not the big hit in America that it was in the U.K. It was certainly not my favorite song on *The Rise and Fall of Ziggy Stardust and the Spiders from Mars.* I found it embarrassing, especially the line "let the children boogie," with Bowie's inauthentic Brit inflection of "bew-gie." Even at fifteen and sixteen, I knew he was ripping off American culture, that he was goofily winging it.
>
> But I loved that you *could* wing it. I felt, in a way I couldn't yet define, that even if I hated a Bowie song, the strong response it generated in me was a creative spark. For a '70s girl in California, who very badly wanted to be a writer, it wasn't just about the lure of kinky sex or his pretty-boy looks or being an outsider. He allowed me to imagine being a boy *or* girl, grabbing the microphone myself.

Our past experiences do imprint who we become and how we perceive the world. More than that, the world itself is always changing, and it's hard to know what any of it means. In trend stories, journalists use anecdotes and credible factual information to explain why such changes matter. And in first-person trend features, writers connect cultural shifts over time with personal changes, often illuminating what it means beyond a dry recitation of data.

Some first-person trend stories are topically driven. Abrahm Lustgarten's "How Climate Migration Will Reshape America," a lengthy 2020 *New York Times Magazine* feature (in partnership with ProPublica), includes reams of climate-change data to indicate sobering environmental trends. But he makes it personal by weaving research about people moving to avoid drought or rising sea levels with his own experiences as a California homeowner in 2019:

> Three of the largest fires in history burned simultaneously in a ring around the San Francisco Bay Area. Another fire burned just 12 miles from my home in Marin County. I watched as towering plumes of smoke billowed from distant hills in all directions and air tankers crisscrossed the skies. Like many Californians, I spent those weeks worrying about what might happen next, wondering how long it would be before an inferno of 60-foot flames swept up the steep, grassy hillside on its way toward my own house, rehearsing in my mind what my family would do to escape.

Lustgarten's time traveling allows him to extrapolate from the data to projections for the future, too, imagining outcomes that are hard to grasp without such subjective specifics:

> I live on a hilltop, 400 feet above sea level, and my home will never be touched by rising waters. But by the end of this century, if the more extreme projections of eight to 10 feet of sea-level rise come to fruition, the shoreline of San Francisco Bay will move three miles closer to my house.

Other trends can be more personally evoked through a writer's exploration of a topic. In "The Weight of James Arthur Baldwin," Rachel Kaadzi Ghansah opens her 2016 first-person feature with her decision to visit Baldwin's house in Saint-Paul-de-Vence near Nice before it was sold and developed into luxury apartments. She does report on going there, meeting his surviving descendants, and digging into why the house didn't end up preserved as a monument. But this personal feature also time travels into her past, contending with Baldwin's vexed legacy for a Black writer like herself:

> What I resented about Baldwin wasn't even his fault. I didn't like the way many men who only cared about Ali, Coltrane, and Obama praised him as the black authorial exception. I didn't like how every essay about race cited him. How they felt comfortable, as he described it, talking to him (and about him) "absolutely bathed in a bubble bath of self-congratulation."

Ghansah sets up what she used to feel as a counterpoint to the general applause for Baldwin, noting that she still has "no idea" why she decided to take that trip from London to Nice. And still, she writes, she "fell in love with Baldwin all over again in France."

We can forecast some trends, personal or cultural, but others shift for more complex reasons. Trend stories aren't the equivalent of weather reports. As Lustgarten's data-driven feature or my own essay about a long-ago hurricane makes clear, even something as seemingly banal as the weather isn't just a fact of existence. In addition to orienting readers about *when*, timing in feature storytelling—especially personal storytelling—involves interpreting change and the way new attitudes shape who we become. As Ghansah concludes in her essay:

> Because I am telling this now, writing it all down, I am finding time to regard memory and death differently. I'm holding them up in the light and searching them, inspecting them, as they are not as what I want them to be. . . . I wanted to alter fate and preserve things. But why? He did not need me—Baldwin seemed to have prepared himself well for his black death, his mortality, and even better, his immortality. Indeed, he bested all of them, because he wrote it all down.

All lives are finite, which means we're always negotiating our past, present, and future—and, ultimately, the end of our own story. *Time is an arrow. Time waits for no one. Time is a river.* Or it's smoke in a bottle we trap and reflect on. Countless writers, philosophers, physicists, and humans have mused about time's passing, but whether what's lost can be regained depends on the self-reporting you're willing to do.

Personal trend story: Write about changes in food, music, or weather

1   **Trend list:** In your notebook, list five trends in food, music, or weather that interest you. They should reflect how your own tastes have changed. Items can refer to a whole genre (blues, Italian food, snow) or a specific focus (mac 'n' cheese, Lady Gaga, Hurricane Sandy).
2   **Trend tracking:** Choose one list item. In your notebook, do the following timed exercises:

   a   Describe how you used to feel about this item (3 minutes).
   b   Describe how you feel about it now (3 minutes).
   c   Reflect on why you feel differently and any related cultural trends (5 minutes).

3   **Trend story:** Write a short first-person feature (from 500 to 800 words) about your changing attitude toward a food, music, or weather trend. The story could take the form of a review, an opinion piece, a topical feature,

or a personal essay—it's your choice. If you include research information about the topic or other people's attitudes, attribute your outside sources and quotes.

Hint: Be sure to keep readers oriented in time when you travel between past and present, whether in your memory or in describing historical events.

Sources

"My Inner Nature" by Martha Nichols, *Talking Writing*, April 15, 2013 (Albert Einstein quote). www.talkingwriting.com/my-inner-nature

"Timing of Boston Marathon Bombing Events" by Sara Morrison and Ellen O'Leary, *Boston Globe*, January 5, 2015. www.boston.com/news/local-news/2015/01/05/timeline-of-boston-marathon-bombing-events

"Beirut Blast Timeline: What We Know and What We Don't" by Michael Safi and Andrew Roth, *Guardian*, August 6, 2020. www.theguardian.com/world/2020/aug/06/beirut-blast-timeline-what-we-know-and-what-we-dont-explosion-lebanon

"I Was Bloodied and Dazed. Beirut Strangers Treated Me Like a Friend" by Vivian Yee, *New York Times*, August 4, 2020. www.nytimes.com/2020/08/04/world/middleeast/lebanon-explosion-beirut.html

"Don't Take Away My David Bowie" (review of Paul Trynka's *David Bowie: Starman*) by Martha Nichols, *Talking Writing*, October 3, 2011. www.talkingwriting.com/dont-take-away-my-david-bowie/

David Bowie: Starman by Paul Trynka (Little, Brown, 2011).

"The 1980 Floor Show" (David Bowie's 1973 performance on NBC), *The Bowie Bible* website. www.bowiebible.com/albums/diamond-dogs/2/

"On Keeping a Notebook" in *Slouching Towards Bethlehem* by Joan Didion (Farrar, Straus and Giroux, 1968; 2008 edition), p. 139.

"The Falconer: What We Got Wrong About Joan Didion" by Nathan Heller, *New Yorker*, February 1, 2021. www.newyorker.com/magazine/2021/02/01/what-we-get-wrong-about-joan-didion

"How Climate Migration Will Reshape America" by Abrahm Lustgarten, *New York Times Magazine* (in partnership with ProPublica and the Pulitzer Center), September 15, 2020. www.nytimes.com/interactive/2020/09/15/magazine/climate-crisis-migration-america.html

"The Weight of James Arthur Baldwin" by Rachel Kaadzi Ghansah, *BuzzFeed*, February 29, 2016. www.buzzfeed.com/rachelkaadzighansah/the-weight-of-james-arthur-baldwin-203

10 Organizing a story

How do I mix everything together?

My first job as a magazine editor was at the *Harvard Business Review* in the early 1990s. I started a few months after moving across the country to Boston, puffed with confidence that I knew everything there was to know about editing. At the time, my background was in book publishing, but I'd also done an array of freelance writing, software-development, and arts administration jobs while getting my master's degree in San Francisco. All of which is to say I knew a lot of things but very little about editing features for a slick magazine.

Some of my story arc is predictable. I started out brash, made mistakes, learned quickly, got a promotion, and left *HBR* within two years for another editing job. I'd found my calling, becoming a magazine editor and feature writer. I can almost imagine it as a movie with Anne Hathaway playing young me, another riff on *The Devil Wears Prada*. Almost. But captivating (and dysfunctional) as *HBR* seemed at the time, it was far from a stylish slick like *Vogue*. And while I went on to launch my own digital magazine, I have yet to win a Pulitzer or lasting fame, something the Movie of Me would have to fictionalize to make my life more dramatic.

Why am I telling you this? Because some of my story doesn't fit a predictable arc—especially all the idiosyncratic, subjective parts that drive first-person features. I started out brash and stayed brash. There was no moment of comeuppance, just feedback from helpful mentors. The backdrop for everything I learned had me doing research, nose in archives, about business and organizational psychology. Sure, I can ask you to picture me as a character back then: in my early thirties, defiantly underdressed in a madras blouse and khaki skirt, flashing my California cred on the Harvard Business School campus, refusing to move out of the way of the big-shouldered male suits who almost crashed into me. What I learned from the experience, however, also requires a different story structure than a single dramatic arc.

In journalistic shorthand, we often talk about "stories" in a generic way. But the information presented in a feature is organized differently than in a straightforward news story. While telling a personal story may sound easy at first glance, constructing a first-person feature often involves reverse engineering to figure out what all the component parts are. That's why this chapter focuses on

DOI: 10.4324/9781003132189-14

the mix, the element that nods to the many shifts in stance, timing, reporting, cultural references, and personal anecdotes typical of a magazine feature article.

You could say editors are the mechanics of this process, tuning up and rebuilding stories that writers turn in, and sometimes that's the case. In my first features, editors taught me the hard way with red ink and reorganizing. Yet I came away not only learning about feature structure but also wanting more control over the construction of my own stories.

The mix doesn't give you permission to be random. Learning to take apart a story and to reconfigure it is often necessary for embracing your own active "I" voice. This crucial aspect of first-person writing, in turn, helps you to figure out the main point of a story. There's usually no way around questioning and remixing with a longer feature, which is why I introduce a few specific mix tools here rather than detailing every format for a magazine article.

In *On Writing Well*, William Zinsser referred to the choice of first- or third-person voice as one of the most unifying decisions a writer makes. "Unity not only keeps the reader from straggling off in all directions," he noted, "it satisfies your readers' subconscious need for order and reassures them that all is well at the helm." That's an excellent description of the active "I" voice in first-person journalism. As a writer, you steer through what might otherwise seem to be an odd assortment of information and personal quirks.

But how are we supposed to find out all this stuff? I've heard students wail such questions when reviewing work by a master. For example, in Malcolm Gladwell's 2004 *New Yorker* feature "The Ketchup Conundrum," he wrangles the backstory of a Grey Poupon TV ad, the history of ketchup, a market researcher who owns a parrot, and more. The answer comes in the particular interests of Gladwell or any other nonfiction writer who is passionately curious. The mix reflects the active "I" telling the story—and that "I" will come up with a mix nobody else could.

The story arc still matters, but the action in a feature article or essay isn't like a chase scene in a movie or the birth-youth-adulthood-death sequence of real life. The story arc, as it's usually conceived, amounts to an action narrative with an emphasis on dramatic turning points. But topical magazine features reframe what constitutes action and turning points. While tension may build toward a revelation (or climax), feature writers often hook readers by making a provocative argument, mixing up the factual material presented, and keeping them guessing.

Back in the 1980s, when I was getting that master's degree in creative writing, I first read E.M. Forster's *Aspects of the Novel*. Originally published in 1927, this classic has greatly influenced my thinking about story structure, especially because I've come to realize that his famous contrast of plot-versus-story applies to nonfiction features as well. In Forster's formulation, a *story* is "a narrative of events arranged in their time-sequence." But he contrasted this with a *plot*, which emphasizes why events happened, not just the fact that they did. His definition:

> "The king died, and then the queen died" is a story. "The king died, and then the queen died of grief" is a plot. The time-sequence is preserved,

but the sense of causality overshadows it. Or again: "The queen died, no one knew why, until it was discovered that it was through grief at the death of the king." This is a plot with a mystery in it. . . . It suspends the time-sequence, it moves as far away from the story as its limitations will allow.

Forster was talking about fiction writing, where authors can make up events to build a plot. And yet, his emphasis on causality, memory, and intelligence are relevant to a nonfiction writer's need to make meaning out of real events.

In this chapter, we'll think of first-person features, particularly longer features, as mystery stories. The mix of material you come up with is the plot. We'll explore one classic feature formula, identifying leads and nut grafs, and you'll try your hand at outlining to help organize scenes in a story. But first, you need familiarity with the construction materials.

What's in the mix?

One of the best ways to see how the mix works in features is to identify the components in a published article by another author. Once you look at a feature story as a mix, you'll find a surprising number of components. Not every feature or essay includes every type, but in general, feature writers do mix together at least a few statistics, quotes, and anecdotes in an article or essay. That's why I often ask students in my classes to *map the mix* in a published feature, instructing them to highlight and label the different components in a given article (Box 10.1).

Box 10.1 Map the mix

anecdotes—personal or otherwise
place descriptions
capsule profiles
historical background
factual information
attribution context
cultural references—movies, pop music, celebrities
expert quotes and other sources
counterpoints
personal reflection/opinion
time tags and time shifts

For example, in "Don't Take Away My David Bowie," the review of mine discussed in the previous chapter, I obviously included cultural references to a celebrity. But my feature is not just a mélange of trivia or a book report. I mixed in a summary of Bowie's life as a musician, quotes from rock critics at the time, critical assessment of some of his most famous songs, my own anecdotes and memories about his music, and self-reflection. If you mapped the mix in my feature, you'd highlight these as separate components. They offer different perspectives on a celebrity and an opportunity for me to reflect on more than Bowie or the specific book. (You might want to do a mini-map of the excerpt included in the last section of Chapter 9.)

A variation of this mix-mapping exercise is to mark all time tags and timing cues in a published feature. Still another variation is to mark all the quotes and attribution tags. Each kind of mix map provides insights into how writers arrange the information they've collected. It can also help you think through why the narrative scenes are presented in a certain order.

One of my favorite first-person features for mix mapping is nature writer Sy Montgomery's "Deep Intellect." This article about the intelligence of octopuses first appeared in *Orion* magazine in 2011. (Montgomery later went on to publish a whole book on the subject, *The Soul of an Octopus*, in 2015.) She opens with a vivid first-person anecdote about meeting Athena the octopus at the New England Aquarium in Boston. She observes not only the octopus in action and her keepers but also self-reports on her own experience of touching Athena in the tank. The rest of Montgomery's lengthy piece mixes in profiles of octopus researchers, facts based on research studies, counterpoints, expert quotes, and more of her personal reflections.

Now it's your turn to do some mix mapping. Before we turn to one of your own features, let's dive "inside the mind of an octopus," as the blurb for Sy Montgomery's article puts it.

Voice Lesson 1

1 *"Deep Intellect" mix:* Based on the list in Box 10.1, highlight and label the different components of Sy Montgomery's *Orion* magazine article. You can print it out and mark the mix by hand or you can annotate a digital version. If you can't access her feature online, then map the mix in another magazine article (2,500 words or longer).

2 *Timing cues:* If you haven't already, mark all the time tags and other cues in Montgomery's article. *Hint:* Use a separate color to indicate timing cues, one that makes them stand out on their own. In your process notebook, reflect on the way this writer organizes the time sequence of different anecdotes and how often she uses time tags.

3 *Direct quotes:* If you haven't already, mark all the direct quotes in anecdotes and from outside experts in Montgomery's article. In your notebook, reflect on the way this writer organizes quotes from different people and how they function in the mix.

Classic feature formula: Lead + nut graf

Say you've witnessed a disaster or had a harrowing accident, dramatic events in their own right. You decide to write a first-person feature about, for instance, the dangers of surfing because you almost died during a local contest. You start by describing your younger self wiping down a special, handcrafted board. You go on to relate how you almost drowned.

As we discussed in the last chapter about time travel, merely relating the story as "first this happened, then this happened" won't necessarily make events meaningful or comprehensible to anyone else. As a first-person writer, it helps to provide personal context through memory or self-reflection. As a first-person journalist, you can also present evidence and counterpoints.

This all sounds good in theory. But the reality of constructing a feature story often feels more like a trip to Trash Mountain. *One person's trash is another person's treasure.* The familiar adage has ironic resonance here. Rarely does the prospect of sorting through your own notes inspire excitement. Fortunately, if you've done good reporting, there will be plenty of treasure. But what if there's too much treasure? Your mountain of capsule descriptions, anecdotes, quotes, and statistics, may only be a little smaller, but this is where reverse engineering comes in.

If you were a fiction writer, you might try the old technique of writing each paragraph (or scene) on an index card. Then you'd shift the cards around, arranging and rearranging, until the paragraphs and scenes cohered into a dramatic narrative. Some writers have been known to print out a first draft, then cut it up, shifting the pieces of paper into a different order.

As a nonfiction writer, you can do this, too, with the equivalent of mix component cards on a tabletop, trying out new arrangements. But most of us digital writers have gotten so used to cutting and pasting on-screen that all the shifting around can just seem to tangle things more. Creative writing as a discipline nods to impulses that are unconscious, as if the right story structure will emerge through emotional sleight of hand. But the Ouija-board approach isn't enough to organize most feature articles, especially think pieces, explainers, or trend stories.

In the magazine and news trade, there are some standard formulas, including the inverted pyramid for a breaking news story, in which the most relevant information comes in the lead. In earlier chapters, I've introduced feature formulas for how-to and opinion pieces. We've discussed the tick-tock narrative, where key events (turning points) in a time sequence are detailed, sometimes with headings to pin down the chronology. Any of these might fit the components you've gathered, depending on the type of feature you're writing.

Yet for magazine articles, one classic formula is often still used to organize component parts: an *anecdotal lead* followed by a *nut graf.* This format is sometimes called the *Wall Street Journal* feature, because it became a fixture in the *Journal's* long print news features in the latter half of the twentieth century. It was popularized by William Blundell, an influential *Wall Street Journal* reporter and bureau chief who explained theme statements, various kinds of leads, and other approaches in his 1988 guide *The Art and Craft of Feature Writing.*

I think of the lead + nut graf combination as the one-two punch in an article. The lead is the emotional hook, and the nut graf explains why readers should care, even if they aren't initially drawn to a topic. Keep in mind that anecdotes are mini-stories: capsule descriptions of something that happened. So, an anecdotal lead (or "lede" in old-style manuscript markups) means the feature starts with a narrative. In the heyday of *Wall Street Journal* features, such as the lighter, oddball stories labeled "A-Heds" on the print front page, that anecdote often involved a tale about some regular person observed by the reporter. The anecdote might run for a number of paragraphs, perhaps even the whole first scene; the articles could be 2,000 words or longer. That's still the case for many topical articles and essays, from the *New Yorker* to *Vanity Fair*.

But however long the anecdotal lead is, the classic formula places the nut graf after it. A good nut graf conveys, in short order, why the opening anecdote is relevant to the topic, what provocative question the writer is posing, and what's at stake. In practice, the "graf" of this typographic shorthand can be longer than one paragraph. For longer magazine features, it's often two or three short paragraphs. And yet, nut grafs are a form of capsule description, too. Think of such theme statements as the "nut" of the story—what matters in a nutshell. They're not just abstract or boring summaries, especially in first-person features.

Blundell called "the main theme statement the single most important bit of writing I do on any story. . . . Frequently, it's the basis for my lead." His version of a theme statement (which he called on "our reporter" to do before a disoganized, rambling story ever crossed an editor's desk) isn't always the same as the final nut graf. But I'd argue that once you get your nut graf right, the rest of a feature becomes easier to organize. Beyond spotlighting the main point for readers, you'll have a clearer sense yourself of what you want to say. As in shorter opinion features, point-counterpoint often structures the evidence.

Another way to think of it: the classic nut graf is an intellectual hook after the first emotional punch, a presentation of the mystery afoot. In a nonfiction feature, the mystery won't be solved as it is in a plotted novel. But this formula does conclude by circling back to the opening anecdote, revealing to readers the outcome of the problem described or the question posed. As Blundell underscored, the writer will at least indicate implications for the future.

Box 10.2 Structural components in the mix

lead
nut graf
evidence
scene breaks
conclusion

You can break down this feature formula into a few basic structural components (Box 10.2). You'll find many examples of deconstructed articles on journalism sites that indicate how feature writers have used these components.

Some students find those examples useful, although they often seem more complicated than the formula. I think it helps to get hands on, so I encourage you to identify the structural components in published features and your own stories, as you did in mapping the mix. In particular, look for the lead + nut graf combination.

I've adapted the *Wall Street Journal* formula for first-person features in Box 10.3, because anecdotes as opening hooks are so well suited to personal non-fiction. If you mapped the mix in "Deep Intellect," for instance, note that Montgomery's first paragraph is an anecdotal lead. It's also followed by a classic setup for a first-person feature article of this length: the second paragraph fills in her own fascination with octopuses to explain why she's at the aquarium. That moves right into her nut-graf section, starting with the third paragraph:

> Many times I have stood mesmerized by an aquarium tank, wondering, as I stared into the horizontal pupils of an octopus's large, prominent eyes, if she was staring back at me—and if so, what was she thinking?

Her nut graf goes on to refer to a counterpoint—"Not long ago, a question like this would have seemed foolish, if not crazy. How can an octopus *know* anything, much less form an opinion?"—then quickly returns to her main point: Octopus researchers are starting to discover, she writes, that these invertebrates have "developed intelligence, emotions, and individual personalities. Their findings are challenging our understanding of consciousness itself."

Box 10.3 First-person feature formula

1 *Anecdotal lead*—a personal mini-story to hook readers
2 *Nut graf*—explain your main idea and why it matters
3 *Evidence*—point/counterpoint, outside sources, capsule descriptions
4 *End with a follow-on story*—circle back to your opening anecdote

---

My description of Montgomery's nut graf has been compressed to highlight her use of point-counterpoint in presenting evidence. Regardless, her lead + nut graf combo takes up only the first five paragraphs of a long article. The bulk of her feature is filled with vivid descriptions of her own experience with Athena the octopus as well as profiles of researchers in the field.

Point: Opening with a story about yourself not only humanizes the question you'll pose but also positions your "I" as the one interpreting the unique mix of information you've gathered. It allows you to get across what's at stake in a personal way. By the end of "Deep Intellect," Montgomery circles back to the octopus she touched in the first scene, grappling with her own tears when she learns that Athena has died:

> Why such sorrow? I had understood from the start that octopuses don't live very long. I also knew that while Athena did seem to recognize me, I was not by any means her special friend. But she was very significant to me, both as an individual and as a representative from her octopodan world. She had given me a great gift: a deeper understanding of what it means to think, to feel, and to know.

Counterpoint: Montgomery cuts to the chase in her lead + nut graf, but for the digital generation, many magazine classics of the *New Yorker* or *Wall Street Journal* school take far too long to get started. Leads and nut grafs now come in many forms. Hooking readers fast has become an immediate business, with a digital article's title and blurb (or searchable summary with image thumbnail) now doing the same work the lead + nut graf combo used to.

Point: Impatient as we digital readers are, plenty of us still want to know more about a topic than *who-what-when-where*. Readers can be hooked by a title and blurb yet need more prompting to start the actual story. As feature writers, our job is to keep readers following the breadcrumbs of our plot. A good anecdotal lead + nut graf remains an excellent opening combo in a topical article, especially if part of your mix is a personal story. Another way to provide guideposts is to break your story into shorter scenes, which we'll address in the next section.

Voice Lesson 2

1 **Structure map:** In a published magazine article, highlight the main structural components: anecdotal lead, nut graf, evidence, scene breaks, and conclusion. You'll challenge yourself more by mapping the mix in a longer article. Suggestions: Malcolm Gladwell's "The Ketchup Conundrum" (*New Yorker*, 2004); Michael Lewis's "Wall Street on the Tundra" (*Vanity Fair*, 2009); or Rachel Kaadzi Ghansah's "A Most American Terrorist: The Making of Dylann Roof" (*GQ*, 2017).

2 **Your own mix:** For the personal trend story you wrote in Chapter 9, map the mix, noting as many of the classic *Wall Street Journal* structural components as you can. If your draft doesn't conform to that formula, be sure to reflect on this in your notebook, discussing how you might use the classic feature formula to rearrange the mix.

3 **Your own nut graf:** Chances are, you haven't yet written a nut graf (or theme statement) for your personal trend story. If not, write one now—or write several versions to see which one feels the most focused.

4 **Bonus response:** In the published article you mapped earlier, how and when does it diverge from the classic magazine formula? In your notebook, consider why the author may have shifted or revised the formula and whether that was effective for you, the reader.

Scene breaks and dramatic tension

Confession: I'm an outliner. My tendency to outline a feature, an essay, or a chapter I'm planning goes back at least as far as my days as a failed science-fiction novelist. I can still visualize the elaborate outlines I scrawled on legal pads in the 1980s. The scribbled yellow pages with cross-outs and additions were taped on the wall beside my splintery desk in San Francisco, including everything from character lists to scene descriptions for my tome about life on a new colony world. Those old outlines are now squirreled away in filing cabinets in what my husband and I euphemistically call the "sunroom" (a weatherized porch). Yet the physical outlines don't matter as much as the process of making them and using them to think through a story.

Not every writer finds outlining helpful, but don't dismiss this tool too fast. These days, you're no longer stuck with paper and tape. You'll find many apps or programs for organizing story components, often drawn from the world of screenwriting. Or you can go with the outlining format of a live Google doc, revising and reworking as you proceed. Whether you construct a starting outline on your mobile device or a legal pad—or opt for the standard outline format—it might become one of your best tools for organizing feature stories and essays.

Outlining highlights another key structural component: *scene breaks.* While the material a writer gathers for a first-person story is rarely the same as anybody else's, using scene breaks provides an organizational foundation for almost any topic-driven feature. More important, outlining with scenes highlights the value of inserting a break before a new scene begins.

Scene breaks in magazine articles can be indicated by extra line spacing, asterisks, bullets, other text ornaments, or a heading—as with the headings that open each section of my chapters in this book. Once you start mapping the mix in published articles, you'll see many typographic versions of scene breaks.

When I'm planning a feature or personal essay of 1,500 to 2,000 words, I start with five scenes, although I may end up adding more later (Box 10.4). The opening scene—or introduction—can be taken up entirely with an anecdotal lead, but usually it includes my nut graf, too. The next two scenes present historical context or other evidence. The fourth scene discusses at least one counterpoint, and the concluding scene circles back to the opening.

Box 10.4 Five-scene feature

1 *Introduction:* lead + nut graf
2 *Background:* historical or research evidence
3 *Context:* more evidence and anecdotes
4 *Counterpoints:* who disagrees and why
5 *Conclusion:* circle back to opening anecdote

My five-scene diagram is a variation on the classic feature formula. Like all schematics, the way an outline evolves in practice may not fit the formula by the time you're done. Here's another process-driven rule: *Story outlines aren't set in stone.* I start with five scenes because conceptualizing a feature this way helps me determine what can be cut from a story.

If, for example, I've crammed too many expert quotes, research studies, or anecdotes into one scene, I know I should delete or move some of it in the outline. My rule of thumb for a 1,500-plus article is no more than three double-spaced pages of material per scene (and even that may be too much). Other times, I end up combining two scenes into one. In any case, I plan to insert a *visible break* after each scene, as you'll find in many longer news or magazine features. Thinking of scenes as another form of capsule description helps underscore how much information a general reader can absorb at a time. Scene breaks introduce a pause.

Structural components like scene breaks developed in the print world: headings, subheadings, chapters, and other organizing elements direct readers through books, magazines, or newspaper columns. A table of contents *is* an outline. If done well, readers can tell at a glance from the table of contents what a book includes and where to find specific topics. In the digital realm, there's also a practical reason for breaking a story into shorter scenes or "chunks," not to mention breaking up long paragraphs: readability.

Scene breaks in magazine articles aren't just practical, however. As in a plotted novel, they build dramatic tension by spotlighting the *why* of a story and keeping readers guessing. Joan Didion's most famous essays, in which she collaged together sections of previously published magazine articles with additional material, use quick cuts ("flash cuts," in her phrasing) to jump between components of her mix. Her quick-cut style has filtered well beyond literary nonfiction into many types of magazine articles. Study her "On Keeping a Notebook" or "The White Album" to see how she builds tension with seemingly random scene breaks.

Or take that hypothetical feature about the dangers of surfing. You've done a first draft of this personal narrative about almost drowning. You've completed the reporting and research—you think—but you're stumped about how to lead readers through everything else in your note pile. Time for a five-scene outline. (See my sample outline at the end of this chapter.)

Scene breaks also help with transitions, chopping out the need for boring expository verbiage. Instead of writing "Here's what I remember, but now let's look at a few facts," just break the scene. After a break, you can open with historical background, changing your stance from that of a personal story. You can switch points of view from yourself to that of an interview subject or another source. And you can travel backward or forward in time when you break a scene, keeping readers oriented. The break signals that a shift in stance or timing is coming.

It's true that in a long article, breaking the story flow is also a risk. Readers may not jump to the next scene. And yet, a pause in the action helps build tension. You might end your opening scene with a provocative question, then leap to background information, carrying readers along because they want to know the answer. If your personal story is the focus, you can create a cliffhanger at the end of the first scene (*did she survive the surfing accident? what happened afterward?*), a tried-and-true approach in fictional stories and blockbuster movies. You break in the middle of the action and don't reveal the outcome until the end. In nonfiction writing, a cliffhanger is sometimes referred to as the "kicker" into the next scene or section.

Regardless, don't let the messiness of factual information hold you back in organizing your material dramatically. Almost any topic is fascinating if you provide the right context with your active "I" voice. Readers are hooked by the tension between competing ideas and experiences, too. Tapping into the oppositions in your topic—the disagreements, the cognitive dissonance you or your subjects feel, the conflict between cultures or personal perspectives—builds real-world tension. Scene breaks help engage readers by changing things up, and to my mind, that's exciting. As is this rule: *All good stories involve change.*

Voice Lesson 3

1   **Response paper:** For the published magazine article you mapped in a previous voice lesson, identify the scene breaks, if you haven't already. Then write a response to the article, discussing how the author structured the scenes and whether dramatic tension is created for the reader.

2   **Your outline:** For the personal trend story you wrote in Chapter 9, create a five-scene outline. It may not be long enough yet to include five scenes, but in your outline, indicate where you might add material based on additional reporting or more personal anecdotes. (Refer to my sample outline for one possible template.) You don't have to keep everything you initially put in such an outline. Like the first draft of a story, outlines are works in progress.

Essays: Emotional journeys

While I've provided mix tools for structuring feature stories, first-person journalism is also unruly, prone to multiple storylines and sub-topics. Tools help, but analogies sometimes convey more. Other guides to narrative journalism or literary nonfiction describe the braided narrative, in which scenes alternate between two or more storylines like woven threads. The collage-like cuts between scenes in movies and documentaries offer another analogy. Joan Didion's essays, as I noted earlier, are classics of the film-cut school.

My own analogy for feature writing is more prosaic: a slice of lasagna. The pasta layers are the equivalent of a set number of scene breaks; the filling between each layer can vary (a lot); but in a good lasagna, it all coheres in a piquant taste when you bite in.

With personal essays, though, the lasagna analogy breaks down. Essays lie at the other end of the first-person journalism spectrum from topical features.

While essays often include scene breaks to help with transitions, time traveling, and stance shifts, the filling between those scenes won't necessarily conform to expository information or counterpoints. Essays have a start and a finish, but in between, their idiosyncratic structure more closely resembles a winding road.

If nothing else, doing a five-scene outline will indicate whether any feature formula is right for the piece you're drafting. Yet that doesn't mean personal essays have no story structure or that you write them by dumping whatever comes to mind. I outline scenes for essays, as well as features, because organizing the material in an essay can take longer to figure out. There's no single formula to capture an individual writer's take on the world. Here's how Cheryl Strayed describes it in her 2013 introduction to *The Best American Essays* collection she edited:

> A good essay isn't a report of what happened. . . . Essayists begin with an objective truth and attempt to find a greater, grander truth by testing fact against subjective interpretations of experiences and ideas, memories and theories. They try to make meaning of actual life, even if an awful lot has yet to be figured out.

It's a tall order—making "meaning of actual life"—but before you go running for the hills, let me emphasize that this is the goal for first-person journalism in general. More to the practical point, essays do share many of the same mix components found in magazine features.

By mapping the mix and identifying scene breaks, you can reverse engineer a published essay just as you have with other articles. The more you do this, the better you'll get at seeing the particular mix in each one. There are many hybrids of the two. Think of free-form lasagna or a straight road that occasionally rambles down sidetracks. I suspect you'll also realize many features are called "essays" in magazines simply because they use the first-person voice.

Let's start with one thing feature and essay formats have in common: opening with an anecdotal lead. A first-person lead is one of the best ways to establish your active "I." It signals to readers right away who is telling the story and interpreting the facts. And in the digital era, a personal anecdote often opens an essay in order to hook readers. For that reason, here's another first-person rule: *Open and close a personal nonfiction story in your own voice.*

While many literary authors love to begin with an epigraph by a famous writer, I cut those when it's in my power to do so as an editor. One of the great strengths of first-person journalism is that your "I" voice can unify the craziest mix of material. But if you open with somebody else's words, your voice has been hijacked from the start. You lose the coherence a consistent "I" voice provides. Meanwhile, many journalists like to end topical features with a quote from a source. It's standard practice at many news sites and magazines; I've occasionally done this at the ends of sections in this book. And yet, closing with your own reflections is a powerful takeaway for readers—a variation on circling back to your opening anecdote.

The main way features and essays diverge structurally is in the nut graf. Classic feature formula has writers put their theme statement close to the beginning so that readers know what's to come. But for literary essayists, this can seem as if they're giving away everything before conveying how they arrived at what they know. For instance, James Baldwin's "Stranger in the Village" opens with his anecdotes about being the only Black person in a remote Swiss village. He doesn't shift into his powerful interpretation of what this means until a few pages in.

Essays are internal explorations, as well as analyses of real-world issues, but essayists are intentional about the way they structure the journey for readers. No matter how sensational, personal narratives that proceed as if on a tick-tock timeline often don't help readers understand or empathize. In E.M. Forster's terms, they're the story rather than the plot. In contrast, essayists have enough self-awareness and distance on their own experiences to give them meaning.

And so, we've wound around to the distinction Vivian Gornick draws between the *situation* and the *story* in a personal narrative. Gornick's dichotomy is not the same as Forster's story-versus-plot for a novel, in part because her influential 2001 book *The Situation and the Story* focuses on essays and memoirs. Some of her arguments about artistic license in memoirs don't sit well with first-person journalism. Yet, as with Forster's *Aspects of the Novel*, Gornick gets across an essential idea for writers of all genres:

> Every work of literature has both a situation and a story. The situation is the context or circumstance, sometimes the plot; the story is the emotional experience that preoccupies the writer: the insight, the wisdom, the thing one has come to say.

Here's another way to envision an essay: its journey, twisty and wandering as it may seem, takes readers to "the thing one has come to say." To get there, writers need to challenge themselves, to get past the curse of unconscious feeling, to determine what they *really* have to say about a topic. Until they do so, they won't get the mix right for readers.

Consider Gornick's situation-versus-story for some of the essays and articles mentioned in this chapter. The situation for James Baldwin's "Stranger in the Village" is being the only Black person in the Swiss town of Leukerbad; the story is the impact of racism on history and Baldwin's justifiably outraged response. The situation in Joan Didion's "The White Album" is a particular time period—the amoral end of the 1960s—but the story is her realization that no absolute meaning can be made of such a chaos of events, no matter how hard she tries. The situation in Sy Montgomery's "Deep Intellect" is the topic—new research about octopus intelligence—but the story is the way she ends up questioning the nature of consciousness.

In each case, the emotional experience of the writer not only drives the mix; it also determines what the story is about, whether it's stated in an explicit nut graf up front or a realization that slowly emerges as the essay follows its winding road to the end.

Just as I am, at last, circling back to Forster's dead queen. If the queen were telling her own story, we'd want to know why she died of grief and what it felt like to be so bereft. I also want to know why the queen didn't decide to rule in the king's stead—and whether the narrator explaining her grief is male. I love stories of all kinds, but I'm most engaged by real-world questions about cultural and political change. That's how personal truth-tellers make an impact, the element we'll focus on in the final practice chapter of *First-Person Journalism*.

New mix: Feature or essay?

1   ***Remix:*** Revise your personal trend story by rearranging the components in a new file. If you've already changed the mix in the outline you made, then follow that order. Otherwise, change the way you present your ideas and information in the new version.
2   ***New opening scenes:*** Based on your remix, write two completely new opening scenes for your trend story. Try rewriting your new openings to set up different types of first-person stories. *Hint:* As a topical feature, craft your new opening to include the lead + nut graf combination. As a personal essay, write a new opening narrative.
3   ***Self-reflection:*** In your notebook, discuss whether your personal trend story will work better as a topical feature or an essay. Be sure to identify the *situation* as well as the *story*, in Vivian's Gornick's terms. Do you like your remix and one of the new openings you wrote for that format? Or do you have something else in mind to hook readers?

Sample outline
Why I'll Never Surf Again (working title) *

Scene 1

- Lead: personal anecdote about almost drowning while surfing
- Nut graf: a few facts about drowning while surfing; why it's a trend— what nobody's talking about and why we should

Scene 2

- Historical background about surfing (the romance of it)
- Cultural references—*Endless Summer, Point Break*, other surfing movies
- Expert quote from Center for Surf Research
- Expert quote? (gung-ho extreme sportscaster—still need to interview)

Scene 3

- Personal reflection: how I was drawn to surfing; the danger beneath the romance hooked me, too
- Expert quote? (counterpoint: surfing is more dangerous than . . .?)

Scene 4

- Direct observation of a recent surf competition
- More anecdotes about famous surfers (quote from *Tapping the Source*)
- Capsule profile: Dukie J, former surf star ("I never even saw that wave coming, dude")

Scene 5

- Personal anecdote: how I was saved from drowning, the aftermath
- Self-reflection: the takeaway (why I changed my mind about surfing)

* The personal anecdotes are fictional, so the outline is hypothetical. As of this writing, there is a Center for Surf Research (at San Diego State University), and the book and movie references are real, but "Dukie J" is fictional.

Sources

"Unity" in *On Writing Well: The Classic Guide to Writing Nonfiction* by William Zinsser (HarperCollins, 1976; anniversary edition, 2006), p. 50.

"The Ketchup Conundrum" by Malcolm Gladwell, *New Yorker*, August 30, 2004. www.newyorker.com/magazine/2004/09/06/the-ketchup-conundrum

Aspects of the Novel by E.M. Forster (originally published 1927 by Edward Arnold; Penguin Books, 1987), p. 87.

"Deep Intellect" by Sy Montgomery, *Orion*, October 2011. www.orionmagazine.org/article/deep-intellect/

The Art and Craft of Feature Writing: Based on the Wall Street Journal Guide by William E. Blundell (Plume/Penguin Books, 1988), p. 27.

"The Nut Graf Tells the Reader What the Writer Is Up To" by Chip Scanlan, Poynter Institute website, May 19, 2003 (from Scanlan's *Reporting and Writing: Basics for the 21st Century*, Harcourt, 1998). www.poynter.org/archive/2003/the-nut-graf-part-i/

"What Is an A-Hed?" by Barry Newman, *Wall Street Journal*, November 15, 2010. www.wsj.com/articles/SB10001424052702303362404575580494180594982

"Introduction" in *The Best American Essays* 2013 by Cheryl Strayed (Houghton Mifflin Harcourt, 2013), p. xvii.

The Situation and the Story: The Art of Personal Narrative by Vivian Gornick (Farrar, Straus and Giroux, 2001), p. 13.

11 Revising for impact

What do I really want to say?

In writing this book, I changed the mix of chapters several times. Years before, I had come up with the elements of first-person journalism based on classroom teaching with real, live students. (In fact, there was originally a tenth element in my series—*exposure*—that I decided to fold into the nine elements in this book.) Yet even after I'd written half the manuscript and had a working table of contents, I shifted the order of elements and their related chapters again.

While I would have loved to work with a perfect template from the start, one in which I could plug in what the outline told me to, the reality I've described so far didn't faze me. I've been a professional writer and editor for decades. I'm used to revising.

But one chapter of *First-Person Journalism* did give me unanticipated trouble: Chapter 2 on "The Ethics of Personal Reporting." Early on, I'd outlined sections and roughed out a placeholder draft. *Piece of cake*, I thought. *I'll finish it after I get the tough stuff done.* When I finally did get back to Chapter 2, however, I realized why I'd avoided it for so long.

I hadn't figured out what I really wanted to say.

Therein followed a good week of hair-tearing and second-guessing. I certainly had a lot to tell readers about ethics and reporting, but that was the problem. I had *too* much to say without enough focus in the chapter draft to highlight what mattered.

That's why I connect *impact*—my ninth and final first-person element—with revising. You're also revising when you make an outline. You'll revise your idea of a story as you're doing the reporting, too. I won't claim that every author revises as much as I do, but as an editor, I know how common it is to write a lousy first draft, tear it apart, then go back to writing—and repeat. Writing is an iterative process. Or as Anne Lamott, Stephen King, and many others have put it: "shitty" or "crummy" first drafts rule.

And yet, pinning down what you really want to say sometimes happens only after you've done most of the reporting, written a first draft, maybe even more than one lousy draft. In my own case, the challenge of writing a nut graf for Chapter 2 was the turning point. I'd left space for adding one in my original draft. But when I sat down to write it, under deadline pressure, no piece of cake

DOI: 10.4324/9781003132189-15

was in sight. At first, that section looked more like a cross between a muddy milkshake and a sugar cookie with too many bright sprinkles. It tasted all right, until I thought about what I wasn't saying and needed to, which brings up one more first-person rule:

> *It can be hard to figure out the main idea of a story, but put in the work to have an impact.*

Forcing myself to focus did get me to the main idea of Chapter 2: don't fake yourself. My earlier version had contained a section about the ethical problem of fictionalizing your own voice, but I'd thrown in more material to make a case for the value of first-person journalism in general. It took me awhile to realize I was avoiding my own competing impulses about art and journalism: I admire many literary nonfiction writers. I'm cynical about the truthfulness of anyone's story. Yet I love personal essays and stories. I had to wrestle with this cognitive dissonance before I made any headway. But once I came up with a focused nut graf, I could see cuts to make in the original draft.

And I homed in: when personal storytellers disguise their own uncertainty behind a well-told tale, they end up fictionalizing their "I," not to mention what actually happened. If the ethics of personal reporting is the topic, this is the moral: when you fake your own voice, you undercut the truthfulness of everything else you say. That's a key concept I hope readers take away from *First-Person Journalism*. It also led me to revise the opening anecdote in this chapter.

Box 11.1 Guidelines for first-person impact

- Make sure the story is about more than you.
- Determine which parts of the story relate to you—and which don't.
- Use meaningful personal anecdotes that illuminate the larger subject.
- Direct the story—don't let other people tell it.
- Ask questions and anticipate the reader's questions —don't play expert.
- Verify everything—don't trust your memory or a single source's opinion.
- Attribute information, where appropriate, to sources.
- Include counterpoints to your argument.
- Limit TMI storytelling and snarkiness but . . .
- Go deep: Make clear why you believe what you do.

Ultimately, having an impact in first-person journalism involves connecting to something larger than yourself. You write about what you think, feel, and observe from your perspective—but you're responding to the world. When feature writers and essayists can link individual experience with universal concerns, their work has real impact on those who read it and continue to read it. Few of us have the staying power of James Baldwin or Joan Didion, but you don't need to reach for the literary stars to affect other people. Impacting readers *is* the goal, not just getting published or the catharsis of telling your own story (Box 11.1).

The sections that follow touch on three approaches to focusing a story: testing ideas in pitches, coming up with a tagline as a quick hook, and directing readers by paraphrasing in your own voice. In practice, freelance writers often test ideas, pitch to editors, and come up with taglines before writing or reporting a story. Selling ideas to editors to get feature assignments is part of the profession, and some writers may find the tips for crafting a pitch letter helpful long before they get to revising a story. But I've also found that pitching (and re-pitching) is a useful exercise for students at all points in the process. If you're having trouble coming up with your nut graf, consider writing a new pitch. Then try it out on anyone who will listen.

Test your idea: Pitching

So, you're sitting around your firepit with friends. Or you're catching up with family members scattered around the country during a weekly Zoom chat. Maybe you're eating bag lunches with a couple of colleagues. Why not tell them about a story idea you have?

Their response will give you immediate feedback. If they're hooked by the topic or problem you're posing, you'll see it in their faces. You'll hear it in the enthusiastic questions they ask or the stories they relate about a time *the very same thing happened to me, Martha, oh my God*. If your idea isn't yet focused, you'll be met with polite silence or tentative questions.

Testing story ideas like this may feel risky, especially with people you want to impress. As with identifying trustworthy readers to provide feedback on a story draft, you need to feel psychologically safe around the people you're sharing an idea with. But if you do like and trust them, an informal test drive is one of the best ways to find out if your idea is focused.

I conduct oral pitching sessions in my classes, often with students in small groups so it feels more informal. For those who want to pitch an idea to the whole class, I ask them to do a timed *elevator pitch*—that is, what they would say if they happened to meet an editor in an elevator and had one minute to get their idea across. A timed elevator pitch requires more advance preparation. (I suggest they practice in front of a mirror, timing themselves before presenting it.) While I discourage students from reading a written version out loud as a pitch in class, the main goal is to create a well-focused, written pitch that can be sent to editors.

Box 11.2 Pitch letter formula

1 Lead paragraph

Dear [insert editor name]: I'm contacting you to propose an 800-word feature about . . .

2 Nut graf

My story matters because. . . . It's relevant to readers because . . .

3 Reporting approach

Here are possible sources [name one or two] and why I'm the writer to tell this story . . .

4 Closing paragraph

Here's how to contact me, my recent publications, thank you.

Pitch letters—also known as queries—come in many varieties. I've listed one basic formula in Box 11.2, but you'll find other examples on writing sites and in resource guides about freelance journalism. The four-paragraph setup is my starting place, one that emphasizes brevity and clarity. No need to stick with the exact wording in the italicized sections. They're placeholders to indicate the content in each paragraph, and you should frame the pitch in your own voice. There's plenty of room for changing the formula to suit your particular topic and point of view, and many pitch letters are longer than four paragraphs. You can also insert links to recent publications—your "clips"—at the end of the pitch rather than in the text. (But don't attach files with an email pitch, because messages with attachments are often filtered as spam.)

Keep in mind that your aim in pitching an editor, as in testing out the idea with friends, is to spark curiosity immediately. We editors tend to be tired and impatient when opening pitch letters, most of which pile up in email inboxes or submissions queues. That doesn't mean we aren't hoping to find the next great voice or investigative reporter. But we read and decide fast. We skim for the big idea, which is why writing a pitch letter is an excellent exercise for focusing your story.

It's no coincidence that the pitch formula resembles the classic feature formula discussed in Chapter 10. Yet in a pitch, you aren't telling the whole story. An anecdotal lead rarely works in a short pitch note, unless you can compress it to a couple of sentences. And if you're pitching an 800-word feature, your pitch shouldn't be more than a page long. The whole point is to boil down what you want to say. That in itself demonstrates your skills as a writer.

Voice Lesson 1

1   *Elevator pitch:* With a small group of family members or friends, describe the idea for your personal trend story from Chapters 9 and 10. If possible, keep your oral pitch no longer than one minute. (Practice first and time yourself.) Alternatively, you can test another story idea.

2   ***Feedback review:*** In your process notebook, jot down the responses you heard after explaining your idea out loud. Did your group of sympathetic listeners seem confused by anything—or did they leap right in with questions or ideas of their own? Has the feedback sparked a new way of focusing your trend story or new angles to report?

3   ***Pitch letter:*** Based on the feedback, write a short email pitch letter to an editor. Be sure to identify *a real editor at an actual magazine or news outlet to whom you can email this pitch*—even if you don't intend to send the pitch letter right away. Selecting a publishing venue for your pitch will help determine the audience for your feature.

Focus your idea: Taglines

In his 2013 book *How to Write Short*, Roy Peter Clark calls *SVO*—subject, verb, object—the "secret formula" for online headlines, which on digital sites now often function as a story's lead. While many digital publishers emphasize SEO (search engine optimization), Clark writes:

> No newfangled formula can replace the one-two-three power of essential reporting and storytelling. In the end, someone does something to somebody, and we want to know more about it, a form of reader interest optimization.

Clark, a journalist and longtime teacher and mentor at the Poynter Institute, has published many other writing guides, and he's a go-to source for story focus. We'll return to some of his advice in a moment. But for now, let's stick with headlines, because that's another crucial part of a pitch letter. A good headline boils down your story even more. Arguably, it's the most important part of your pitch. In an email query, it's the subject line—the thing that hooks an editor and often determines whether the message gets opened at all.

And yet, headlines for feature articles often flag the situation or topic rather than the emotional core. For that reason, try homing in on what you really want to say with a *tagline:* a brief blurb—just a sentence or two—that conveys your story. Think of it as a capsule version of the nut graf or theme statement. The goal is to get across, in a few words, why the story will matter to readers. A tagline can be like a topical headline, but it's also supposed to sell an idea. Screenwriters call this the log line; some marketers refer to it as a one-liner. If the lead of many online stories is now the headline, the nut graf is the tagline (or blurb) before the story starts.

Is writing a tagline hard? Yes. But writing a good one helps focus the story, even if you don't end up using it in the piece itself. Although a tagline may seem melodramatic or reductive for a personal essay, coming up with one can help pinpoint your key opposition and what readers need to know. Essays do more wandering, but they still need an emotional focus.

If you can tolerate a brief foray into marketing, consider business author Donald Miller's tips to "clarify your message" in his 2017 guide *Building a Storybrand*. For Miller, it's about getting customers to understand what you can do for them immediately. In his "one liner" exercise, he proposes this formula (I'm paraphrasing): *business problem + your plan to solve it + success*. Miller's exercise is meant for entrepreneurs who need to get across their business in one line—or at most, two sentences—and then repeat that line endlessly for marketing purposes. He's not interested in factual accuracy or letting readers know who the "I" telling the story is.

Yet when you pitch a feature idea to editors (or potential readers), you *are* selling it to them, and you need to hook their attention fast. The point of such tagline exercises is not to turn yourself into a marketer but to try journalistic variations on the basic three-point formula:

1   *The problem I'm wrestling with is . . .*
2   *Some possible solutions are . . .*
3   *But the thing that really matters is . . .*

In this formula, the first point is the equivalent of the situation and the third is the real story. For instance, here's a one-liner for a 2014 feature of mine:

> *Entrepreneurial language has coopted the business of being a writer—so I've learned the hard way to focus on stories that matter, not selling my work to the highest bidder.*

You may recognize this from Chapter 5 and the excerpts of a first draft I included there. The final version was published in *Talking Writing* with the following title and blurb:

The Trouble With Being an Entrepreneur
Why Business Thinking Messes up a Writer's Head

But if I'd pitched it to another editor at, say, the following hypothetical magazine, I would have put my tagline in the first paragraph of my pitch letter:

> *Dear Ms. Editor:*
>
> *I'm contacting you to propose a 1,000-word feature about a real hazard for your* Digital Freelancing *readers. Entrepreneurial language has coopted the business of being a writer—so I've learned the hard way to focus on stories that matter, not selling my work to the highest bidder.*

Regardless, writing a tagline will give your story idea more impact in revising the feature for publication. Feel free to come up with your own combinations of the three-point formula. Here are a few tagline setups to get you started:

1   *TV viewers recently protested when . . .*
2   *The producers have countered with . . .*
3   *But recent historical evidence shows that . . .*

-or-

> 1   *The trauma I experienced was . . .*
> 2   *I tried to recover by . . .*
> 3   *But I was surprised to discover that . . .*

Voice Lesson 2

1   **Practice headlines:** In your notebook, list three good examples of SVO—subject, verb, object—in headlines from the daily news. Resist the temptation to make up your own "Man Bites Dog" headlines. Pay attention to actual examples of SVO and whether they hook you.
2   **Your headline:** Compose several possible headlines for your personal trend story using the SVO formula.
3   **Your tagline:** Based on one of the three-point setups in this section (or your own combination), write a tagline for your story. If you come up with something longer than two sentences, try again—and again.

Focus your voice: Cutting and selecting

When it comes to pitching or revising a draft, there's plenty of advice out there about chopping down words, getting rid of passive constructions, fixing flabby leads, and so on. Do all this, please. William Zinsser's chapters on "Clutter" and "Unity" in *On Writing Well* should still be mandatory reading for any magazine writer, not to mention social-media influencers.

In *How to Write Short*, Roy Peter Clark includes a chapter titled "Cut It Short," examining Strunk and White's famous dictum from *The Elements of Style*: "Omit needless words." Whether you think "needless" is necessary there, Clark emphasizes cutting more than words: "I am on the prowl for big things to take out. Omitting or cutting words is nickeling-and-diming a text. I want to cut big pieces if I can—twenty-dollar bills, not dimes and nickels."

In other words, before you cut for the sake of cutting, first figure out why you're doing it. Revising a feature to increase its impact may mean cutting whole quotes from outside experts or paragraphs of background, even an entire scene. It could mean chopping any reference to some sources—or deleting an evocative capsule profile you're attached to. In revising this book, along with a jingling heap of dimes and nickels, I ended up cutting a whole chapter and one of my first-person elements.

The goal is to be a "disciplined cutter," in Clark's phrasing. He and other journalists advise cutting 25 percent of a first draft. For a wordy novelist like Stephen King, it's a "10 percent rule." Regardless of the percentage, forcing yourself to make cuts will help identify what you really need to keep. Clark has also referred to this as trimming branches from the tree, not just picking off a few leaves.

Effective paraphrasing helps focus a story, too, especially in cutting down on long expert quotes. You can rephase tedious explanations or arguments in your own words to clarify them for readers. Sometimes you need to include direct quotes as corroboration; news writing differs from feature writing and essays in this regard. But for first-person storytelling, putting information from other sources into your own words is a powerful tool. For readers, it establishes who the active "I" is and helps direct them through a story to what matters (Box 11.3).

Note that paraphrasing for focus doesn't involve simply changing a few words of the original or claiming someone else's ideas as your own. That's an unethical shortcut and should never be considered as a workaround to get away with fabrication or plagiarism. When you paraphrase an expert quote to tighten and decode it for readers, you should still add an attribution tag to indicate where the idea or information comes from.

Box 11.3 Paraphrase power

Increase the impact of what experts say.

Explain an event more dramatically.

Clarify the time sequence.

Specify how something works.

Summarize key facts and other information.

Establish your own expertise and authority.

Highlight what matters and why.

Good paraphrasing not only avoids word bloat and voice hijacks—it also focuses your voice, which in turn unifies everything you present to readers. Focusing your "I" does come down to choices, and some choices may involve losses of nuance, precision, or context. But as long as the loss doesn't make a first-person account inaccurate, there's liberation in cutting away distractions, both in life and in writing. It can be painful to lose stories that are personally meaningful, yet acknowledging what's been lost may have the most impact of all.

Voice Lesson 3

1   ***Cutting:*** Delete at least 25 percent of the draft of your personal trend story. Alternatively, you can delete 25 percent from another short feature or essay you've written (that is, reduce it to 75 percent of its original length, in Clark's version of the cut rule). Consider making the cutting process visual by annotating your file with strikeouts on-screen or marking them by hand on a printout of your draft.

2   ***Paraphrasing:*** Select at least one outside expert quote in your trend story to paraphrase—and write two different versions of it in your own words. (If you've chosen to cut most or all of a quote, even better.) Alternatively, you can select long expert quotes in a published article or book and

practice paraphrasing them in your own words. See my sample paraphrase of an academic quote in the "Danger! Avoid Voice Hijacks" section of Chapter 7.

Connect to the world: Your impact

When we include our own stories in a work of nonfiction, there's no guarantee every reader will connect with the particular details of setting, time period, or culture. There are different audiences for different features. Some readers only want to be informed of current events. Some want an explanation of how a complex sequence of events happened, but they don't care about the reporter. Other readers do want to know the "I" who's interpreting information for them. More than that, they're looking for illumination in a messy world.

The audience for first-person journalism is varied, but the stories that drive many longer personal features and essays may require more ungainly branches than a tight news article. Consider Carvell Wallace's "Trying to Parent My Black Teenagers Through Protest and Pandemic," a close to 5,000-word essay that appeared in the *New York Times Magazine* in June 2020. The title is followed by an evocative blurb:

> This is the world I let be created. They know this. They blame me for it. They are right. Also, would you like dinner? What movie should we watch?

It's certainly a title + tagline hook, yet the combo didn't satisfy all the students in a feature-writing class I taught in the fall of 2020. I asked them to write response papers for Wallace's piece, and the reaction seemed evenly split. Half the students loved the essay and his conversational voice (he's also an accomplished podcaster). The other half thought it was too long and didn't pay off on the practical advice they said the title implied.

That's the real risk we take in writing first-person stories with an impact: exposing ourselves, especially our uncertainties and mistakes, to public scrutiny. Wallace's essay provides no easy answers to readers looking for solutions. Yet he connects his individual story to the larger world that affects his family. I've encountered few other essays that combine the impact of racism on Black families with the daily grind of parenting in such a convincing way. For instance, Wallace recalls chatting about relationships on a walk with his teenage son:

> He had questions about what to do with another person's feelings. I started by trying to tell him what I know, which I quickly realized was not much. So I ended up telling him what I don't know, what I struggle with—how much time I've spent trying to control what others think of me, or treating every opportunity at intimacy as though it were life or death. I told him how I did not know how to love myself, so I looked to other people to love me. And how rarely that worked.

Some of my students felt Wallace exposed too much here or was being too hard on himself. But for me, his admission of "I did not know how to love myself" is a brave one—the kind of risk that matters. It rings true. It's personally honest, the opposite of an attempt to fake the "I" voice or to perform emotions for self-serving reasons. More than that, Wallace conveys to readers what he tells his son without revealing too much about the boy or any other family member. As a first-person journalist, the person Wallace exposes to public scrutiny, warts and all, is himself. He takes the risk on his own chin and nobody else's chin.

Back in Chapter 2, that tricky chapter about ethics and reporting, I listed several "true questions" that I've touched on throughout *First-Person Journalism*. It should be obvious by now they have no set answers. The answers will differ for every "I" interpreting what they see, from Carvell Wallace to so many other nonfiction storytellers who connect their personal lives to universal experiences. The point is to ask the questions (Box 11.4).

Box 11.4 True questions

What makes a personal voice believable?
What makes my first-person story accurate?
What will readers expect when they read this story?
How do I know what I know?

As truth-tellers, the best tool we have is to keep asking, "How do I know what I know?" This central philosophical question will push you to be accurate in reporting factual information. It will nudge you to admit what you don't know and to reflect on the consequences. Making a traditional reporting plan or source list is helpful, too. But the "Impact Plan" at the end of this chapter encourages you to do more than note down which facts are still missing or your interview contacts. The five items on the worksheet focus on the quality of your information.

Achieving impact with personal features has as much to do with reflecting on what a story means as it does with identifying additional outside sources or what can be cut. As soon as I finish this book, I'll want to revise it. I'll see the errors, the places where I still have doubts. I'm human, imperfect, prone to fooling myself. And yet, I aspire to an honest recounting when I sit down to write—and so can you. That's the nature of first-person journalism. We may come to the end of one story or book, but then we start again.

Story revision: Complete a feature or an essay

1 *True questions:* As a warm-up in your notebook, respond to the four true questions in Box 11.4 one more time. If you've answered them previously, how do your responses differ now?

2   ***Your impact plan:*** Consider how to focus the trend story you began in Chapter 9 about a change in food, music, or the weather. (Alternatively, you can revise another feature or essay.) Complete the "How do you know?" items in the Impact Plan worksheet that follows. Provide as much detail as possible about factual evidence and sources, as well as anything that may still be missing.

3   ***Your revision:*** Based on your impact plan and the remixing and editing you've already done, complete a new draft of your trend feature or essay.

4   ***Bonus motivator:*** Revise your pitch letter to match the focus of your new draft—and send it to an editor.

Impact plan: *How do you know?*

1 *Personal anecdotes: Fact checking the basics*

For personal anecdotes in this feature, list all the who-what-where-when *facts that can be checked and describe how you'll verify them.*

2 *General assumptions: Fact checking what "everyone knows"*

List any general statements you make about humanity or the world. Are these sweeping claims—or reasonable assumptions based on what you've observed? List counterpoints to your assumptions, too.

3 *Orienting details: Describing your "I"*

List all the basic details readers need to know about you to understand your POV, personal experience, and why you believe what you do.

4 *Uncertainty: Acknowledging what you don't know*

List what you don't know and may never know—and why. Then draft three different sentences that explain why the facts are slippery.

(Hint: In at least one sentence, connect your inability to pin down what happened with what that makes you feel.)

5 *Mistakes: Reporting on what you got wrong*

After you finish fact checking and pinning down your "I," list all the facts you got wrong when you first came up with this idea—or that don't match what you originally assumed.

What do you think that means?

Sources

How to Write Short: Word Craft for Fast Times by Roy Peter Clark (Little, Brown, 2013), pp. 123, 228.

"Let Your Lead Be Your Flashlight and Nine Other Ideas for Focusing a Story" by Roy Peter Clark, Poynter Institute website, December 10, 2015 (adapted from *Help! For Writers* by Roy Peter Clark, Little, Brown, 2011). www.poynter.org/newsletters/2015/let-your-lead-be-a-flashlight-and-9-other-ideas-for-focusing-a-story/

Building a Storybrand: Clarify Your Message so Customers Will Listen by Donald Miller (HarperCollins, 2017).

"Storybrand One Liner Exercise" (video) with Donald Miller, *EntreLeadership Master Series*, October 16, 2017. www.youtube.com/watch?v=HFergI0UOAs

On Writing: A Memoir of the Craft by Stephen King (Scribner, 2000).

"Trying to Parent My Black Teenagers Through Protest and Pandemic" by Carvell Wallace, *New York Times Magazine*, June 15, 2020. www.nytimes.com/2020/06/15/magazine/parenting-black-teens.html

Endnote

Witnessing the world with empathy

In an iconic image from Vietnam, a young Vietnamese soldier leads a captured U.S. pilot. The Vietnamese soldier is a woman—small, barefoot, forthright—while the male pilot is so large he seems alien. The camera stares at her head-on rather than down from a height.

The female soldier with the defeated American man contrasts sharply with some of the most familiar 1960s Vietnam images from Western news sources: villagers fleeing napalm attacks, monks on fire. Yet this photograph, taken by Phan Thoan of the Vietnam News Agency, has been incorporated into Vietnamese war memorials, as shown on the cover of anthropologist Christina Schwenkel's 2009 book *The American War in Contemporary Vietnam*.

Writing about wars inspires partisan views. In the United States, it's been the Vietnam War for half a century; in Vietnam, it's the American War. To ignore this under a cloak of objectivity is to deceive on a grand scale. Emphasizing competing points of view rather than disguising them has other implications as well. War has long been thought of as the province of muscular male reporting. But consider a reversal on a par with that photo of the Vietnamese woman soldier. The subjective, personal, seemingly inconsequential aspects of the soft realm may really matter in getting the truth out about wars or anything else.

In December 2009, I attended a seminar at Harvard University led by Christina Schwenkel, in which she showed pictures taken by North Vietnamese photojournalists during the war. Many weren't widely available in Vietnam or elsewhere until the late 1990s. One of a young couple looking after a baby in the remains of a blasted American tank still haunts me.

"Contrary to representations of violence and suffering portrayed in the United States," Schwenkel writes in her book, the images by Vietnamese photojournalists, many of whom lived with their subjects in infamous holdouts like the Cu Chi tunnels, "also provide insights into more sanguine and leisurely moments in war, and occasionally even fleeting romantic encounters."

Some of her most thought-provoking points involve which ideas of professional journalism dominate and shape history. Western journalists are often celebrated as "detached moral witnesses," she notes, while the socialist press are derided as unprofessional propagandists. Schwenkel isn't defending the Vietnamese Communist Party; clearly, the North Vietnamese government used war photos as propaganda. But she argues that the North's photojournalists weren't just government stooges, either. She likens them to ethnographers, doing the kind of work that anthropologists do, in close contact with their subjects.

Shifting points of view

Many decades after that war in Southeast Asia, views of who won and lost remain contested, especially among those who were part of the Vietnamese diaspora of refugees to other countries. More than ever, our complicated times call for empathy in interpreting perspectives other than our own. I began this book by emphasizing how first-person journalism can build trust with audiences who are wary of the press. Now, as I come to a close, I'll highlight why looking both inside and outside ourselves can make us more humane writers.

Empathy begins with witnessing your own shifting attitudes. In *First-Person Journalism*, I've underscored the value of self-examination, asking you to be a rigorous self-reporter. In writing an opinion piece or essay, for instance, you may start out furious or shocked by an event that intersects with your personal life. Yet as a good self-reporter, you step back to examine your response and to check the facts. More than that, you acknowledge your biases and mistakes, exposing yourself to public scrutiny—that's part of the rigor, the honesty, the journalism.

Self-examination doesn't mean, however, that you become detached from your feelings or ignore them in order to sound objective. It's also not a self-criticism session focused on changing "bad thoughts" to "right thinking." Just as I don't believe reporters should function as detached witnesses of other people in pain, I think empathy for your own messy self is required.

Here, I'm nodding to the divisions inside we all feel—those key oppositions that fuel personal nonfiction. They spark questions and shifts in perspective. They're uncomfortable, prickly, itches we can't stop scratching. In "Montaigne on Trial," a close reading in the *New Yorker* of the sixteenth-century essay master's work, Adam Gopnik observes:

> Montaigne animates for the first time an inner human whose contradictions are identical with his conscience. "If I speak diversely of myself, it is because I look diversely upon myself," he writes, in "On the Inconstancy of our Actions."

Literary essays often read as if they emerged full-blown from a writer's head, but Michel de Montaigne, originator of the form, was famously revising his prose right up to his death. The process of accumulating a big nest of thoughts, then cutting it down, then adding something back, then whittling away more, creates a final product that mimics the mind at work.

It also calls forth the heart and its many vicissitudes, especially when faced with a world in constant flux. As a writer, it's easier to fake yourself—to pitch your voice to what an audience wants to hear or to create the illusion of authority—than to admit your own confusion. But empathy for that uncertainty has to be the starting point for witnessing others. Not all pain is obvious to outsiders, not unless self-reporters can see beyond their limited points of view.

Consider how Damon Young's "Racism Made Me Question Everything. I Got the Vaccine Anyway," a 2021 *New York Times* opinion piece, upends the liberal white perspective of an emergency. Young lays out why public-health measures can seem threatening to Blacks such as himself, noting that evangelical anti-vaxxers aren't the only ones reluctant to try a new drug. He cites many current and historical reasons to be suspicious of a medical system that favors whites. Of his own decision, he acknowledges mixed feelings:

> The trust still isn't there. Will never be there. But the negotiation that placed me in that vaccination line last month required me to weigh that distrust against all that I miss. I miss the year we just lost. I miss playing basketball. I miss watching it with my dad. I miss barbecues. Malls. Movie theaters. . . . With the disproportionate havoc this plague has wreaked on Black and brown people, my desire to return to a semblance of normalcy and prevent more death is a force greater than my cynicism.

An opinion piece isn't news, but it can change the lens through which a problem is viewed. From my perch in the world, I trust public-health experts. Yet Young's piece pushed me to examine my point of view on this topic as a white woman. The perspective of an African American in Pittsburgh is not mine—nor is that of a well-to-do Frenchman like Montaigne, who could retire to write his *essais*. But as a reader, I benefit from these different first-person voices. As a writer, I feel empowered by their willingness to change their minds.

In his 2017 *New Yorker* article, Gopnik quotes a long paragraph by Montaigne that lists an array of opposing feelings in "the writer's soul"—"bashful, insolent, chaste, luxurious, peevish, prattling, silent, fond, doting, laborious, nice. . . ." Then Gopnik, an accomplished essayist himself, follows up with an evocative passage of his own:

> Lists are the giveaways of writing. What we list is what we love, as with Homer and his ships, or Whitman and his Manhattan trades, or Twain and steamboats. That beautiful and startlingly modern list of mixed emotions suggests a delectation of diversities . . . insulated by nothing but a comma, anchored together in one soul's harbor. They bang hulls inside our heads.

I think of Young's list of what he misses or all the individual lists of what we want and loathe and fear. Witnessing those hulls banging together, perhaps even loving our inner mess, can be the impetus for understanding that other people feel divided, too. Such empathy allows us to shift points of view and to recognize struggles that differ from our own.

Witnessing a fragile world

At the bitter end of 2020, Margaret Renkl opened another *New York Times* opinion piece by reacting to a major news event that had just occurred in her Tennessee town:

> It's hard to know, in the midst of sorrow, exactly which brand of anguish is lodged in the human soul. I do know this, though: It's been a miserable year here, a year that tore our hearts to pieces even before a bomb reduced a historic part of this city to rubble on Christmas Day.

In "The Bomb That Struck the Heart of Nashville," Renkl fills in details known at the time: A lone man set off a bomb in his RV, killing himself and damaging nearby buildings. But a recorded voice from the car warned people away, alternating with Petula Clark's 1960s hit "Downtown." The frothy song is ironic, but Renkl suggests another interpretation: a response to that Nashville street being taken over by neon-lit tourist traps like Hooters. "In that sense," she writes, "the bomb that went off on Christmas morning feels like a visible manifestation of a quiet alienation that has been growing here for more than two decades."

An essayist as well as a *Times* contributor, Renkl goes beyond her initial reaction and the coronavirus crisis to observe other tensions. She balances strong feelings with relevant facts and local twists for those who don't live in Nashville. Instead of dispassionately presenting both sides of a story—or deciding which side deserves the most space—the balance of facts with feeling yields a compassionate view of all this writer observes.

Since first reading her piece, I've thought about how much to share of my own distress. A few months later, when I saw the first reports about a supermarket shooting in Boulder, Colorado, I kept hitting refresh on various news feeds, hoping a feature would pop up to explain what motivated the shooter. Weeks passed, yet no motive emerged. In 2021, seemingly senseless acts of violence in the United States keep unfolding: eight people shot to death in and around a Georgia massage parlor; ten people murdered by that Colorado shooter; a Capitol police officer dying after he was rammed by a car. In all cases, a mentally ill perpetrator apparently acted alone, and we're left with few answers for such internal disintegration.

I'm struck by how fragile the sense of self can be. The edges play out in our lives in particular ways but ripple through all stories in times of trouble. With my own family, I have more than a passing experience with mental illness and the distortions of paranoia. Such illness is no excuse for harming others, but living with yourself can require strength that's hard to muster once you feel broken. There may be no safe harbor within or capacity to listen to anyone else.

The classic essay is woven with shiny scraps of memory, fact, argument, and self-observation. It takes existential leaps amid personal ruminations. Centuries later, Montaigne is still the model for embracing uncertainty. In "On Liars," he begins: "There is nobody less suited than I am to start talking about memory. I can hardly find a trace of it in myself. . . ." This short essay moves from his skeptical self-observations to the crucial distinction between not remembering and deliberately lying. Montaigne's conclusion: "Lying is an accursed vice. It is only our words that bind us together and make us human."

Speaking to readers as an unflinching witness is part of what binds us. Near the end of "The Bomb That Struck the Heart of Nashville," Renkl writes, "I am grieving as much as anyone over what he did to our city. But I am also thinking of the weight we've all carried this hard year, in Nashville and everywhere. There are times when it feels too heavy, no matter how resilient we are determined to be."

In acknowledging her sorrow, Renkl gives readers like me permission to feel our own. And she addresses the very human need for meaning when the *why* of what happened may remain a mystery. She closes by comparing the resilience of survivors to an insect's carapace, a surface shell that hardens in times of stress but also covers up vulnerabilities we need in order to stay open to other people. First-person journalism at its best is based on such empathetic witnessing. It opens up other points of view at the same time that it challenges readers to open their hearts, too.

Sources

The American War in Contemporary Vietnam: Transnational Remembrance and Representation by Christina Schwenkel (Indiana University Press, 2009).

"Montaigne on Trial" by Adam Gopnik, *New Yorker*, January 8, 2017. www.newyorker.com/magazine/2017/01/16/montaigne-on-trial

"Racism Makes Me Question Everything. I Got the Vaccine Anyway" by Damon Young, *New York Times*, April 9, 2021. www.nytimes.com/2021/04/09/opinion/racism-covid-vaccine.html

"The Bomb That Struck the Heart of Nashville" by Margaret Renkl, *New York Times*, December 30, 2020. www.nytimes.com/2020/12/30/opinion/nashville-bombing-covid.html

"On Liars" in *Michel de Montaigne: The Complete Essays*, translated by M.A. Screech (Penguin Books, 1991/2003). Also see "Of Liars" in *The Essays of Michel de Montaigne*, translated by Charles Cotton, edited by William Carew Hazlitt, 1877 (first published in 1580; Project Gutenberg, 2006). www.gutenberg.org/files/3600/3600-h/3600-h.htm#link2HCH0009

25 Rules: First-person journalism

1 Do not knowingly change facts or the sequence of what happened.

2 Don't bore yourself.

3 The process of telling your story is not the same as the end result.

4 No first drafts.

5 Spend 15 minutes a day researching a topic you like.

6 Memories are not facts.

7 We all have biases, and it's important to acknowledge what they are.

8 Hiding who you are and what you feel isn't a simple style choice.

9 The best feature ideas make writers uncomfortable.

10 "I don't know" doesn't excuse lazy reporting or thinking.

11 Your emotional motivation is not the same as the story.

12 Specific details matter more than vague generalities, as long as the details are relevant.

13 Attribute everything you can with context, even if it seems like too much.

14 Tell stories that not only move readers but also make sense of why people disagree.

15 Don't isolate facts from emotional consequences—connect them when reporting.

16 Don't be a mouthpiece.

17 Don't confuse readers about when something happened.

18 Narrative chronology is not the same as the actual timeline of what happened.

19 Whenever you narrate an event, stamp it with a date or approximate time period.

20 Establish how much time has passed between your active "I" and your younger self.

21 Start with five scenes.

22 Story outlines aren't set in stone.

23 All good stories involve change.

24 Open and close a personal nonfiction story in your own voice.

25 It can be hard to figure out the main idea of a story, but put in the work to have an impact.

Index

194   *Index*

Printed in Great Britain
by Amazon

15965199R00120